P-30 N
35
37

Sam Houston with the Cherokees
1829–1833

Diana Rogers, Cherokee wife of Sam Houston. Painting drawn from contemporary accounts by the Creek-Cherokee artist Joan Hill.

SAM HOUSTON with the Cherokees 1829–1833

By JACK GREGORY *and*

RENNARD STRICKLAND

UNIVERSITY OF TEXAS PRESS, AUSTIN AND LONDON

Library of Congress Catalog Card No. 67–25326

Printed by the University of Texas Printing Division, Austin
Bound by Universal Bookbindery, Inc., San Antonio

FOR

CAROLYN THOMAS FOREMAN

AND

NETTIE WHEELER

in appreciation of their work in the preservation of the history and the art of the American Indian

AN INTRODUCTION

. . . Sam Houston was . . . one of the most independent, unique, popular, forceful and dramatic individuals ever to enter the Senate Chamber. . . . Although there are available endless collections of diaries, speeches and letters . . . Houston himself remains shadowed and obscured . . . a mystery to the careful historian of today. . . . sometimes spectacular, sometimes crude, sometimes mysterious, but always courageous.

JOHN F. KENNEDY, *Profiles in Courage,* pp. 101, 105, 106

I had . . . Sam on his way to join the Indians after the crash of his first marriage; and there was opposed by a blank wall. About a dozen printed pages was all the reliable material I could scare up in New York or in the Library of Congress on the four years he spent in exile. . . . [T]hat blank wall of the Indian years was what treed me.

MARQUIS JAMES, "On the Trail of Sam Houston," *The Texas Monthly,* VI (July, 1930), 3–4

Sam Houston, in the minds of the American people, symbolizes the movement for independence in Texas. More than Stephen Austin, Jim Bowie, or Davy Crockett, Houston personifies the spirit of that struggle. He has become the folk hero of a romantic epoch in the westward expansion of the United States. Much of Houston's career prior to the Texas Revolution, however, remains "a blank wall" colored with legend and darkened with mystery.

Unquestionably, the most mysterious years are those immediately preceeding Houston's arrival in Texas. In most of the fifty biographies of Houston only slight reference is made to the years between 1829 and 1833, which Houston spent in "exile" with the Cherokee Indians. Even Marquis James in his prize-winning biography *The Raven* was forced to prune out "about one-third of those . . . Indian Chapters" and "to kill entire episodes or compress them into sentences or clauses."[1] Ignored or romanticized by Houston's contemporary historians, these years have become a "mysterious" interlude in Houston's life.

Nonetheless, these three and one half years have produced violent controversy among Houston biographers. Political biographer C. Edwards Lester romanticized, ". . . his history during this period is filled with stirring and beautiful incidents . . . [which] afford the finest pictures of the lights and shadows of forest life."[2] Another biographer, concluded, ". . . it would be neither interesting nor pleasant to dwell . . . upon . . . his experiences among the Indians. It is properly considered a blot upon his life."[3]

Where some biographers have seen Houston's retreat to the Cherokee Nation as an escape from the shock of failures in Tennessee, others have seen the retreat as a cold-blooded design to enlist Cherokee support in making himself emperor of an independent Texas. In the same manner, Andrew Jackson has been pictured both as Houston's conscious partner in this Texas plot and as Houston's determined adversary attempting to preserve the integrity of the Mexican provinces.

To the authors one of the most interesting conflicts is contained in the legends of Houston's Indian wives and children, but more important for a study of Houston's personality are questions concerning the commercial and political relationships between Houston and his Indian colleagues. With facts pointing in many directions it might be fruitful to ask whether Houston was ever respected by the Cherokees or whether they were only seeking his personal influence with President Jackson. Another question raised is whether Houston could have been advancing the Indian's cause only to gain a national platform to rebuild his political power.

To reconstruct these years, Indian Agency records, maps, congressional documents, traders' account books, contemporary diaries, un-

[1] Marquis James, "On the Trail of Sam Houston," *The Texas Monthly,* VI (July, 1930), 5–6.

[2] C. Edwards Lester, *The Life of Sam Houston: The Only Authentic Memoir of Him Ever Published,* p. 52.

[3] Alexander Hynds, "General Sam Houston," *The Century Magazine,* XXVIII (August, 1884), 500.

published letters, shipping records, missionary reports, and newspapers, combined with Houston's letters and speeches, have been examined. In seeking solutions to the mysteries, however, the authors have also included much that is "legend" or "speculation." In apology, we must state that these Cherokees whom we are seeking to portray are a people of oral tradition. Our purpose in offering these legends is not to answer the questions raised, but to narrate the story of the years Houston spent with the Cherokees, hoping the reader will draw his own conclusions. The author's own theories may reveal themselves in some chapters and for this we do not attempt to apologize.

JACK GREGORY

RENNARD STRICKLAND

Fayetteville, Arkansas

CONTENTS

ILLUSTRATIONS

MAPS

A BIBLIOGRAPHICAL NOTE

More than fifty biographies of Sam Houston have been written, and hundreds of articles have centered around his life. Most of these contain only slight reference to his years with the Cherokees. Because this is the first attempt at a detailed examination of Houston's life with the Cherokees, the authors have provided detailed notes upon the sources from which material was drawn. Undoubtedly, many interpretations of this material are possible. Hopefully, others will choose to test the authors' interpretations against the original sources.

The first source to which any student of Southwestern history must turn is the writing of Grant and Carolyn Foreman. The value of the Foremans' work is clearly expressed by Marquis James:

> I had begun writing and had Sam on his way to join the Indians . . . and there was opposed by a blank wall. . . . [Then] I met Grant Foreman, and it was lucky that I did. Mr. Foreman is a retired lawyer of Muskogee, Oklahoma, who devotes his time to . . . original research into southwestern history. . . . Although interested in Houston only incidentally he knew more about his Indian years than everyone else put together had found out up to that time; and he knew the sources bearing upon that period and place. With these he acquainted me in a spirit of unselfish scholarship.[1]

Fortunately for research historians, the Tulsa oilman and philanthropist Thomas Gilcrease acquired the Foreman collection of Indian documents, photostats, typescripts, and handwritten notes. The collection, which includes thousands of unpublished letters, reports, and accounts of Indian and pioneer history, was presented to the Thomas Gilcrease Institute of American History and Art in Tulsa, Oklahoma, where the materials are available for historical research. The Oklahoma Historical Society also has a large collection of Foreman materials which are rich in unpublished sources on Houston's years with the Cherokees.

[1] Marquis James, "On the Trail of Sam Houston," *The Texas Monthly*, VI (July, 1930), 3–5.

ABBREVIATIONS

Abbreviations of frequently cited correspondents and archival locations are used in the notes as follows:

AJ—Andrew Jackson
GBF—Gilcrease Biographical File, Thomas Gilcrease Institute of American History and Art, Tulsa, Oklahoma
GFP—Gilcrease Foreman Photostats, Thomas Gilcrease Institute of American History and Art, Tulsa, Oklahoma
GFT—Gilcrease Foreman Typescripts, Thomas Gilcrease Institute of American History and Art, Tulsa, Oklahoma
GMC—Gilcrease Map Collection, Thomas Gilcrease Institute of American History and Art, Tulsa, Oklahoma
GRL—Gilcrease Reference Library, Thomas Gilcrease Institute of American History and Art, Tulsa, Oklahoma
GSHBF—Gilcrease Sam Houston Biographical File, Thomas Gilcrease Institute of American History and Art, Tulsa, Oklahoma
JE—John Eaton
JP—James Prentiss
MA—Matthew Arbuckle
OBF—Oklahoma Biographical File, Oklahoma Historical Society, Oklahoma City, Oklahoma
OFP—Oklahoma Foreman Photostats, Oklahoma Historical Society, Oklahoma City, Oklahoma
OFT—Oklahoma Foreman Typescripts, Oklahoma Historical Society, Oklahoma City, Oklahoma
OIA—Oklahoma Indian Archives, Oklahoma Historical Society, Oklahoma City, Oklahoma
OMC—Oklahoma Map Collection, Oklahoma Historical Society, Oklahoma City, Oklahoma
ORL—Oklahoma Reference Library, Oklahoma Historical Society, Oklahoma City, Oklahoma
OVF—Oklahoma Vertical File, Oklahoma Historical Society, Oklahoma City, Oklahoma

PC—Phillips Collection, University of Oklahoma, Norman, Oklahoma

SH—Sam Houston

UOL—University of Oklahoma Library, University of Oklahoma, Norman, Oklahoma

Sam Houston with the Cherokees
1829–1833

1. Houston Returns to the Cherokees

> Mr. Houston's strange retirement from the office of Governor of Tennessee to take up his home among the Indians west of the Mississippi, leaving a wife whom he lately married, has caused much surprise among the people.
>
> *Niles' Weekly Register,* May 29, 1830, Vol. 38, p. 258

In the spring of 1829 the steamboat *Facility* brought more than her usual cargo of blankets, whiskey, tomahawks, and trade pipes to the community around Webbers Falls in the Cherokee Nation West. Standing on board was Sam Houston, former governor of Tennessee —"an exile" returning to the Cherokee Indians. Houston, after resigning from the governorship in April, came immediately to make the Cherokee Nation his home.[1]

The man who disembarked from the *Facility* was no ordinary trader or speculator who had come to the Indian country to make a fortune trading mackinaws and "Mongahala" whisky. This was a governor of the state of Tennessee, who described himself to President Andrew Jackson as "the most unhappy man now living";[2] a man in "the darkest, direst hour of human misery."[3]

Sam Houston was expressing the bitter shock of marriage failure. As governor of Tennessee and Jackson's anointed successor-heir apparent to the Presidency of the United States, he was probably the most desirable bachelor in the South. Four months prior to this departure for the Indian country, Houston had married Eliza Allen, daughter of

[1] SH, Resignation as Governor of Tennessee, April 16, 1829, Sam Houston, *The Writings of Sam Houston,* Amelia C. Williams and Eugene C. Barker (eds.), I, 131; *Niles' Weekly Register,* May 9, 1829; *Nashville Republican,* April 17, 1829.

[2] SH to AJ, May 11, 1829, Houston, *Writings,* I, 132–134.

[3] SH to John Overton, December 28, 1829, Houston, *Writings,* I, 144–145.

a wealthy and politically powerful Tennessean, Colonel John Allen of Gallatin. The young Eliza, described as a beautiful girl with a refined, gentle, and cultured nature, seemed an ideal hostess for the governor's mansion and perhaps even the White House.[4]

On the afternoon of the marriage, Houston recalled, a raven had fluttered and died in the dust on the road as he approached the Allens' house. Houston considered the raven his bird of destiny, and its cries of distress were later interpreted as a note of forewarning to this short marriage.[5] But there were no notes of distress that afternoon. The extravagent celebration was said to have combined the splendor of a medieval jousting tournament with the spirit of the Andrew Jackson inauguration.

Gossips have circulated rumors. Close friends and relatives have told "the true story." But neither Sam Houston nor Eliza Allen ever discussed the separation. When Phil Sublett asked Houston for his version, the General stormed from his friend's home into a blinding East Texas rainstorm shouting, "Sir, you violate the laws of hospitality by seeking to tear from my bosom its secret!" Traditionally, Eliza's conduct is reported as equally violent. She is said never to have mentioned Houston's name, but to have read every notice of his career and to have answered every harsh reference to him by turning her back on the speaker.[6]

This marriage has produced speculation as unreliable as it is varied. Eliza is said by some to have loved a cousin.[7] Others think that Houston married Eliza with the intention of leaving her, deliberately creating an excuse to go to the Indian country and revolutionize Texas.[8] It is

[4] Ernest Shearer, "The Mercurial Sam Houston," *The East Tennessee Historical Society's Publications,* No. 35 (1963), 8–9.

[5] A. W. Terrell, "Recollections of General Sam Houston," *Southwestern Historical Quarterly,* XVI (October, 1912), 132–133.

[6] Terrell, "Recollections," pp. 132–133. Before her death Eliza Allen supposedly had all likenesses of herself destroyed. The unavailability of photographs of Eliza only adds to the mystery surrounding her relationship with Sam Houston.

[7] Mrs. Gail Ward (an Allen cousin), Interview, June 26, 1964. This is suggested also in articles found in the William Weaver Scrapbook, Microfilm Division, University of Arkansas Library, Fayetteville.

[8] Daniel S. Donelson to AJ, May 22, 1829, Robert H. White (ed.), *Messages of Governors of Tennessee,* II, 251–253.

said also that Houston charged her with infidelity or even caught her in compromising circumstances, charges which Houston denied in a letter to Eliza's father.[9]

Members of the Allen family and descendants of Houston's physician insist that Houston's frontier crudeness, combined with his wounds, proved intolerable to Eliza. Moreover, Houston was almost twice Eliza's age and accustomed to bolder tavern maids and Indian women. A barbed arrow had pierced Houston's leg during the Battle of Horseshoe Bend and the injury never completely healed. According to Houston's physician, Dr. W. D. Haggard, who later married a daughter of Eliza's second marriage, the arrow produced in Houston's "groin" an offensive "running sore," which repulsed the young girl.[10]

A letter written by Emily Drennen to Emily Austin Perry at Potosi, Missouri Territory, reflects the interest and speculation surrounding Houston. She wrote:

> There is a dreadful stir in the country and town about our governor—he was married two months ago and is now parted from his wife. There is a thousand diferent tails afloat. He has resined, and poor fellow is misearable enough. I never can believe he has acted ungentlemanly untill I see him and know the trouth from himself for he was a man so popular I know it must be some thing dreadfull or he never would have left her. He is very sick and has been ever since. As soon as he gets well enough he intends leaveing the country never to return.[11]

Regardless of the reason, the separation was a shattering blow to Houston's manly pride, a blow which his friends said changed his life.[12] After Eliza returned to her father's home, Dr. William Hume, who had performed the marriage ceremony, and Obadiah Jennings, of the Nashville Presbyterian Church, refused Houston the rite of baptism. Houston then escaped public pressure by hiding. Finally, accompanied by two friends, Dr. John Shelby and Sheriff Willoughby

[9] SH to John Allen, April 9, 1829, Houston, *Writings,* I, 130.

[10] Louise Davis, "Mystery of the Raven," *The Nashville Tennessean,* August 5, 12, 19, 1962.

[11] Emily Drennen to Emily Perry, n.d., 1829, cited in Llerena B. Friend, *Sam Houston: The Great Designer,* p. 22.

[12] Terrell, "Recollections," pp. 117–118.

Williams, the former governor left his secluded hideaway.[13] It is said that Houston's separation from his friends as he left Nashville "was a touching scene" of a man who "seemed to be casting from him the palm of victory." Describing him as a man who had won the "myrtle wreath of fame," Houston's friends openly predicted that he would rise "to a higher and fairer eminence than before."[14]

Houston went from Nashville to Little Rock by way of Cairo, Helena, and the mouth of the White River—partly by boat, on foot, and on horseback. Houston was a drifter in disguise, known by the assumed name "Samuels." *Red Rover*, the name of the boat on which Houston left Cairo, is symbolic of Houston's drifting during these weeks. H. Haralson, known as a "light-hearted-Irishman," seems an ideal traveling companion in the river-drifter, rover tradition. Drunk most of the trip, the two sought to avoid any outside companionship, although they are said never to have refused to join in the shipboard gambling. The slave who accompanied Houston on the first phase of the trip seems never to have reached the Cherokee Country and it is thought he may have been lost in one of these poker games.[15]

On the *Red Rover* Houston met a man who was to play a significant role in the development of Texas: Jim Bowie. Bowie was not headed for Texas, however, but was returning to his Arkansas cotton plantation and sawmill. Older accounts establish this meeting as the first moment when Houston began to think of Texas, and it is true that Bowie, who had visited Texas several times, encouraged others to look there for rich land. Since both men were visionaries, excitement for Texas must have run high as they planned and dreamed.

Houston stopped for several days in Little Rock. News from President Jackson reached him there and so distressed him that he replied immediately. Rumor of a plan to revolutionize Texas had reached Jackson, and the President demanded reassurance. Assurances, Hous-

[13] Friend, *Sam Houston*, pp. 22, 23.

[14] C. Edwards Lester, *The Life of Sam Houston: The Only Authentic Memoir of Him Ever Published*, p. 49.

[15] Marion Karl Wisehart, *Sam Houston: American Giant*, p. 51. The Wisehart account is perhaps the best written of the stories of Houston's trip to the Cherokees. See also Lester, *Authentic Memoir*, pp. 49–51, and Marquis James, *The Raven: A Biography of Sam Houston*, pp. 89–92.

ton was willing to give, although he denied any knowledge of the plan or even of the nature of the rumors.[16] Afterward, he went back to the taverns and boasted of his plans to form a "Rocky-Mountain Alliance."[17]

From Little Rock, Houston, Haralson, and their friend John Linton went to Fort Smith, where their drinking contest became so heated that they transformed it into a "bacchian celebration." Each of them, as they danced around a large fire, was required to sacrifice clothing to the god of wine, Bacchus. Houston and Haralson, who had another suit of clothes, thought it a great joke to depart, leaving the sleeping Linton without a place to go or clothing to wear.[18]

The *Facility,* on which Houston traveled as a first-class passenger, was one of a fleet of steamboats which regularly traveled between New Orleans, Little Rock, and Fort Gibson, stopping at the small Mississippi and Arkansas river towns to take on cargo, distribute newspapers, and circulate the latest gossip. Advertisements in the *Arkansas Gazette* drew sizable cargoes from the entire Mississippi Valley. The Indian traders traveled to Fort Smith, Little Rock, or New Orleans and purchased goods, which they shipped up river on these boats.[19]

The steamboat *Facility* was overloaded when Houston boarded it at Little Rock. While the *O'Hara* generally made this trip up river to the Cherokee country, the water was so low that Houston was boarded on the *Facility,* which could pass through the low channels.[20] The *O'Hara* then returned to New Orleans and the *Facility* brought Sam Houston upstream to join the Cherokee Indians. Houston's trip was delayed, however, when the channels became so low that Captain Philip Penny-

[16] SH to AJ, May 11, 1829, Houston, *Writings*, I, 132–134.

[17] See letter of Charles Noland to his father about his observations of Houston in Little Rock, cited in Wisehart, *Sam Houston,* p. 52.

[18] James, *The Raven,* pp. 90–91.

[19] *Arkansas Gazette,* March 5, 1828, and January 6, 1829. An excellent analysis of Indians and the riverboat trade is Grant Foreman, "River Navigation in the Early Southwest," *The Mississippi Valley Historical Review,* XV (June, 1928), 34–55.

[20] *Cherokee Phoenix,* June 24, 1829. In an article dated May 20, from Little Rock, Arkansas, the *Phoenix* reported: "The late Governor of Tennessee, Gen. Samuel Houston, arrived at this place a few days since, and after two days' stay, took passage in the Steamboat *Facility,* ascending the river." See also *Arkansas Gazette,* May 20, 1829; *Muskogee Daily Phoenix,* January 10, 1932.

wit was forced to abandon cargo at the mouth of the Sallisaw. Only a small part of the consignment of goods and supplies which were boarded with Houston left the ship, several members of the crew were killed and much of the remaining cargo was destroyed when a signal gun used to draw the attention of the soldiers and Indians at Cantonment Gibson exploded as one of the soldiers attempted to light it.[21]

The *Facility's* arrival on a moonlit spring evening was as dramatic as if Houston had staged it. The arrival was what the Indians would have expected of a former United States congressman and governor of Tennessee, a man known reverently among the Cherokees as "Great Chief" of the whites.[22] Houston did not ride exhausted into the settlement and collapse at the feet of the Cherokee chief, nor did he come on foot, dragging himself the last ten miles, as the tale is often told.[23] Houston stepped from the ship into a clearing lighted with torches carried by the Negro slaves of the Cherokee Chief John Jolly.

The return is pictured in the *Authentic Memoirs*:

> It was night when the steamboat which carried Houston arrived at the Falls, two miles distant from the dwelling of the Cherokee Chief. As the boat passed the mouth of the river, intelligence was communicated to the old man that his adopted son Coloneh (the Rover—the name given him on adoption) was on board. . . . [T]he chief came down to meet his son.[24]

Little imagination is required to see the Cherokee Indians gathered at the river with their bright torches held high, as the stoic fullbloods shout "Coloneh! Coloneh!" The women in back whispering about Houston's marriage and his separation must have wanted to know more. Jolly stepped forward to welcome his adopted son.

At last he was home. Houston had anxiously awaited this return to his Indian friends and the pleasant memories of his early days among the Cherokees. His early years with these Indians had been

[21] *Muskogee Daily Phoenix,* January 10, 1932. Arrival at the Steamboat landings is vividly portrayed in Muriel H. Wright, "Early Navigation and Commerce along the Arkansas and Red Rivers in Oklahoma," *The Chronicles of Oklahoma,* VIII (March, 1930), 65–88.

[22] Lester, *Authentic Memoir*, pp. 49–53.

[23] William Weaver Scrapbook, Microfilm Division, University of Arkansas Library, Fayetteville.

[24] Lester, *Authentic Memoir,* p. 50.

the happiest of his life, and it was natural that he wanted to return to them during this blackest period in his life.

Perhaps he was trying to recapture his youth when he had run away from his home to live with Chief Jolly and his people on the banks of the Hiwassee River in Tennessee. Then he sat under the forest trees and read from the Greek classics, spoke Cherokee, played in the ball games, and joined in the dances. He was a part of this Cherokee society, more than just a tolerated white man. He *was* a Cherokee, the adopted son of John Jolly—"Oo-loo-te-ka" or "Arl-tek-ka," the "Man-who-beats-his-own-drum."[25]

He may have been trying to relive the adventure of a young soldier fighting beside the Cherokees in the Creek-Cherokee Battle of Horseshoe Bend in the War of 1812. The excitement of battle and the warm friendship which developed with General Andrew Jackson created a nostalgia for those days.[26]

Still more likely, Houston probably remembered the satisfaction he had felt while he served as subagent to the Cherokees during the period when Jolly and his tribe had left the country in Tennessee and had come West. He had conducted much of the negotiation during this period of profound change in the Western Cherokees and had felt considerable pride in removing them to a land which he thought was beyond the encroachment of white society. He may have wanted to feel once again the satisfaction of ministering to their needs.[27]

The sentiment of Houston's reunion with his foster father is pictured in the *Authentic Memoir*:

> The old chief threw his arms around him and embraced him with great affection. "My son," said he, "eleven winters have passed since we met. My heart has wandered often where you were; and I heard you were a great chief among your people. Since we parted at the Falls, as you went up river, I have heard that a dark cloud had fallen on the white path you were walking, and when it fell in your way you turned your thoughts to my wigwam. I am glad of it—it was done by the Great Spirit. . . . We are in trouble and the

[25] James, *The Raven*, pp. 18–23.

[26] Alexander Hynds, "General Sam Houston," *The Century Magazine*, XXVIII (August, 1884), 495–498.

[27] John P. Brown, *Old Frontiers: The Story of the Cherokee Indians from Earliest Times to the Date of Their Removal to the West, 1838*, pp. 463–477.

Great Spirit has sent you to us to give us council, and take trouble away from us. I know you will be our friend, for our hearts are near to you, and you will tell our sorrows to the great father, General Jackson. My wigwam is yours—my home is yours—my people are yours—rest with us."[28]

[28] Lester, *Authentic Memoir,* p. 51.

2. Houston's Indian Brothers

> Living Witnesses among the Cherokees have seen the Old Chief and Houston seated on the floor . . . feeding each other in the aboriginal fashion of friendliness with the common spoon.
>
> Alfred M. Williams, "Houston's Life among the Indians," *Magazine of American History,* X (November, 1883), 403

The Cherokee Nation, which Houston declared was his home, and the red men, whom he claimed as his brothers, were paradoxical in denouncing the "white man's civilization" but freely accepting it. While condemning the white man, many lived in feudal splendor, identical in almost every respect to the Southern white planter. They owned magnificent plantations and homes copied from their white neighbors in Georgia, Mississippi, and Tennessee.[1] They kept Negro slaves,[2] and traveled to New Orleans, Baltimore, or Philadelphia for goods to stock their stores.[3]

Jolly's celebration of Houston's arrival was more like something one would expect to see in the Mississippi delta country than in a Western Indian village.[4] Houston remembered it in his memoirs:

> This venerable old chief, Oo-loo-te-ka [John Jolly] . . . had the most courtly carriage . . . and never a prince sat on throne with more peerless grace than he presided at the council fire of his people. His wigwam was large and comfortable, and he lived in patriarchial simplicity and abundance. He had ten or twelve servants, a large plantation, and not less than five

[1] The state of Oklahoma has opened one of these homes, "The Hunter House" or Murrell Home, to the public. A picture of the Hunter House as it looks today suggests the distinction between a Plains teepee and a Cherokee plantation house. See Carolyn Thomas Foreman, *Park Hill,* pp. 104–105.

[2] The most authentic and detailed picture of the Indian as a slaveholder is Annie H. Abel, *The Slaveholding Indians,* especially I, 22, 292.

[3] John Drew Papers and Accounts, GRL.

[4] Marquis James, *The Raven: A Biography of Sam Houston,* pp. 98–100.

hundred head of cattle. The wigwam of this aged chieftain was always open to visitors, and his bountiful board was always surrounded by welcome guests. He never slaughtered less than one beef a week, throughout the year for his table.[5]

This "wigwam" was not the teepee or thatched-hut wigwam of the Plains tribes[6] but a large "comfortable home,"[7] not unlike Jolly's home in Tennessee, which Agent Return J. Meigs described as "one of the largest . . . finest homes in the South."[8] The Cherokees who owned these "wigwams" were often classed with the wild Plains tribes, who still lived a nomadic life chasing the buffalo and raiding white settlements, but even as early as the mid-eighteenth century the Cherokees were cultivating fields and could correctly have been described as "the most ingenious Indians."[9]

It is impossible to characterize Houston's Cherokees as a uniform people. There were two distinct groups. Many of the full bloods sought to avoid the white man's ways, while a considerable number maintained a way of life surprisingly close to that of the Southern planter. Their leaders were generally of the mixed-blood class, whose fathers or grandfathers had been white traders who settled among the Cherokees.

The Indians with whom Houston most closely associated operated large plantations and mercantile establishments. These men, such as John Jolly, Walter Webber, Captain John Rogers, and John Drew, cultivated cotton and corn tended by Negro slaves under the supervision of overseers. Their rich bottom land was ideal for growing large crops, which were transported down to New Orleans by the Arkansas River steamboats.[10] At one time in the Cherokee Nation

[5] C. Edwards Lester, *The Life of Sam Houston: The Only Authentic Memoir of Him Ever Published,* p. 51.

[6] The wigwams or teepees of the Plains Indian and of the early Cherokees are clearly described in M. Jourdan Atkinson, *Indians of the Southwest,* pp. 289–290, 304.

[7] Alexander Hynds, "General Sam Houston," *The Century Magazine,* XXVII (August, 1884), 500.

[8] Return Jonathan Meigs Papers, OFT, OIA.

[9] See Wilbur R. Jacobs (ed.), *Indians of the Southern Colonial Frontier: The Edmond Atkins Report and Plan of 1775,* p. 49.

[10] Grant Foreman, "River Navigation in the Early Southwest," *The Mississippi Valley Historical Review,* XV (June, 1928), 34–55.

there was more than one slave for every ten Indians, and several Indians owned as many as one hundred slaves.[11] The account books of John Drew and the warehouse receipts of the Arkansas shippers testify to the prosperity of the native merchants. They imported silk coats and fine glass from England and France to sell to these Indian planters.[12]

Chief John Jolly, Houston's adopted father and chief of the Western branch of the Cherokees, was typical of this group. Oo-loo-te-ka, or John Jolly (Jol-lee or Col-lee) as he was known to the whites, was described by George Catlin, the famous painter, as "a dignified chief . . . a mixture of white and red blood, of which . . . the first seems decidedly to predominate."[13] Catlin, who visited among the Cherokees and painted Jolly's portrait on one of these visits, wrote that "Six or seven thousand of the tribe (Cherokees) have several years since removed to the Arkansas, under the guidance and control of . . . Jollee."[14]

Even before his removal to the West, Jolly was the leader of the plantation element of the Cherokees. Chief from 1818 until his death in 1838, he was a popular figure with the full bloods. Agents feared Jolly's shrewd diplomacy, which was made even more forceful by his inability, or refusal, to speak English, and his appearance in the traditional buckskin, hunting shirt, leggings, and moccasins.[15] In Tennessee he operated a trading establishment, which made him so wealthy that Meigs described him as "possessed of considerable personal property besides his plantation here [Tennessee]."[16] His wealth as a planter was shown by the many slaves he owned and the large fields which he had under cultivation.[17]

[11] See David Brown, "Views of a Native Indian, as to the Present Condition of His People," *The Missionary Herald,* XXI (November, 1825), 354–355.

[12] John Drew Papers and Accounts, GRL.

[13] Thomas Donaldson, "The George Catlin Indian Gallery in the United States National Museum (Smithsonian Institution) with Memoirs and Statistics," *Annual Report,* July 1885, p. 207.

[14] Donaldson, "The George Catlin Indian Gallery," *Annual Report,* pp. 207–208.

[15] Cherokee Leaders Files, OFT, OIA.

[16] Return J. Meigs Papers, OFT, OIA.

[17] Morris L. Wardell, *A Political History of the Cherokee Nation 1838–1907,* p. 12.

Even the most prosperous and educated of these Cherokees, however, maintained many of the old customs. Men such as Webber and Rogers, who were educated and who visited New Orleans, Washington, and St. Louis on Indian business, still made war upon their neighbors when it was profitable to their interests. On a raiding party to the Osage Nation, Colonel Webber and his party killed a trader and then murdered several young Osage children.[18]

Houston wrote of attending the Indian Green Corn Dance and of the frenzy as the "civilized" Cherokees danced around the fire in a ceremony which still retained the primitive religious significance of cleansing the body and protecting the crops.[19] The missionaries complained that they were never able to convert this band of Cherokees from the practices of the tribal dance. When the hot summer months began to turn the corn for harvest, the Cherokees felt that they must also start life anew by discarding all their sins of the past year. The summer dances provided the chance to begin again with the new crop of corn.[20]

Fear of witches persisted among these Cherokees, who were free until as late as 1824 to kill any "witch" in the tribe.[21] It was only three years before Houston came to the Indian country that the Committee and Council had made the killing of an alleged witch a punishable crime. The Reverend Cephas Washburn, an early missionary, reports the murder of a number of witches by Cherokees whom he was never able to convert from their belief in the "dark spirits."[22]

As late as 1832, three years after Houston's arrival, large segments of the Cherokee population had never seen the new alphabet invented by Sequoyah. The Cherokee syllabary, invented by a mixed blood who could neither read nor write English, was composed of symbols repre-

[18] Carolyn Thomas Foreman, "Early History of Webbers Falls," *The Chronicles of Oklahoma,* XXIX (Winter, 1951–1952), 446; John P. Brown, *Old Frontiers: The Story of the Cherokee Indians from Earliest Times to the Date of Their Removal to the West, 1838,* p. 475.

[19] SH to MA, July 8, 1829, Sam Houston, *The Writings of Sam Houston,* Amelia W. Williams and Eugene C. Barker (eds.), I, 136–139.

[20] "Indian Dances," *National Intelligencer,* April 4, 1849.

[21] See Cherokee murder laws, Emmett Starr, *An Early History of the Cherokees,* pp. 141–142.

[22] Emmett Starr, *Cherokee "West" 1794–1839,* pp. 53–57.

senting each of the Indian sounds. The alphabet enabled a Cherokee to learn to read and write in less than a week and is said to have advanced the tribal civilization by over a hundred years.[23] Houston knew Sequoyah during these years and was remembered by him as late as 1846, when Sequoyah told a visitor that "General Houston told him it [the syllabary] was worth more than a double handful of gold to each of the nation."[24]

Despite the establishment of mission schools, such as Dwight and Fairfield, Agent George Vashon was compelled to request the secretary of war to transfer funds to eliminate illiteracy among these Cherokees. In answer to Vashon's request, the National Committee and Council of the Cherokee Nation passed a resolution that "Mr. George Guess [Sequoyah] be employed . . . to teach a school in the Cherokee language."[25]

It would be a mistake to imagine from Houston's letters that the places he visited in the Cherokee Nation were villages even in the sense of a frontier town. These five to six thousand Cherokees lived in small settlements ranging "from the Verdigres to the S. W. corner of Missouri to the Canadian [River] Fork, and thence westwardly to the Forks of the Canadian, nearly . . . up to the old territorial line between the Arkansas and the Canadian." They were so scattered that an attempt to vaccinate them in the autumn of 1832 failed because of the cost of employing additional doctors to visit their villages.[26]

Houston was keenly aware of the problems of his Cherokee brothers. He had been in the Arkansas country only a few days when he saw that the Indians were being victimized by their own agents, who knew

[23] The full scope of Sequoyah's contribution to the advancement of the Cherokee Nation can be seen in the two excellent biographies of this "American Cadmus." See Grant Foreman, *Sequoyah,* pp. 6–40, and George E. Foster, *Se-Quo-Yah: The American Cadmus and Modern Moses,* pp. 96–178.

[24] Journal of John Alexander, cited in Grant Foreman, *Advancing the Frontier, 1830–1860,* p. 322.

[25] George Vashon to Secretary of War Cass, July 12, 1832, and Resolution of the Cherokee National Committee and Council, July 11, 1832, in "Cherokee Agency, West," Letters Received by the Office of Indian Affairs. Microfilm Publications, Microcopy No. 234, Roll No. 78, The National Archives of the United States.

[26] Vashon to Cass, August 7, 1832, "Cherokee Agency, West," Microcopy No. 234, Roll No. 78.

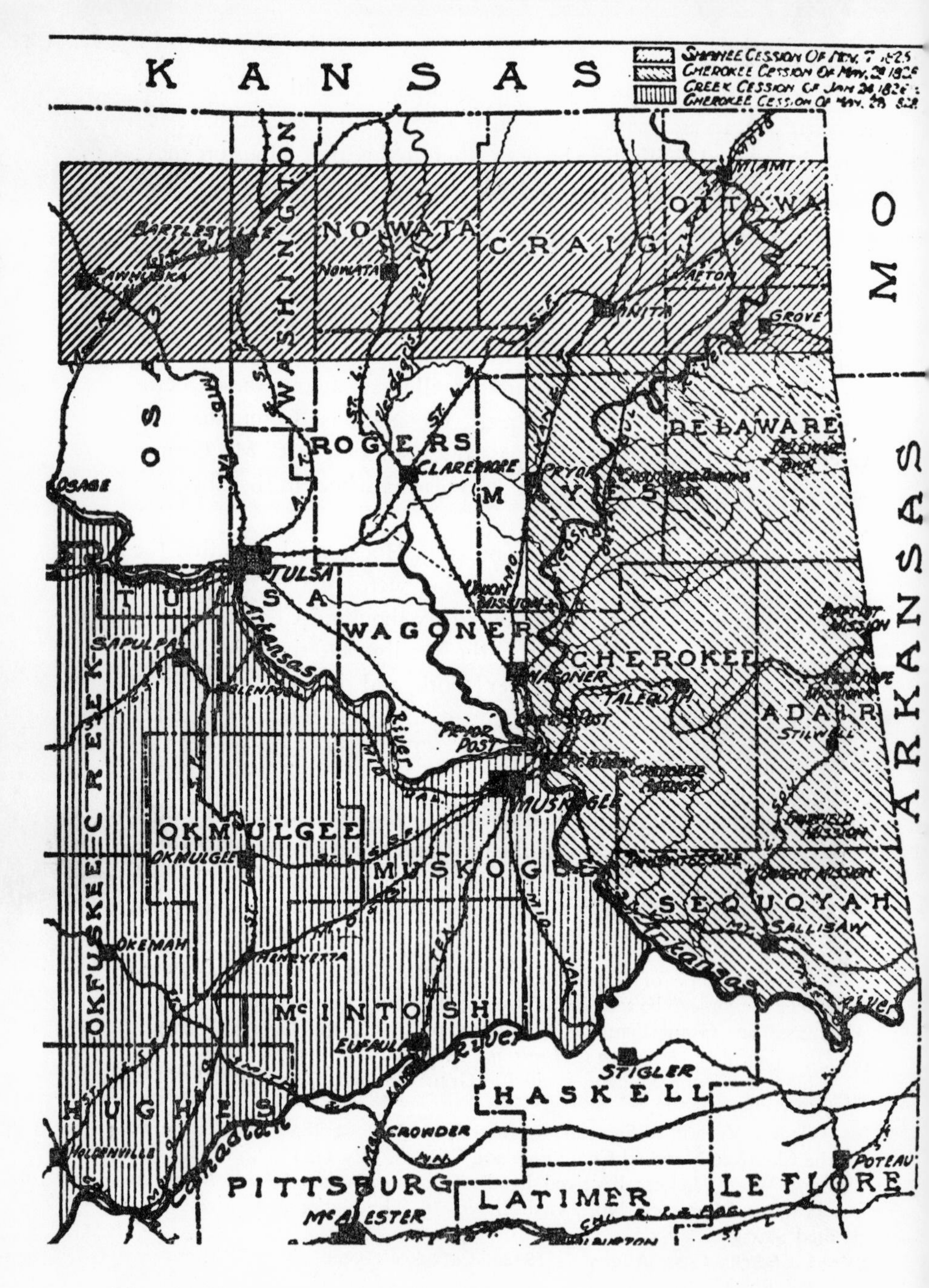

Map 1. CHEROKEE NATION WEST, 1832. Drawn by Emmett Starr.

that many Cherokees did not understand paper money and who took the specie certificates, issued in lieu of the gold payments to which they were entitled under the treaty of 1828, in exchange for "whiskey and mackinaws."[27]

These were the Indians whom Houston had encouraged to move westward voluntarily in order to escape the pressures of the Southern whites trying to force the Cherokees from their native homes. He had hoped that by encouraging them to take land in the Arkansas Territory in exchange for their old lands in Tennessee he would enable them to escape white encroachment forever.

When Houston was Cherokee subagent in Tennessee, the United States government sought to encourage the Cherokees under the leadership of John Jolly to join their brothers who had already come West. Some of these "Western Cherokees" had migrated as early as 1782, when they received permission from Don Estevon Miro, governor of Louisiana, to locate in the Spanish territory west of the Mississippi. There were records of the success of the "Cheraquis" Indians over a group of miners at Mine de Mota [Mine La Motte] Missouri, in 1775; and "The Bowl" came West after an encounter between the Cherokees and a group of whites in 1794. The Indian chiefs "Dutch," Tallantusky, and Doublehead were located in the West when Houston became subagent in 1818, and the government thought that Jolly would leave the Hiwassee country for new lands.[28]

Thomas Jefferson had suggested as early as 1803 that all Southern Indians be moved west of the Mississippi, and in 1809 a delegation of Indians had visited these Western lands. General Andrew Jackson pushed the plan and in 1816 announced that all of the Cherokees would soon offer to move West.[29]

When the offer did not come, General Jackson suggested to Secretary of War John C. Calhoun that a young officer of his acquaintance who had lived with the Cherokees and spoke their language be ap-

[27] Lester, *Authentic Memoir,* pp. 51–63.

[28] Starr, *An Early History of the Cherokees,* p. 114–125.

[29] Annie H. Abel, "The History of Events Resulting in Indian Consolidation West of the Mississippi," in *Annual Report of the American Historical Association for the Year 1906,* I, 241, 245–249, 276–295.

pointed their subagent.[30] Houston was appointed on October 21, 1817, with most of his assignments devoted to encouraging the Indians to move westward. This was not a betrayal of his Indian friends, who were themselves eager to leave Tennessee and be free from the influence of the white man. This white encroachment threatened their way of life, and to them removal from their homes seemed inevitable.[31]

Although Houston did not sign the removal treaty, he conducted most of the affairs connected with the removal. This treaty, which was signed in 1817, was considerably more favorable than the removal treaties ratified when the largest portion of the Cherokees were forced from their homes. The treaty of 1818 provided for the selection in equal amounts of suitable land in Arkansas in exchange for Indian land in Tennessee; payment for all improvements to land and real estate; reservation of all head rights; compensation in rifles, guns, ammunition, traps, and household goods; and free navigation of waters in the new country.[32]

In December of 1817, Houston went to Lookout Mountain, ". . . in consequence of the Arkansas delegation having arrived" to go to Washington, and accompanied them on the trip.[33] There he appeared in the native Indian costume of the Cherokees and so angered John C. Calhoun that he sought Houston's dismissal.[34] Houston, however, remained in complete charge of this delegation, which came to Washington to implement the removal treaty of 1817. During the Cherokee

[30] See John P. Brown, *Old Frontiers,* pp. 463–477. Jackson later recommended Houston "as a proper person to fill the appointment of Agent for the Cherokees on the Arkansas," but he "declined acceptance to the office." AJ to John C. Calhoun, January 17, 1820, Cherokee West. Removal Papers, GFT, GRL.

[31] The Cherokee historian Emmett Starr has written the best account of the attitude of the "Old Settlor" or Western Cherokee in his *Early History of the Cherokees,* pp. 114–179, and *Cherokee "West" 1794–1839,* pp. 9–22.

[32] Charles Keppler (ed.), *Indian Affairs, Laws and Treaties,* II, 140–144, 177–181; Cherokee Nation, *Treaties between the United States of America and the Cherokee Nation from 1785,* pp. 41–50. The 1817 treaty was signed by Major General Andrew Jackson, Joseph McMinn, who was Governor of Tennessee, and the "Chiefs and Headmen of the Cherokees on the Arkansas," John Rogers and John D. Chisholm.

[33] J. McMinn to John Calhoun, November 24, 1817, OFN, OIA.

[34] Marion Karl Wisehart, *Sam Houston: American Giant,* p. 22–24; Margaret Coit, *John C. Calhoun,* p. 122.

visit in Washington, Calhoun wrote to McMinn that the department worked with much zeal to assure execution of "the late treaty which contains stipulations so important to Tennessee and the rest of the Union."[35]

McMinn and Calhoun were convinced that the wisest Indian policy to assure performance of the treaty was "bribery" of the leaders of the delegation. The Indians were each given "very considerable presents." Tallantusky, the leader, was given one thousand dollars, and each of the others were given five hundred dollars. That these were bribes is unmistakably apparent from Calhoun's statement that "this will no doubt have important effects in aiding preparations now going on."[36] Whether Houston approved of the bribery is unknown, but Governor McMinn defended it as the only sound Indian policy.[37]

The wisdom of the early removal policy which had brought these Cherokees to the Western territory is shown by contrasting the "Trail of Tears," by which in 1838 the major body of the tribe was forced from the Southern states, with these Western removals of 1817 and 1818. The early Cherokee removal advocated by Houston involved no forced march, and little starvation and suffering; these were well-organized, well-managed, and orderly trips by river boat. The suffering of the "Trail of Tears" and the futility of the policy of resistance which was advocated by John Ross are well known. These were brutal experiences of forced marches, starvation, and agonizing death.[38]

Captain John Rogers was one of the first of the group of Cherokees to leave for Arkansas. Thirty-one were in his party when it left Knoxville in October of 1817, and they all arrived safely in Arkansas by April of 1818. Governor McMinn wrote the secretary of war that "Rogers, a white man of more than forty years residence in the Chero-

[35] John Calhoun to J. McMinn, March 1818, OFN, OIA.

[36] Brown, *Old Frontiers,* pp. 476–477; Charles C. Royce, "The Cherokee Nation of Indians," *Fifth Annual Report,* Smithsonian Institution, pp. 209–223.

[37] McMinn wrote, "I am truly pleased to learn that the usual plans have been taken with the chiefs in purchasing their friendship, for such has been the course pursued with the natives from time immemorial, and corrupt as it may seem, we are compelled to such measures." Cited in Brown, *Old Frontiers,* p. 477.

[38] For more information on this period see Grant Foreman, *Indian Removal: The Emigration of the Five Civilized Tribes of Indians,* pp. 229–312.

kee Nation had removed to Arkansas with a very numerous tribe of connections."[39] Rogers was furnished with boats and provisions for the trip, but in 1821 was still making demands for payment of $171.08 for his expenses "for bringing 31 emigrants, 182 days at 94 cents per day for provisions."[40]

While Houston was subagent in Tennessee, John Jolly left for the Arkansas region with a party consisting of sixteen boats of Cherokees and their possessions. The agency estimated their needs and gave them rations for seventy days, in addition to providing boats, which remained the property of the United States. Of the 333 under Jolly's care, 108 were warriors, who had each been supplied with a new rifle under the provisions of the treaty of 1817. The agency estimated that this group, which left on February 7 and 16, consisted of "almost the whole of the Cherokees from this section" and that it was expected that "more would join" as they "passed through the Cherokee River Settlements."[41]

Once settled in Arkansas, the Cherokees tried to recapture the life they had known before the white man came to America. They soon learned that conditions had changed. Their new homes in Arkansas were different from their old ones in Tennessee. The United States had placed them on the historic hunting grounds of the savage Osage and Quapaw Indians.[42] The Cherokees, who had almost forgotten how to fight, were forced into open warfare with these savage tribes, and the United States was forced to open Cantonment Gibson to protect the Cherokees. White men were all around the Cherokees and pushing constantly westward through their new land. The peace and happiness which they had been promised was not found in Arkansas.[43]

[39] J. McMinn to John Calhoun, February 19, 1818, OFN, OIA, Oklahoma Historical Society.

[40] J. McMinn to John Calhoun, November 11, 1817, OFN, OIA; Power of Attorney, John Rogers to James Rogers, March 22, 1821, Captain John Rogers Papers, GFT, GRL.

[41] R. J. Meigs to John Calhoun, February 19, 1818, OFN, OIA.

[42] The missionary accounts of the hunting habits and savage nature of the Osages clearly show the problems faced by the Cherokees. See "Osages," *The Missionary Herald,* XXV (April, 1829), 123–126.

[43] Lonnie J. White, "Arkansas Territorial Indian Affairs," *The Arkansas Historical Quarterly,* XXI (Autumn, 1962), 193–212.

The hostilities with the Osages and the constant encroachment of white men living in Arkansas compelled the Cherokees to move into what is today the state of Oklahoma.[44] Having twice been forced from their homes and the graves of their loved ones, the Cherokees were determined that they would never be driven from this land.[45]

In short, Houston's Indian brothers were a dissimilar tribe composed of mixed and full bloods who, while they differed in education and in economic levels, were more decidedly Indian than white. Even the planter element, which enjoyed the advantages of the gracious, cultured ante-bellum life, followed the ancient Cherokee religious celebrations and openly made warfare upon their Osage enemies. These paradoxical Western Cherokees were more civilized than any Indian tribe and yet more savage than any white man. They were fearful of white encroachment and equally unwilling to have the Cherokees who remained in Georgia and Tennessee come into their nation. They were a people who were running from the white man but who had run as far as they could.

[44] See Ina Gabler, "Lovely's Purchase and Lovely County," *The Arkansas Historical Quarterly,* XIX (Spring, 1960), 31–32.

[45] John Jolly to Great Father [Andrew Jackson], December 3, 1829, Letters Written for John Jolly, GFT, GRL.

3. Sam Houston: Cherokee Citizen

> In consideration of . . . [Houston's] former . . . Services . . . to the Indians, and his present disposition, to improve their condition . . . we . . . grant to him for ever all the rights, privileges, and Immunities of a citizen of the Cherokee Nation . . . as tho he was a native Cherokee . . .
>
> Houston's Certificate of Citizenship in the Cherokee Nation, October 21, 1829, *Writings,* I, 143–144

Citizenship in the Cherokee Nation was the most important single factor in the relationship between the Indian tribes and Sam Houston. The game of "power politics" which Houston played rested upon the fact that he was a Cherokee citizen. His trading activities, ambassadorial duties, and even his marital status revolved around Indian citizenship.

During his boyhood years Houston became a "blood brother" of the Cherokee tribe.[1] However, Houston's claim to Cherokee citizenship did not rest on these early years, for as a boy Houston did not renounce his United States citizenship but only visited his Indian friends. He fought with his Indian brothers in the War of 1812 as a soldier of the United States, and later served as a representative of the United States to the Cherokee as subagent. The oaths of office as a United States congressman and a governor of Tennessee both required citizenship in the United States. His claim to the rights and privileges of a Cherokee citizen extended only from 1829 and his resignation as governor of Tennessee. Houston not only resigned "the office of chief magistrate" but also dissolved "the political connection which has so

[1] C. Edwards Lester, *The Life of Sam Houston: The Only Authentic Memoir of Him Ever Published,* p. 22.

long in such a variety of forms existed between the people of Tennessee and myself."[2]

Even before he had reached the Indian country Houston was considering resigning his United States citizenship and therefore wrote to Andrew Jackson that he was an "exile." "What am I?" Houston asked. "An exile from my home; and my country, a houseless unshelter'd wanderer, among the Indians. . . . I will love my country; and my friends."[3]

At the moment of Houston's arrival, John Jolly again took him into the tribe. The chief, according to stories, grasped him in his arms and said, "My wigwam is yours—my home is yours—my people are yours—rest with us."[4] Less than six months after his arrival Houston was formally adopted as a Cherokee. A committee appointed by John Jolly considered the contributions which he had made to the Cherokees, as well as his plans for their improvement, and on October 21, 1829, passed a resolution admitting Sam Houston to Cherokee citizenship:[5]

> Whereas an order has been published by the agent of the Cherokee Nation requiring all white men who reside in the Nation without the consent of the Chiefs of the said Nation to comply with certain rules and regulations set forth in Said *order* Now be it know by these presents, that Genl. Samuel Houston, late of the State of Tennessee, has been residing in the Nation for Some time past, and has manifested a disposition to remain with us. In consideration of his former acquaintance with and Services rendered to the Indians, and his present disposition to improve their condition and benefit their scircumstances [*sic*], and our confidence in his integrity, and talents, if he Should remain among us; we do as a committee appointed by order of the principal chief John Jolly; Solemnly, firmly, and unrecovable [*sic*] grant to him for ever all the rights, privileges, and Immunities of a citizen of the Cherokee Nation and do as fully impower him with all rights and liberties as tho he was a native Cherokee, while at the Same time the Said Houston will be required to yield obedience to all laws and regulations made for the government of the Native Citizens of the Cherokee Nation.

[2] Sam Houston, *The Writings of Sam Houston,* Amelia W. Williams and Eugene C. Barker (eds.), I, 12, 26, 131–132.

[3] SH to AJ, May 29, 1829, Houston, *Writings,* I, 133–134.

[4] Lester, *Authentic Memoir,* p. 51.

[5] "Certificate of Citizenship in the Cherokee Nation," Houston, *Writings,* I, 143–144.

In Witness whereof, we have this day Set our hands this 21st day of October 1829
Cherokee Nation

his
Illenois [*sic*] Walter X Webber President Comte
mark
Aaron Price vice
his
Jno Brown [*sic*]) John X Jolly Chief principal
) mark
Nation Com[tee])

[Endorsed]: Admission letter from the Cherokee Chiefs to Houston 21st Oct. 1829.

The procedure followed in conferring citizenship was invalid because the act was never approved by Council, and because the chief was himself a party to the resolution. To correct any possible legal defects in the resolution, on October 31, 1831, Houston was again adopted into the Cherokee tribe. This act was signed by the same parties, but passed by the National Committee and Council and approved by John Jolly as chief:[6]

Resolved by the National Committee and Council in General Council Convened, That in consideration of his former acquaintance with, and services rendered to the Cherokees and his present disposition to improve their condition and benefit their circumstances, and our confidence in his integrity and honor, if he should remain among us, we do solemnly, firmly, and irrevocably grant to Samuel Houston forever, all the rights, privileges, and immunities of a citizen of the Cherokee Nation.

Walter Webber,
President of Committee
William Thornton,
Clerk of Committee
Aaron Price,
Speaker of Council
John Brown,
Clerk of Council

Tah-lon-tee-skee, October 31, 1831

Approved—John Jolly

[6] Emmett Starr, *An Early History of the Cherokees*, pp. 156–157.

A controversy over Houston's citizenship began in the summer of 1830 when the goods for a proposed trading establishment began to arrive. Houston, as an adopted citizen of the Cherokee Nation, claimed the same rights to trade which had always been granted to the native merchants. Such prosperous traders as John Drew and Walter Webber were Cherokees by blood and were neither required to obtain a license to trade nor regulated by the Intercourse Acts. Houston outlined his position in a letter to Commandant Matthew Arbuckle:

My situation is peculiar and for that reason, I will take pains to obviate any difficulty arising from a supposed violation of the intercourse laws. I am a citizen of the Cherokee Nation, and as such, I do contend that the intercourse laws have no other bearing upon me, or my circumstances, than they would have upon any native born Cherokee! As I exercise all the rights, which any-one is enabled to do! The letter of my adoption, and the evidence of my citizenship I have the honor of enclosing to you![7]

Within two days this letter was forwarded by Arbuckle to the secretary of war with a strong recommendation that Houston be required to obtain a license to trade. The General threatened to seize all of Houston's goods unless a pledge was given that when the new Cherokee agent arrived Houston would obtain a license. The pledge was made, but Arbuckle concluded, ". . . it is obvious that he expects his rights to trade with the Indians will thereafter [when the agent arrived] be greatly relieved from that trouble."[8]

Arbuckle was certain that Houston could not "absolve himself from his allegiance to the United States, by becoming a citizen of the Cherokee Nation." But an opinion was requested because of threats which the politically powerful Houston had made against Arbuckle and the fear that a newspaper controversy, similar to one in the *Arkansas Gazette* in which Houston was involved, might result and that all that Houston had "done in this country to which exception could be taken" would be brought "before the public."[9]

Houston's right to operate without a trader's license was quickly denied by G. P. Randolph, the acting secretary of war. If Houston's

[7] SH to MA, July 21, 1830, Houston, *Writings,* I, 185–187.
[8] MA to Randolph, July 23, 1830, Matthew Arbuckle Papers, GFT, GRL.
[9] MA to Randolph, July 23, 1830.

argument was to be accepted, the entire trade regulations system with the Indians would be destroyed, because a trader could escape regulation by becoming an Indian citizen. "An Indian tribe did not have the right to confer on such citizens any privileges incompatible with the law of the United States."[10]

Randolph was acting upon the advice of the Office of the Attorney General, which rendered an opinion on "Whether a citizen of the United States by entering an Indian territory . . . and becoming one of them by adoption, can claim to be exempt from the laws of the United States which regulate intercourse with them?" The opinion, issued by Attorney General John MacPherson Berrien, was published on December 21, 1830, and dealt directly with Sam Houston, "a citizen of the United States having established himself in the Cherokee nation, and been adopted by them, [who] claims the privilege of trading in that nation without a license from the agent of this government."[11]

The Attorney General concluded that:

> . . . a citizen of the United States cannot divest himself of his allegiance to this government, so long as he remains within the limits of its sovereignty . . . that nothing can be more clear than that a citizen of the United States cannot, by establishing himself with the limits of this tribe, and incorporating himself within it, by whatever form, withdraw from the operation of the laws of the United States. I think, that it is only as a citizen of the United States . . . that the individual [Sam Houston] whose case has given rise to your inquiry can take license to trade.[12]

Despite his protestations to Colonel Arbuckle that "I am a citizen of the Cherokee Nation," Houston was ready to exercise the rights of a United States citizen when they were to his advantage. When he left for Texas to visit with the Indian tribes, Houston carried a passport dated August 6, 1832, issued by Acting Secretary of War John

[10] Randolph to MA, Matthew Arbuckle Papers, GFT, GRL.

[11] Opinion, Attorney General John MacPherson Berrien to Secretary of War, December 21, 1830, in Benjamin F. Hall (comp.), *Official Opinions of the Attorneys General of the United States Advising the President and Heads of Departments in Relation to Their Official Duties; and Expounding the Constitution, Subsisting Treaties with Foreign Governments and with Indian Tribes, and the Public Laws of the Country,* I, 404–405.

[12] Hall, *Official Opinions of the Attorneys General,* I, 404–405.

Robb to "General Sam Houston . . . a citizen of the United States."[13]

In an ironic bit of nineteenth-century oratory, Houston adopted the arguments of Secretary of War Randolph and Attorney General Berrien when he appeared before the House of Representatives charged with assault of Representative Stanbery of Ohio. He began by stating that he appeared "for the first time in my life on a charge of violating the laws of my country." And he concluded:

> American citizen! It is a sacred name! Its sanctity attaches itself alike to his person, whether he journeys over the scorching sands of Florida or wanders in the deepest forests of our Northern frontier; throughout the republic, or in his native State; in the bosom of civilization, or in the wildness of savage life: still he is an American citizen.[14]

Houston was not the only person in the Indian country seeking the advantages of both United States and Cherokee citizenship. The problem was so serious, especially with the white men intermarried into the Cherokee Nation, that it threatened the entire federal Indian policy and endangered tribal government. Elbert Herring, commissioner of Indian affairs, began considering a new system of Indian law after George Vashon wrote him that:

> The whites who are intermarried with the Indians seem to consider themselves thereby exempt from the operation of the laws of [the] United States until the Indian law is attempted to be enforced against them for some misdemeanor, and then they seek the legal protection due to United States Citizens in shielding them from the operation of the Indian Law.[15]

An interesting sequel to the conflict of Cherokee–United States citizenship could have been written if Houston had returned to Tennessee and run for Governor as he often suggested that he might.[16]

[13] Passport, SH, August 6, 1832, Houston, *Writings*, IV, 11; Marion Karl Wisehart, *Sam Houston: American Giant*, pp. 82–83. See also "Application for Headrights in Austin's Colony," December 24, 1832, Houston, *Writings*, I, 271–272.

[14] "Houston's Defense in the Stanbery Case," May 7, 1832, Houston, *Writings*, I, 207–226.

[15] Vashon to Herring, October 12, 1833, in "Cherokee Agency, West," Letters Received by the Office of Indian Affairs. Microfilm Publications, Microcopy No. 234, Roll No. 78, The National Archives of the United States.

[16] SH to Major William B. Lewis, May 20, 1830, Houston, *Writings*, I, 151–152; SH to John R. Houston, December 2, 1832, VI, 1–2.

Houston went to Texas, however, and became a citizen of Mexico and then the Republic of Texas, regaining his United States citizenship only by the Texas Admissions Act.

That Houston's Cherokee citizenship was deeper to him than the advantages which came to him as a trader is shown by the fact that he actively entered into the business of his Nation. As a council leader, interpreter, peacemaker, and ambassador he "exercise[d] all the rights which anyone is enabled to do."[17] The letters of merchants, agents, soldiers, and Cherokees themselves show that Houston's interest and participation in the affairs of the Nation was as a Cherokee citizen, not an outside advisor.

It is alleged that Houston became the most influential man in the Cherokee Nation.[18] This may be true, but it was the unusual influence of a man with special knowledge and talent. This position as a Cherokee citizen who understood the white man and knew the "Great Father" appears in John Jolly's letters which Houston carried to Washington and presented to his friend President Jackson.[19]

By an act of the National Committee and Council all Cherokees were entitled to seek a position on the National Council, which governed the affairs of the tribe. The Cherokee government in the West was organized in 1824 into four districts, with two persons elected to serve from each district on the National Council for one year. This group met with the General Council and constituted the legislative branch of the Cherokee Nation.[20] As an adopted citizen, Houston placed his name in nomination during the spring of 1831. Houston's defeat in this race for elective office in the Cherokee Nation probably demonstrates the "native jealousy of the members of an alien race which is characteristic of the Indian." The defeat was such a shock that, according to the *Cherokee Phoenix,* Houston considered abandoning his Indian wife and moving to the Choctaw Nation.[21]

[17] SH to MA, July 23, 1830, Matthew Arbuckle Papers, GFT, GRL.

[18] Sam Houston, *The Autobiography of Sam Houston,* Donald Day and Harry Herbert Ullom (eds.), p. 52.

[19] John Jolly to Great Father [Andrew Jackson], December 3, 1829, Letters Written for John Jolly, GFT, GRL.

[20] Morris L. Wardell, *A Political History of the Cherokee Nation, 1838–1907,* p. 6.

[21] *Cherokee Phoenix,* May 28, 1831, p. 2, col. 4; Alfred M. Williams, "Hous-

Knowing that the Cherokees did not trust white men and wanting to become as much like his Indian brothers as possible, Houston adopted all of the manners of the Cherokees. He is said to have refused to speak English during his stay in the Cherokee Nation and to have used an interpreter upon occasion when he talked with other white men.[22] In fact, Judge W. S. Oldham, who had known Houston in Tennessee, was a judge in Arkansas and visited Fort Gibson, where "he saw him [Houston] dressed like a Cherokee." Judge Oldham reported that Houston "would never then speak English to anyone and a deep melancholy caused him to avoid all intercourse with white men. . . . He was seen armed only with the bow and arrow with which he had become dexterous when a boy."[23]

Houston, however, may have tired of his Indian costume while visiting his old friends in the national capital. The *Cherokee Phoenix* reported on his visit in 1830 and concluded: "It is stated that Governor Houston, who, as has been mentioned, is now at Washington, has abandoned entirely assumption of the Indian costume and habits, and mingles in social intercourse and gaiety as freely as formerly."[24]

Houston did begin to wear the Cherokee-style turban, which he continued to use after the Texas Revolution and in which he was pictured by a New York cartoonist as late as 1836.[25] He so completely adopted the Indian ways that one visitor to the Cherokee Nation recorded, "Living witnesses among the Cherokees have seen the old chief [John Jolly] and Houston seated on the floor . . . by the wood trough of ka-nau-ha-na, hominy cooked to the consistency of paste . . . and feeding each other in the aboriginal fashion of friendliness with the common spoon."[26]

---

ton's Life among the Indians," *Magazine of American History,* X (November, 1883), 404.

[22] *Cherokee Advocate,* November 25, 1893, p. 4, col. 1.

[23] A. W. Terrell, "Recollections of General Sam Houston," *The Southwestern Historical Quarterly,* XVI (October, 1912), 118.

[24] *Cherokee Phoenix,* March 4, 1830, p. 3, col. 2.

[25] A cartoon drawn by H. R. Robinson and published in New York in 1836 shows Houston in his turban costume with Santa Anna bowing before him. A copy of this print, entitled "Gen. Houston, Santa Anna, and Co.," is printed following page 82 in Llerena B. Friend, *Sam Houston: The Great Designer.*

[26] Williams, "Houston's Life among the Indians," p. 403.

On occasions of state Houston is said to have "arrayed himself with the best." While visiting in Washington, Houston had a miniature painted of himself in his formal Indian attire which was the "Oriental style" adopted by a number of Cherokees.[27] On other occasions:

> . . . he has been described as wearing, in full dress, a white hunting-shirt brilliantly embroidered, yellow leggings and moccasions elaborately worked with beads, and a circlet of turkey feathers for his head. He let his hair grow and braided it in a long queue, which hung down his back, and wore his beard upon his chin in a "goatee," shaving the rest of his face.[28]

The Indians considered Houston's costumes to be almost theatrical and are said to have arranged a trick to show him the humor of his "dignity and splendor." At one council meeting a negro slave was dressed in Houston's theatrical style and placed behind him to imitate his pose and manner. The council was delighted and Houston seemed to view this imitation with shrewd indifference.[29]

Nevertheless, the Cherokees considered Houston a Cherokee citizen. Today in the old Cherokee country the stories of Sam Houston's visit are told and retold.[30] That Houston was a Cherokee citizen none doubt, and that he was loved and respected is almost the universal story. That Houston is remembered is obvious from the names of many prominent Cherokees—Sam Houston Benge, Houston Shaw, Samuel Houston Smith, and Samuel Houston Mayes.[31] The *Cherokee Advocate*, official newspaper of the Cherokee Nation, proudly reported that Sam Houston "lived with the Cherokees as their chief."[32]

Houston never forgot his friendship with the Cherokees. As presi-

[27] The miniature was painted of Houston at Brown's Hotel in Washington and is reproduced in this volume. The "Oriental influence" can be seen in pictures of early Cherokee Chiefs, such as Attackullocullla, who visited England with Sir Alexander Cummings. Sequoyah is generally pictured in a turban.

[28] Williams, "Houston's Life among the Indians," p. 403.

[29] Williams, "Houston's Life among the Indians," p. 403.

[30] The best collection of these tales is found in the "Indian-Pioneer Papers." Typescripts of Interviews of the Works Progress Administration. 116 vols. OIA, PC, UOL. The authors found their interviews with old settlers and their descendants interesting in that each person seemed to have a different tale of Houston's life in the Cherokee Nation.

[31] See generally the genealogical tables in Emmett Starr, *History of the Cherokee Indians,* pp. 303–446.

[32] *Cherokee Advocate,* November 25, 1893, p. 4, col. 1.

dent of the Republic of Texas and later as a United States senator he championed the cause of justice for the American Indian.[33] Houston is said to have remembered his days as a citizen of the Cherokee Nation with nostalgia. Charles Edward Lester who wrote the *Authentic Memoir* captured this feeling. "Houston . . . has been heard to say that when he looks back . . . there's nothing half so sweet to remember as this sojourn he had among the untutored children of the forest."[34]

[33] See "Speeches on Indian Policy," Houston, *Writings,* VI, 111–156, 487–501; "Remarks on Indian Appropriations Bill," V, 155–161; "Speeches on Boundary of Texas," V, 29–37; "Lecture on Trials and Dangers of Frontier," V, 267–281; 341–349; 349–354; 397–404; 428–432; 433–440.

[34] Lester, *Authentic Memoir,* pp. 13–23, 62, 384–386.

4. The Legend of Talihina

> He took an Indian girl to wife and lived with her quite happily. . . . Very little, however, is known of her life with Houston.
>
> Lyndon Orr, *Famous Affinities of History,* III, 19

Whether from need of comfort and reassurance, from fear and anxiety over his manliness created by the rejection of his first wife, or from sheer physical lust, Sam Houston "took an Indian girl." The relationship was so open that Houston was called the "Squaw Man" by his enemies and labeled a man so low that his only company was a savage—an Indian squaw. The picture conveyed by these openly partisan attacks in newspapers and magazines was that of the former governor of Tennessee living at the lowest depths of humanity with a filthy Indian squaw.[1]

This is a picture so black that many historians have strongly denied the existence of an Indian woman, while others, who because of historical accuracy refuse to deny her existence, asserted that there was "no instance of quite so conspicuous an abandonment of . . . honor."[2] There is no mention of this woman in Houston's official biography, *The Authentic Memoir*, or in early biographies, such as William Crane's *Life and Select Literary Remains of Sam Houston of Texas.*[3] Even today many Texans refuse to acknowledge her or discuss this

[1] Alfred M. Williams, *Sam Houston and the War of Independence in Texas,* p. 51; also see Alfred M. Williams, "Houston's Life among the Indians," *Magazine of American History,* X (November, 1883), 406–408. An open attack was made by Tekatoka in *The Arkansas Gazette* (*Supplement*), October 20, 1830.

[2] Williams, "Houston's Life among the Indians," p. 401.

[3] C. Edwards Lester, *The Life of Sam Houston: The Only Authentic Memoir of Him Ever Published*; William Carey Crane, *Life and Select Literary Remains of Sam Houston of Texas,* pp. 9–266.

"blemish," "scandal," or "blasphemy" on the name of the liberator of Texas.[4]

The fact that Houston lived with an Indian woman is unmistakably documented in the archives of the Bureau of Indian Affairs and the old War Department.[5] The story has been told so often, however, that the legend and the fact have become almost one. The only fact which is certain is that she was not a "Squaw Woman," the savage pictured by Houston's enemies.

She was a tall and beautiful woman, the daughter of Captain John Rogers, one of the most prominent white men in the Cherokee Nation.[6] Far from being an Indian squaw, she could more accurately be described as a "white woman" because she was less than a quarter Cherokee Indian, probably closer to "one-sixteenth Cherokee and fifteen-sixteenths Scotch and English."[7] Her mother was the part-Cherokee sister of two prominent Cherokee chiefs.[8] While there are no pictures of her, Amos Williams came to Indian Territory and recorded descriptions which he published in an early magazine article. She was, according to those who knew her, "a half-breed [she was considerably less than half Cherokee], of great personal beauty, and as tall and stately for her sex as Houston himself."[9]

[4] The authors were warned when they began the book that Houston's Indian wife was not accepted in many circles and that they would receive little co-operation from certain individuals. Discussions with some have become so heated that physical violence seemed almost imminent. Because of the openly partisan feelings toward an Indian wife most of this material was gathered from older printed sources. The interviews which were taken proved clearly that the stories of Houston's Indian wife have become legends, expanded with each telling.

[5] Grant Foreman, "Some New Light on Houston's Life among the Cherokee Indians," *The Chronicles of Oklahoma,* IX (June, 1931), 148–152.

[6] See generally Jessie Dawson Blackwell, *Families of Samuel Dawson and Polly Ann Rogers,* pp. 16–19; Emmett Starr, *History of the Cherokee Indians,* pp. 305–307, 466–476 (notes A1, A5, A6, A7, A41); Narcissa Owen, *Memoirs of Narcissa Owen, 1831–1907,* pp. 100–101.

[7] Emmett Starr, *Cherokee "West" 1794–1839,* pp. 142, 143.

[8] Starr, *History of the Cherokee Indians,* pp. 305, 307.

[9] Williams, "Houston's Life among the Indians," p. 406. Travelers in the Cherokee country made similar observations of Cherokee women. William Bartram noted that "the women of the Cherokees are tall, slender, erect, and of a delicate frame, their features formed with perfect symmetry, their countenance cheerful and friendly and they move with a becoming grace and

The mystery and legend surrounding her extend even to the name by which she is known. She has been called by many names—Talhina,[10] Talihina,[11] Tallahina,[12] Talihena,[13] Tahlihina,[14] Titania,[15] Talhina,[16] Talahina,[17] Tyania,[18] Tenia,[19] Tiana,[20] Teeanna,[21] Tyenia,[22] Diana,[23] and Dianna.[24] Her name was actually Diana (or Dianna) Rogers, but she may have been known among the Cherokees as Tiana Rogers.[25]

---

dignity." William Bartram, *Travels through North and South Carolina, Georgia, East and West Florida, the Cherokee Country, the Extensive Territories of the Muscogules, or Creek Confederacy, and the Country of the Choctaws; Containing an Account of Those Regions, Together with Observations on the Manners of the Indians, 1791,* p. 484.

[10] "Tragic Romance of General Sam Houston and Talhina Rogers," *The American Indian,* IV, No. 9 (June 30, 1930), 10.

[11] Thomas Nuttall, *A Journal of Travels into the Arkansas Territory during the Year 1819, with Occasional Observations on the Manners of the Aborigines,* p. 190. Sarah Barnwell Elliott, *Sam Houston,* p. 17; "Indian-Pioneer Papers," Typescripts of Interviews of the Works Progress Administration, Vol. 57, p. 507, OIA, PC, UOL.

[12] George Creel, *Sam Houston: Colossus in Buckskin,* p. 41.

[13] Owen, *Memoirs,* p. 100.

[14] *Fort Gibson Post,* October 15, 1904.

[15] Mabel Washburn Anderson, "Old Fort Gibson on the Grand," *Twin Territories Magazine,* IV, No. 9 (September, 1902), 253.

[16] William Weaver Scrapbook. Microfilm Division, University of Arkansas Library, Fayetteville.

[17] John M. Oskison, *A Texas Titan,* p. 135. *Muskogee Daily Phoenix,* May 30, 1926.

[18] Lyndon Orr, *Famous Affinities of History,* III, 19.

[19] Sam Houston, Selected Letter and Typescripts, OBF, ORL.

[20] Paul I. Wellman, *Magnificent Destiny,* p. 303.

[21] N.A., *Old Fort Gibson,* 7. A copy of this rare little book may be found in IA.

[22] Williams, "Houston's Life among the Indians," p. 406. Also see notes in OFN, OIA.

[23] G. Foreman, "Some New Light," pp. 149–151. Note especially, "Power of Attorney," Diana Gentry to Saml. Houston, June 27, 1833; "Bill of Sale," Diana McGrady to Samuel D. McGrady, August 24, 1836, which are reprinted by Foreman.

[24] G. Foreman, "Some New Light," pp. 149–152. Contrast "Affidavit," Joseph Rogers for Sale of negro slaves "unto my sister Dianna Houston," November 20, 1834, and Gov. M. Stokes, "Report for the decision of the Dept. on a claim of Saml. D. McGrady," November 7, 1836, with the other documents Foreman gathers.

[25] Grant Foreman and Carolyn Thomas Foreman were convinced that her

The name as it appears in the official documents found in the War Department and the Bureau of Indian Affairs is spelled both "Diana" and "Dianna" Rogers. There is a family tradition that the name "Diana" was selected because as a baby Diana was as beautiful as the Greek goddess of the moon and the hunt.[26] But Houston is said to have known her as "Hina."[27]

The many variations of Diana's name are the result of the colorful imaginations of creative historians and the difficulty of the Cherokees in pronouncing the *d* in Diana.[28] The name which appears on the tombstone in the National Cemetery at Fort Gibson is "Talahina."[29] The most popular name, "Talihina," was created in the 1890's by a Tahlequah newspaperman, who, having heard the legends of Houston's Indian wife, went into the hills and interviewed Cherokees to learn the truth behind the legends. He was never able to understand the varied Cherokee pronunciations of Diana and, not being familiar with the language, selected a word which seemed as near as possible to what he heard pronounced.[30] He selected the name Talihina, which is not a Cherokee word but is like the Choctaw word (Talihina) which means "iron road" or "railroad."[31] "It is a sad commentary on the historian's

---

name was Diana, although Grant Foreman has spelled it "Diana" and "Dianna." In his early articles she is called "Tiana" or "Talihina." Carolyn Thomas Foreman, Interview, July 3, 1964. See also *Muskogee Daily Phoenix,* September 29, 1935.

[26] Grant Foreman to D. C. Roberts, July 24, 1934, Grant Foreman Letters, "Arkansas File Box," OIA.

[27] Sam purportedly called her "Hina." Oskison, *Texas Titan,* p. 135. This is supported generally by Mrs. Gail Ward, Interview, July 23, 1964.

[28] Carolyn Thomas Foreman, Interview, July 3, 1964; Jim Lucas, "Fort Gibson Grave Recalls Romance of Houston and Cherokee Maid," *Muskogee Daily Phoenix,* September 29, 1935.

[29] But the name "Tiana" was selected by Marquis James for his Pulitizer Prize winning biography, *The Raven: A Biography of Sam Houston,* pp. 150–152. Phil Harris, "Houston's Life with Cherokees," *Muskogee Daily Phoenix,* February 21, 1965.

[30] W. P. Campbell, "Sam Houston in Indian Territory," *Historical Quarterly,* VIII (July, 1919), 3–4, and (October, 1919), 6–8.

[31] Charles N. Gould, *Oklahoma Place Names,* p. 105; "Report of the Annual Meeting of the Oklahoma Historical Society," *The Chronicles of Oklahoma,* XXII (June, 1934), 127. But see the meaning given by Cyrus Byington, *A Dictionary of the Choctaw Language,* Smithsonian Institution, Bureau of American Ethnology, Bulletin 46, pp. 336–358, 482, 531.

understanding of Indian languages that such a beautiful woman has come to be known by the name 'railroad'."[32]

Another legend without foundation concerns the naming of the town of Talihana, Oklahoma. The legend is found in an interview in the "Indian and Pioneer Papers" compiled by the Works Progress Administration:

> Sam Houston visited the Cherokee people at Webbers Falls and courted and married a young Cherokee girl, according to Cherokee custom. They started South to Texas via Stigler. His young wife grieved over leaving her people or her tribe, sickened and died in the Choctaw Nation and the town of Talihana now stands as a monument to her grave.[33]

There is a persistent belief among the full-blood and old-settlers group of the Cherokees that Sam Houston married Diana Rogers for power and position.[34] It is true that no woman had a more powerful position or family in the Cherokee Nation than Diana Rogers. The matriarchal Cherokee society observed by early travelers had vanished by the 1830's when Houston came to the Cherokee Nation, but Diana Rogers' importance and power came through her kinsmen.[35]

Diana Rogers was the daughter of Captain John "Hell-Fire-Jack" Rogers, a wealthy Scotch trader who had been a Tory captain in the American Revolution, had fought in the Battle of Horseshoe Bend, and later had directed Cherokee emigration to Arkansas. Her uncles were Chief John Jolly and Chief Tallantusky. Tallantusky until his death had been chief of the Western Cherokees and was succeeded by Jolly, who was at this time the most influential man in the Cherokee Nation. Her brothers—Captain John, William, and Charles Rogers—each operated profitable trading establishments and salt works. John Rogers was the official interpreter for the Cherokee Agency and destined to become Jolly's sucessor as chief. Diana's sisters and nieces were married to wealthy Cherokee merchants, such as John Drew,

[32] Muriel H. Wright, Interview, July, 1964.

[33] "Indian-Pioneer Papers," Vol. 76, p. 501, OIA, PC, UOL.

[34] This part of the legend persists and was emphasized to the authors by Oklahoma District Judge Claude Garrett, who has studied the history of Fort Gibson for almost fifty years. Claude Garrett, Interview, August 26, 1964.

[35] See note 6, this chapter.

Ignatius Chisholm, and Peter Harper.[36] She was also related to Sequoyah, whose alphabet had made him one of the most important figures in the Nation.[37] Even today, the descendants of Diana's kinsmen are among the intellectual and social leaders of their people.[38]

A popular tale is that Sam Houston and Diana Rogers loved each other in Tennessee. In the "Nation East of the Mississippi," where he lived as subagent, Houston often visited with Diana's brothers and uncles who served with him in the Creek-Cherokee Battle of Horseshoe Bend during the War of 1812. It would have been almost impossible for the two not to have known each other during these early days in Tennessee. About the nature of their relationship, there can be only speculation, supported by the Cherokee traditions.[39]

It is known that Diana Rogers was married to David Gentry before the removal from Tennessee. Gentry was a white man of considerable wealth and power who removed with the Cherokees in 1817 to the community around Dardanelle, Arkansas, where he practiced his trade of blacksmithing. According to reports of the missionaries, the blacksmiths prospered in this community, having more business than they

[36] See note 6, this chapter.

[37] John Howard Payne, author of "Home Sweet Home," who lived among the Cherokees, wrote that "the family of Gist (Sequoyah), on the Indian side (the mother's) was of high rank in the nation. Two of his uncles were men of Great Distinction—one was Tahlonteeskee." Althea Bass, "Talking Stones—John Howard Payne's Story of Sequoyah," *The Colophon,* Part Nine (1932) (article pages are not numbered). See also Samuel C. Williams, "The Father of Sequoyah: Nathaniel Gist," *The Chronicles of Oklahoma,* XV (March, 1937), 3–20. Carolyn Thomas Foreman, Interview, August 24, 1964.

[38] Three principal chiefs of the Cherokee Nation came from this family, as did dozens of representatives in both the Cherokee and Oklahoma Senate and House of Representatives. The family was especially known for fine orators and entertainers as well as sportsmen. Important families such as the Bushyheads, McSpaddens, Adairs, Vanns, Coodeys, Drews, Gulagers, Martins, Fields, Wests, Foremans, and Hickses are related to this Rogers clan. W. C. Rogers, last chief of the Cherokee Nation, was a collateral of Diana Rogers. Will Rogers was a cousin by three generations. Television and motion-picture actor Clu Gulager is one of these kinsmen. Sequoyah Rogers is one of the few men in America who can yet "make a gun from scratch."

[39] This story is found in most newspaper and magazine articles and is preserved as an old Cherokee legend by Judge Garrett. Claude Garrett, Interview, August 26, 1964.

could manage. The Gentrys had two daughters, but it is frequently asserted that they had no children.[40]

In one of the battles in which the "civilized" Cherokees faced the "savage" Osages, David Gentry was killed. Diana Rogers was not the only Cherokee widowed in these bloody wars, which persisted long after Fort Gibson was established and even after 1828, when the Cherokees removed from Arkansas to Oklahoma.[41]

Very little is known about Diana, "the widow Gentry." She probably visited and lived for a short time at several places in the new country. She could have stayed at her father's home or at Jolly's, which was at Tahlontuskee near Webbers Falls. One of her brothers lived near the old chieftain and also stayed at Fort Gibson at the old Cherokee Agency, where he was official interpreter. Other relatives lived in the scattered settlements within the forty- or fifty-mile radius of Fort Smith, Arkansas. Tahlontuskee, Webbers Falls, Maynard Bayou, and Chouteau's trading post formed a stright line northward. Letters, store accounts, and council records show considerable movement and visitation between these Cherokee kinsmen. Merchant John Drew regularly sold to the inhabitants of each of these communities, and John Rogers is known to have traveled regularly between them.[42]

An "X" of Diana's which appears on a power of attorney in the National Archives has stimulated a controversy over her education. The family tradition is that Diana was educated at a Moravian mission school in Tennessee before the family came to Arkansas, perhaps at Brainerd.[43] The "X" was not a universal sign of illiteracy among

[40] Emmett Starr notes that "David Gentry, a blacksmith" was married to Mary Burrington, who was Diana Rogers' aunt, and "was also the first husband of Tiana Rogers." Starr also reports that Diana and David Gentry had two children, Gabriel and Joanna Gentry, who died without having married and with no children. Starr, *History of the Cherokee Indians,* pp. 305, 307, 317, 467. See also *Muskogee Daily Phoenix,* December 27, 1931. The reports on blacksmiths are taken from Missionary Journals. Cephas Washburn Journals, OFN, OIA.

[41] The authors could find no record of Gentry's death in any reports or correspondence on the Osage wars; however, this is the universal explanation.

[42] John Drew Papers and Accounts, GRL.

[43] Sequoyah Rogers, Interview, July 18, 1964. Brainerd was operating at the time the Rogerses moved to Arkansas and was a most influential mission on the development of the Western Cherokees. That Diana was "mission edu-

the Cherokees, but more often represented the refusal of an Indian to sign his Cherokee name to a white man's document.[44] The daughter of such a prominent family would certainly have been educated at the mission schools if not by a private tutor. The Rogerses, especially old Captain John Rogers, were very interested in education; the scholarship of John Rogers, Jr., is well known, and the records of the early mission schools show the attendance of Diana's sister.[45]

In 1829 the Green Corn Dance was the most important social function in the Cherokee Nation. To the full-blood or old-settler Cherokees, these dances were the major governmental, religious, and social event of the year. The entire tribe gathered for the celebrations, which lasted many days. Thousands participated in the Indian stick-ball games and still larger numbers joined around the fires for dancing.[46] Even today, the Green Corn Dance is an important event in the life of many Cherokees.

Sam Houston knew the dance and its meaning. At this time of the year the Indians came to cleanse themselves of the wrongs of the past year by drinking a vile, bitter liquid, which caused them to expel all foreign and evil substances from their bodies. Celebrating for seven days, ". . . they would, in the first place, expunge from their bodies every vestige of all the colds and disease with which they may have been afflicted during the past winter . . . and, in the second place, they would propitiate the Great Spirit, so as to secure his blessings upon the crops which they . . . deposit in the ground."[47]

As a youth and during his term as subagent, Houston had joined in the celebration, played in the stick-ball games, and even danced

---

cated" is asserted in Jenning C. Wise, *The Red Man in the New World Drama,* p. 358.

[44] George Guess, or Sequoyah, inventor of the Cherokee alphabet, could neither read nor write English. Rather than sign his name in Cherokee, he is known to have made an "X." See "Cherokee Agency, West," Letters Received by the Office of Indian Affairs, Microfilm Publications, Copy No. 234, Roll No. 77, The National Archives of the United States.

[45] Blackwell, *Families,* p. 7; James, *Raven,* pp. 151–152.

[46] Williams, "Houston's Life among the Indians," pp. 405–406. James Mooney, "The Cherokee Ball Play," *American Anthropologist,* III (April, 1890), 105–133.

[47] Preston Skarritt, "The Green-Corn Ceremonies of the Cherokees," *National Intelligencer,* April 4, 1849.

with the Indians. He was now the resigned governor of the state of Tennessee, however, and a man of thirty-six years. Those who lived with Jolly during this period say that Houston did not join in the ball playing or dancing but simply watched with respect and reverence.[48]

It is at this dance that Houston is supposed to have seen Diana Rogers for the first time since his arrival in the Cherokee Nation. Houston unquestionably attended the dances in July of 1829 and it is almost as unquestionable that Diana would have been there. It may be that Diana Rogers Gentry stared from afar at this man whom she remembered and had read of in the papers. It may be that he asked immediately about the young girl he had loved in Tennessee. Or it may be that he admired her beauty from a distance and begged for a meeting.[49] However it was, they did meet, and whether he came to love her upon sight or married her for her position and perhaps later came to love her, Diana became Sam Houston's woman.

[48] Williams, "Houston's Life among the Indians," pp. 405–406.

[49] The stories of their meeting are so varied that the authors have listed only the most popular. Perhaps the most reliable is found in Williams, "Houston's Life among the Indians," p. 406. A more colorful presentation is found in the announcement of the American Indian Theatre Production of Ann Bradshaw Nihell's play, *The Call of the Whippoorwill.* The play is said to tell the story of Houston's "love for the beautiful young Indian maiden, Tiana Rogers . . . how they met . . . and how he laid the sacred white deer at her feet," quoted in Phil Harris, "Play On Houston Life Soon," *Muskogee Sunday Phoenix and Times Democrat,* February 14, 1965. However, the play's Dallas opening was cancelled. Some suggested the difficulty resulted from "changes in the script . . . [which] had been demanded by cast members . . . to make the play more historically authentic," *Muskogee Daily Phoenix,* March 6, 1965.

5. Diana Rogers as Mrs. Sam Houston

> William R. Houston of Dallas, Texas, a son of General Sam Houston . . . was visiting the scene of his father's Oklahoma home . . . The General's son is satisfied now that they were wed by the Cherokee law, and is ready to recognize that Talihina was his father's wife.
>
> "Sam Houston's Cherokee Wife Honored by Son," *Muskogee Times Democrat,* September 26, 1919, p. 1., col. 2

That Sam Houston and Diana Rogers were married under the customary law of the Cherokee Indians is almost universally recognized.[1] Few people realize that according to Cherokee tradition they were married by a civil ceremony, as the laws of the Cherokee Nation required for a white man to marry a Cherokee woman. "In 1830, at the home of Captain John Rogers on Spavinaw Creek now Mayes County, Oklahoma, Sam Houston and Tiana Rogers were married."[2] Tradition in the Rogers family supports this statement that they were united in such a ceremony.[3]

[1] "Sam Houston's Cherokee Wife Honored by Son," *Muskogee Times Democrat,* September 26, 1919, p. 1, col. 2. See also F. N. Boney, "The Raven Tamed," *The Southwestern Historical Quarterly,* LXVIII (July, 1964), 90–92.

[2] "He again met Diana Rogers then widow of David Gentry, in the Cherokee Nation West in 1829 and in 1830, at the home of Captain John Rogers on Spavinaw Creek now Mayes County, Oklahoma, Sam Houston and Diana Rogers were married," in "Three Forks Settlement," Sam Houston Typescript, OBF, ORL. James Carselowey, Cherokee historian of Adair, Oklahoma, has been told this story by many Cherokees. Carselowey has searched for the home but found only ruins (James Carselowey, Interview, December 23, 1964). Grant Foreman, however, noted, ". . . while their cohabitation appears to have been open and notorious, I have never found any evidence of a marriage ceremony, though their relation seems to have had the sanction of the Indians." Grant Foreman, "Some New Light on Houston's Life among the Cherokee Indians," *The Chronicles of Oklahoma,* IX (June, 1931), 148.

[3] Letters of Nan Hainey (Mrs. W. C.) Rogers, Cherokee Collection, Sequoyah Rogers, Tulsa, Oklahoma.

The problem of intermarriage of white men and Indian women had been so serious by 1830 that the National Committee and Council had passed a resolution establishing intermarriage laws.[4] Diana Rogers was only part Cherokee and marrying a white man required a civil marriage ceremony to be performed by a minister or civil authority of the Cherokee Nation.[5]

Whether this law applied to Sam Houston is a matter of considerable doubt, since it was designed to prevent white men from gaining the rights of Cherokee citizens through intermarriage, and Houston, under his "Certificate of Citizenship," had been given all the rights and privileges of a Cherokee citizen.[6] It was the general, almost universal, practice of white men living, even temporarily, in the Cherokee Nation to take an Indian wife; not, generally, "until death do us part," but during the residence of the husband in the Nation. Such marriages had been recognized as valid from the very earliest period of recorded Cherokee history.[7]

For years rumors persisted in Texas that Sam Houston was married to an Indian in the Cherokee country. Members of the Houston family had generally come to accept the fact that he lived with an Indian woman but had never been satisfied whether they had been man and wife in a legal and moral sense. Hoping to find an answer to this question, the General's son, William R. Houston, left his home in Dallas to visit the sites of his father's stay with the Cherokees.[8]

While at Fort Gibson, the sixty-four–year–old son of Sam Houston, visited with newspaperman and historian Colonel J. S. Holden, toured

[4] A. H. Murchison, "Intermarried Whites in the Cherokee Nation between the Years 1865 and 1887," *The Chronicles of Oklahoma,* VI (September, 1928), 299. The Cherokees considered their standards lowered by marriage to most whites. See *Cherokee Phoenix,* March 27, 1828.

[5] Cherokee Nation, *Laws of the Cherokee Nation Adopted at Various Times,* pp. 10, 171.

[6] "Certificate of Citizenship," October 21, 1829, Sam Houston, *The Writings of Sam Houston,* Amelia W. Williams and Eugene C. Barker (eds.), I, 143–144. Emmett Starr, *An Early History of the Cherokees,* p. 156.

[7] Albert V. Goodpasture, "The Paternity of Sequoyah," *The Chronicles of Oklahoma,* I (October, 1921), 129.

[8] The remainder of the account of William R. Houston's visit is a paraphrase of "Sam Houston's Cherokee Wife Honored by Son," *Muskogee Times Democrat,* September 26, 1919, p. 1. col. 2.

the site of Talihina's grave at Wilson's Rock, and visited the National Cemetery. He investigated the area and talked with old settlers until he was so convinced that Houston and Talihina, or Diana Rogers, had been married that he announced plans to erect a monument in her memory at the National Cemetery. A local newspaper reported that "Mr. Houston . . . recognizes that Talihina was really General Houston's wife, though they were married under the Indian custom and not by a minister."

There were two prevailing Cherokee marriage customs. The young man might seek to reward the father with gifts, which was a custom interpreted by white men as a "purchase" of the bride. In truth, this was a reward and compensation made to the father by the husband to pay him for the loss which the father felt when his daughter left him. Or by the second custom, ". . . a young couple will go out and found a homestead of their own on the mountain slopes."[9]

By 1830 both of these customs had begun dying out among mixed-blood families such as the Rogerses. Houston, however, might simply have taken Diana to his home in the frontier fashion and recognized her as his wife. This is a style of "common-law" marriage which is still recognized in Oklahoma, the state which succeeded the Cherokee Nation. In Oklahoma a common-law marriage stands on equal legal footing with a civil or church wedding. The children of these marriages are legitimate and the wife has all the rights of inheritance and support.[10]

The type of ceremony by which Sam Houston and Diana Rogers were married is immaterial. This was recognized by Houston's son, who decided to his satisfaction that they were man and wife. Diana Rogers was known and is still known by the people of the Cherokee Nation as "Mrs. Sam Houston."[11] This name was used in the official

[9] Fred Eggan (ed.), *Social Anthropology of North American Tribes,* p. 503; James Mooney, "Myths of the Cherokees," *Nineteenth Annual Report of the Smithsonian Institute,* pp. 481–482.

[10] The requirements of "common-law" marriage in the state of Oklahoma vary little from those of the Cherokees.

[11] The authors were surprised that they never talked to an individual in the Cherokee country who doubted that Sam Houston and Diana Rogers were man and wife. Diana Rogers was recognized as the wife of Sam Houston in the *Cherokee Advocate,* official newspaper of the Cherokee Nation. See *Cherokee Advocate,* November 25, 1893, p. 4, col. 1.

records of William Armstrong when he reported a controversy over a slave which had been given to Diana Rogers, and is recorded as Diana's name by her brother.[12]

Some question her right to use the name "Mrs. Houston" because Houston was not divorced from Eliza Allen until 1833. This was a marriage between two citizens of the Cherokee Nation, however, and, under the Cherokee law, after the separation from Eliza Allen there was a "divorce," since they had "split the blanket" and no longer lived as man and wife.[13]

In the eyes of the Cherokee Nation, the Rogers family, and the descendants of Houston, Sam Houston and Diana Rogers were married. Today, under the official sanction of the United States government, an Indian woman is buried in the Officers Circle of the United States National Military Cemetery at Fort Gibson, and inscribed on her tombstone is "Talahina, Indian Wife of General Sam Houston."

Life with Sam Houston must have been a change from life in the homes of Diana Rogers' aristocratic kinsmen, such as John Jolly and Captain John Rogers, who had built magnificent homes, "almost palaces," with large porticos and yards tended by slaves.[14] When Houston and his new wife came to Cantonment Gibson to their "Wigwam," the field in which it sat was a prairie, three miles from the Gibson community and directly on the Texas Road.[15]

Even Cantonment Gibson was a wild place and not at all the sort of place that a girl such as Diana Rogers would dream of visiting.

[12] Mumford Stokes, "Report for the decision of the Dept. on a claim of Saml. D. McGrady," in G. Foreman, "Some New Light," pp. 149–152.

[13] Eggan, *Social Anthropology,* p. 503; Mooney, "Myths of the Cherokees," pp. 481–482.

[14] E. C. Hunter, in "An Oklahoma Sketchbook, General Sam Houston," *The Daily Oklahoman,* March 9, 1924, wrote that "Chief Oolooteka [John Jolly] . . . was living like a King, with many servants around him where he conducted a great plantation in the valley. He was rich in cattle and his wigwam was what would be termed a palace in those days." Contrast this with the Sam Houston cabin, as described by Dr. G. W. West of Eufaula, Oklahoma, "Sam Houston sent his man (Shaw) down the Grand River to build a cabin. It was a one room cabin made of rough logs." "Indian-Pioneer Papers," Typescripts of Interviews of the Works Progress Administration, Col. 59, p. 228, OIA, PC, UOL.

[15] *Muskogee Daily Phoenix,* December 27, 1931. See also Chapter 14, "The Wigwam Neosho."

Known as the "Hell Hole of the Southwest" and "Graveyard of the Army," the Cantonment lived up to the name when gamblers, traders, and adventurers came to the "Fort." It was the last frontier, the farthest military outpost in the United States.[16]

Correspondence of soldiers stationed at the Cantonment and journals of travelers in the area record the story of the nightly poker games and drunken celebrations. During the time that Houston and his wife lived near Fort Gibson, professional horse racing and betting were actively pursued, with seven gamblers licensed in the area from 1829 to 1830.[17] Actually the Fort was known as "Cantonment Gibson" and was little more than a collection of log buildings, almost hutlike in appearance. The magnificent stone structures still standing were built much later. The finest building was a boarding house, which was always filled with officers and their visiting ladies. Even the accommodations of the Fort's commandant were cramped by comparison with the homes of Jolly or Rogers. One general refused to remain at the Fort because of these conditions and commanded from the safer and more respectable Fort Smith.

All that is known of life at the Wigwam Neosho are those half-truths, half-dreams of which legends are made. It is said that Diana kept a store for Sam while he played cards and drank with the soldiers and gamblers of the fort; that she went to the Fort and brought him home strapped to his horse, so drunk that he did not recognize her; and that she supervised the fields and orchards. As much as Houston traveled during these years, if a trading post was operated, then she probably did assist one of his partners in running it. The slaves would have required supervision in the farming operation and this also would have been left to her. In the traditional Indian fashion, they kept a small herd of cattle and Houston had a garden. Together

[16] For a picture of Fort Gibson see generally Grant Foreman, *Fort Gibson: A Brief History*; Ethan Allen Hitchcock, *A Traveler in Indian Territory*, pp. 30–63, 87–99; Grant Foreman, "Nathaniel Pryor," *The Chronicles of Oklahoma*, VII (June, 1929), 152–163; Henry Leavitt Ellsworth, *Washington Irving on the Prairie, or a Narrative of a Tour of the Southwest in the Year 1832*, pp. 2–10.

[17] Gambler Licenses, "Cherokee Agency, West," Letters Received by the Office of Indian Affairs, Microfilm Publications, Copy No. 234, Roll No. 77, The National Archives of the United States.

Diana and Sam planted a pear orchard. Houston's interest in these herds and fields seemed no deeper than an outward symbol of his pastoral, agrarian, native Indian existence, and so the wife, in the traditional Indian fashion, would have supervised them.[18]

It is equally possible that Diana did not remain at the Wigwam Neosho "tending the store" while Houston went on his long trips to Washington or to make treaties or land deals with the Chouteau interests at the Grand Saline. In fact, Diana probably accompanied Houston on these trips to Chouteau's and visited with her sister-in-law, as she would have done when her brother was a member of Houston's delegation to Washington.

Life at the Wigwam Neosho was bustling and dynamic. Houston had been the center of political activity too long to become an exile or recluse, for he heard his bugle blow[19] and answered when Indian delegations of Choctaws, Creeks, and Osages, as well as Cherokees, called for advice and for assistance in making their complaints known to President Jackson. The Wigwam was directly on the Texas Road and the caravans of settlers passing must have stopped to talk with Sam Houston, "late governor of Tennessee."

The Cherokee Indians have always been a hospitable people, who graciously entertain their visitors. Missionaries and travelers among the Cherokees noted their hospitality, which extended even beyond the genial receptions of their Southern neighbors. Bartram remembers the Cherokees going into the hills to look for wild strawberries to serve a guest. The Rogers family was especially noted for its entertaining and Diana would have been no exception to the rule of the gracious Cherokee hostess.[20]

[18] There are hundreds of traditions such as these which appear in the biographies and magazine and newspaper articles and which are repeated in almost every interview. One of the earliest and the father of many of the other stories is Alfred Williams' excellent article, "Houston's Life among the Indians," *Magazine of American History,* X (November, 1883), especially pp. 406–408.

[19] SH to AJ, September 19, 1829, Houston, *Writings,* I, 140–143.

[20] William Bartram, *Travels through North and South Carolina, Georgia, East and West Florida, the Cherokee Country, the Extensive Territories of the Muscogules, or Creek Confederacy, and the Country of the Choctaws; Containing an Account of Those Regions, Together with Observations on the Manners of the Indians, 1791,* pp. 350–358. The story of one of Captain John

Entertaining the rough traders and savage Indians, as well as the collection of stray soldiers and frontier gamblers who congregated around the Wigwam, would have been trying to any well-bred woman. The ruckus of drunken laughter and the midnight arrivals and departures combined with the rowdy frontier character and sense of humor must have been offensive to one who was raised among a quiet people and previously married to a gentle artistic craftsman such as David Gentry.

Nevertheless, Diana stayed. Many say she stayed because she wanted to make Sam Houston happy, that she knew their life together was short, and that she felt he had a destiny waiting for him in another land. She must have known that Houston would not stay with the Cherokee Indians forever. He had made too many trips and was too concerned with the activity in Texas to stay away from that struggle for independence. Having been raised among the Western and full-blood Cherokees, who more clearly than any other group realized the irreconcilable nature of the white and the Indian way of life, she must have known also that the life they now lived in the Wigwam could not be recaptured in the white man's land.

Life for her at the Wigwam was not always the struggle which women of her background, whether Indian or white, invariably faced on the frontier. Diggings at the site of the Wigwam have uncovered pieces of blue china export porcelain and glassware, which Diana could have used.[21] These pieces would have been reserved for the special visits from Colonel Arbuckle, A. P. Chouteau, or Washington Irving.

Houston frequently visited in the home of Dr. Baylor and his wife. The Baylors had many associations with Diana's brother, the Chero-

---

Rogers' famous Christmas parties was reported in the Missionary Records. The guests "consumed a number of beeves, two barrells of flour, and two barrells of rum." Over two hundred guests were present. The details of this party are reported in Jessie Dawson Blackwell, *Families of Samuel Dawson and Polly Ann Rogers,* p. 18.

[21] The authors have frequently walked the area of the Wigwam Neosho. The Bolings, who own the site, have themselves found many relics of former inhabitants, including a broad axe, which they have donated to the museum maintained by the state of Oklahoma in the restored stockade at Fort Gibson. See Jack Gregory and Rennard Strickland, "Historical Archeology: Locating Sam Houston's Cherokee Trading Post," *The Northwest Arkansas Archaeological Society Amateur,* IV (August, 1965), 3–6.

kee Interpreter Captain John Rogers, and it is possible that Houston took Diana with him on these visits and that the Baylors may have been entertained at the Wigwam Neosho.[22]

On October 10, 1832, Washington Irving visited with Sam Houston. In his Western journal, Irving records having ridden and visited with Houston, who the next day accompanied Irving as far as the Verdigris River, where he rejoined his party. Irving tells the story of this visit to Fort Gibson and the Indian Territory in *A Tour on the Prairies*.[23]

Houston had apparently already decided to leave the Wigwam and Diana. The picture of this world traveler setting out on a tour on the prairies must have intensified his desire to find destiny awaiting him in Texas. Diana could have sensed his restlessness and suspected, at least, that he was preparing to depart.

Nothing in the story of Sam Houston and Diana Rogers is more colored with legend and romance than the parting. One of the most beautiful of these stories is the entirely imaginative account of her death in his arms at the Wigwam Neosho. Houston buried her by the banks of a clear stream and in his grief left her people forever. This is a variation of the legend that she died in the Choctaw Nation near Talihina, Oklahoma.[24] War in Texas was for Houston the only escape from the haunting memories of his Indian maiden.

Another and more reliable story is that Diana went with Houston as far as Wilson's Rock. Houston begged her to go with him, but she refused. There on the banks of the river they parted . . . he to go to Texas and she to return to her kinsmen.[25] Little imagination is re-

[22] *Cherokee Advocate,* November 25, 1893.

[23] Washington Irving, "Western Journals," Notebook 6, Irving Collection, New York City Public Library; Washington Irving, *The Journals of Washington Irving*, p. 134; Washington Irving, *A Tour on the Prairies,* pp. 10–20.

[24] "Indian-Pioneer Papers," Typescripts of Interviews of the Works Progress Administration, Vol. 76, p. 501, OIA, PC, UOL.

[25] Emmett Starr, *Cherokee "West" 1794–1839,* p. 143. The Cherokee legend was summarized by Phil Harris, city editor of the *Muskogee Times Democrat*: "Among the Cherokees it is told that Houston sent runner after runner to Tiana, urging her to join him in Texas, saying 'I have made for you a kingdom.' Always her reply was that he had returned to his people, and she would stay with her's." Phil Harris, "Houston's Life with Cherokees," *Muskogee Sunday Phoenix and Times Democrat,* February 21, 1965.

quired to picture Diana on one bank of the river as Houston riding on horseback on the opposite bank glances over his shoulder and slowly disappears.

Diana Rogers, according to one of the legends, died "of a broken heart" when Sam went to Texas. She wept, or so the legend goes, when her husband left the Wigwam Neosho, and when she finally realized that he would not return for her, died of sorrow. An equally tragic story is that Diana could not endure life without Houston and that in a moment of despair this lovely "Indian Princess" threw herself over a cliff known today as "Lover's Leap."[26]

It is perhaps unfortunate that these legends are destroyed by documents found in the Bureau of Indian Affairs which prove beyond question that Diana Rogers did not die of a "broken heart" but was married again.[27] The most popular story is that Houston promised to return for Diana when the war in Texas was over and that she refused to leave her people because "she would be a stranger in the white man's land," but hoped that he would return again to the Cherokees.[28] Another version of this same story is that Houston asked her to go with him when he left for Texas and that he continued to ask her to join him until the time of her death.[29]

The facts of Diana's subsequent marriage are recorded by Montford Stokes of the Cherokee Agency at Fort Gibson in the proceedings of a controversy between Samuel D. McGrady and William Rogers over a slave which Diana gave McGrady. Stokes notes that "sometimes . . . say about 1st. April 1836, the said Diana Houston intermarried with the said Samuel D. McGrady."[30] While the details

[26] Jim Lucas, "Fort Gibson Grave Recalls Romance of Houston and Cherokee Maid," *Muskogee Daily Phoenix*, September 29, 1935; "Indian-Pioneer Papers," Typescripts of Interviews of the Works Progress Administration, Vol. 76, p. 501, OIA, PC, UOL. The Indian interest in "Lover's Leaps" and a legend of another Indian maiden, Authula, can be found in Irma Celestine Heard, "Lover's Leap—A Legend," *My Oklahoma Magazine,* I (April, 1927), 37–38.

[27] Foreman, "Some New Light," pp. 148–152.

[28] This story appears in almost every account of Houston and Diana Rogers. It is most dramatically presented in "Indian-Pioneer Papers," Typescripts of Interviews of the Works Progress Administration Interviews, Vol. 76, p. 501, OIA, PC, UOL.

[29] Starr, *Cherokee "West,"* p. 143.

[30] M. Stokes, "Report for the Decision of the Department a Claim of Saml.

of Diana's life with McGrady are unimportant to this story, the fact that she remarried seems final proof that Diana was certain Houston would not return for her.

William Armstrong, acting superintendent for the Western Territory, placed serious doubt upon McGrady's character in the note which he attached to the Stokes report.

> McGrady has intermarried in the nation, doubtless for the property; and whether he may have a legal demand upon the Cherokee nation . . . he has at least produced the difficult breach between a large and numerous connection. In every instance where property is taken from a citizen of the United States and carried to the Indian country, I . . . have it restored, but . . . this case . . . is different, for the property [which] he acquired . . . was the property of an Indian woman, her own and uncontrolled by her husband. McGrady may sell the slave if placed in his possession and leave his wife the late Mrs. Houston to find *another* husband.[31]

Whether Diana and McGrady separated is unknown, as is whether she remained at the Wigwam Neosho or returned to the home of her family. The speculation about her life during these years is probably accurate when it places her at Wilson's Rock, visiting her sister, and staying for a short time at the home of John Jolly. She probably did all the things that are attributed to her, such as looking south toward Texas while wondering what "had happened to her Sam?"

But her life with Sam Houston had ended and her influence upon his destiny and the destiny of Texas was the influence of a memory—a memory of a young woman who had accepted the love which others had rejected. The memory which Houston had of Diana Rogers was so strong that "it is reported to have brought tears to his eyes as late as 1856." W. W. Weaver of Fort Smith reported having spoken to Houston in Philadelphia about the Indian woman and Houston is said to have acknowledged to him that he loved her and always remembered these days.[32]

D. McGrady for a negro taken by Wm. Rogers," in G. Foreman, "Some New Light," pp. 149–150.

[31] Armstrong to C. A. Harris, in G. Foreman, "Some New Light," pp. 151–152.

[32] "Mr. Weaver [W. W. Weaver] talked to Gen. Houston at Pittsburgh, Pennsylvania in 1856 . . . he talked to him for several hours of the Cherokee

Sometime during 1838 Diana Rogers became ill and died of pneumonia. The body was buried, according to tradition, near Wilson's or Swallows Rock.[33] However, the final resting place of Diana Rogers Gentry Houston McGrady is seriously disputed, with at least three grave sites defended as her final resting place.

Perhaps the most famous Cherokee historian, Emmett Starr, wrote that "the location of her last resting place is unknown, but it is generally thought by those most competent to judge, that it is somewhere in the vicinity of her home near Rex, Oklahoma." He takes direct issue with newspaperman J. S. Holden by concluding that "the bones interred in the National Cemetery at Fort Gibson and foisted on the public as those of Samuel Houston's Cherokee wife, were those of a woman whose maiden name was Coody, who was never the wife of Houston."[34]

An equally well-known Cherokee historian, Shorey Ross, "a native of Oklahoma" and member of the famous Ross family, thought that the grave was located on Fourteen Mile Creek.

> A great mistake was made at the time of the reinterment. She died in her early forties [and, according to Ross, is buried] not near Muldrow but in a burial ground not far from the house in which she died, some miles north of Ft. Gibson. Whose bones were buried in the National Cemetery at Ft. Gibson will never be known but Diana or Tiana lies in a forgotten grave near the banks of a small creek which flows through the valleys of the wooded hills north of the old military post at Ft. Gibson.[35]

However accurate it may be, the site at Wilson's Rock has come to be the accepted place of Diana's grave. Colonel J. S. Holden called attention to this grave when he and George Williamson, with the

---

Country, and especially Talihina. Mr. Weaver told General Houston of visiting Wilson's Rock and planting flowers on Talihina's grave. The General's countenance grew sad and tears filled his eyes. He said, there he spent the happiest days of his life." William Wilson, "Talihina's Grave," *The Fort Gibson Post,* July 21, 1904. See also William Weaver Scrapbook, Microfilm Division, University of Arkansas Library, Fayetteville.

[33] Lucas, "Fort Gibson Grave"; Carolyn Thomas Foreman, Interview, August 24, 1964.

[34] Starr, *Cherokee "West,"* pp. 143–144.

[35] Campbell, W. P. "Sam Houston in Indian Territory," *Historical Quarterly,* VIII (July, 1919), 3–4, and (October, 1919), 6–8.

assistance of Judge William Wilson of Fort Smith, found an unmarked grave in 1895. Williamson was an ex-Confederate soldier from Fort Smith who had been with Price's army on retreat after the Battle of Pea Ridge or Elkhorn Tavern in what is now Benton County, Arkansas. The retreating army crossed the Arkansas at Wilson's Rock and, according to Williamson, he then saw the grave of Sam Houston's Cherokee wife and remembered that the location was near a cedar tree. After considerable clearing of brush, the grave was found and identified by Mr. Wilson as the one which he remembered having seen over thirty years before.[36]

Williamson placed at the head and the foot of the grave sandstone slabs, which Holden inscribed with his pocket knife: "Talihina, Cherokee wife of Sam Houston, liberator of Texas." From that time, Holden devoted himself to gathering proof that this was the grave of Talihina. In July of 1895 Holden interviewed W. W. Weaver of Fort Smith, who had visited the grave with Diana's sister, Mrs. John Drew. They came to Wilson's Rock in 1840 and planted shrubs and flowers upon the grave of Houston's Cherokee wife. Weaver went to the graveside and identified this spot at Wilson's Rock as the one which he and Mrs. Drew had decorated some fifty-five years before.[37]

The tradition of this location is also supported by Narcissa Owen, mother of United States Senator Robert Owen. She wrote in her *Memoirs* that:

> Sam Houston, after his painful experience . . . sought comfort with his friend, Charles Rogers, then in Indian Territory, having formed a friendship in Tennessee. Later he married Talihina Rogers, and lived at Skin Bayou Bluff, on the Arkansas River, where I as a young girl often gathered roses near her grave, which was marked by small white marble head and foot stones. In later years the remains of Sam Houston's loving comforter and wife . . . were reinterred at Fort Gibson.[38]

Diana's body lay at Wilson's Rock almost seventy years until Holden obtained permission from the War Department to have the body removed to the National Cemetery. Holden felt that the wife of a gov-

[36] The most detailed account of the visit of W. W. Weaver and Mrs. John Drew to Diana's grave is found in *The Fort Gibson Post,* July 21, 1904.

[37] *The Fort Gibson Post,* July 21, 1904.

[38] Narcissa Owen, *Memoirs of Narcissa Owen, 1831–1907,* p. 100.

ernor of Tennessee and Texas, a United States congressman and senator, and President of the Republic of Texas should have a more prominent resting place. With O. H. Farley, a Muskogee undertaker, and a crowd of people, Holden went to Wilson's Rock to exhume the body.

The most detailed account of the reburial of Diana Rogers is found in the World's Fair Edition of the *Fort Gibson Post.* Colonel Holden was editor of the paper and also the man who had persuaded the United States government to consent to the reburial, and thus covered every aspect of the proceedings.[39]

Having obtained permission of the war department by order of Col. West, general superintendent of the United States army to remove the remains to the U.S. National cemetery at Fort Gibson, the writer in company with O. H. Farley, undertaker at Muskogee, on September 3rd went to Wilson's Rock and exhumed the remains in the presence of a good number of people, and removed the same that day to Fort Gibson. The rest is told in the Post of September 8th as follows:

The closing scene in the often told tale of General Sam Houston's Cherokee wife, Tahlihina Rogers, was enacted in the U.S. National Cemetery, Fort Gibson, Sunday, September 4th, 1904, when the remains were laid to final rest in the most honored and conspicuous place in the cemetery in the circle around the flag, among the army officers and their wives. . . .

The funeral was widely advertised and had it not been for the rainy weather an immense throng of people would have been present, including Co. A of the Territorial Volunteer Militia, and Muskogee G.A.R. Post. The excursion trains also failed to come. As it was a good number drove over later in carriages, so that the attendance numbered four or five hundred people.

The procession started from the Hefferan House at 1:20 p.m. headed by the fine hearse of O. H. Farley & Co. of Muskogee which contained the remains, being in a fine casket enclosed in a metallic lined box, all draped in a fine American flag, loaned by keeper Chapman, of the National Cemetery. The following named gentlemen, members of the Muskogee G.A.R. were the pallbearers:

A. W. Chapman	G. A. Tatome
William Harper	H. R. Estes
J. B. Doyle	J. M. Davis

[39] The remainder of the account of the burial, location, and reburial of the

Secret Service men, and others, followed by a lengthy procession of carriages and wagons, . . . took the line of march to the cemetery, about a mile distant, accompanied by Mayor Munn on horseback.

Arriving at the cemetery the pallbearers placed the casket in position near the grave, when the undertaker, Mr. Farley, opened the box and casket, so that all who wished might view all that is earthly of The Once Beautiful Tahlihina who died in the year 1838. All were surprised that so much remained after a lapse of 66 years. All the large bones were there—lower limbs and arms, with skull in two parts, frontal and back, with portions of upper and lower jaw which contained a number of teeth in an apparently perfect state of preservation.

The bones showed that the woman was of tall if not large stature. The skull was a very fine one, showing a high state of intelligence and moral qualities being very full in the region of benevolence, reverence, and veneration, conscientious and idealty, and of her moral organs according to the science of phrenology, which the writer had studied for years. The skull also showed large social organs, all showing that the woman was a person of much more than ordinary talent, ability, and amiableness.

But one of the great surprises was a large tortorise shell comb in a reasonable state of preservation, circular shape, and about seven inches across.[40] The material was of the finest kind and most of the teeth were intact. . . . The only traces of a coffin was an old-fashioned six-penny nail.

After the remains had been viewed by several hundred people, they were consigned to their last resting place, beneath the stars and stripes, in a beautiful spot midst shade and grassy lawn.[41]

---

body of an Indian woman who is alleged to be Diana Rogers is taken from the "World's Fair—Historic Edition" of *The Fort Gibson Post,* October 15, 1904.

[40] Captain John Stuart noted, ". . . the Cherokees dress precisely as the women of the United States do; and according to their wealth and ability follow them closely through all the European fashions in form and materials, except that they seldom wear a bonnet, but in lieu thereof, after placing their hair up in a most fruitful manner with fine large and side combs, they place over their heads a fine silk handkerchief, in a very tasteful manner, so as to appear quite ornamental. This handkerchief is sometimes so very fine, and of so light a texture, as to show their hair and combs through it." John Stuart, *A Sketch of the Cherokee and Choctaw Indians,* p. 13.

[41] Much of this news story was confirmed in an interview with Robert Langston of Fort Gibson, Oklahoma, who attended the funeral and recalled, ". . . they had preachin' and the real funeral things." Robert Langston, Interview, October 10, 1964.

6. Sam Houston, Alias Tah-lohn-tus-ky, Alias Standing Bear: Newspaperman and Political Writer

> My motive and object in all my political work . . . have been to rescue man from tyranny . . . and enable him to be free.
>
> Thomas Paine, *Rights of Man,* XV

Houston, frustrated by Andrew Jackson's preoccupation with the removal of the Eastern Cherokee and by Jackson's refusal to correct abuses against the Western Cherokee, wrote to Secretary of War Eaton that he was preparing a political tract. Perhaps envisioning himself as an Indian Thomas Paine, he announced that a series of articles would soon appear in the *Arkansas Gazette* signed "Tal-lohn-tus-ky."[1] Like Paine, Houston planned to "rescue man from tyranny . . . and enable him to be free."[2] Freedom in this case required freeing the Indians from the oppression of their corrupt agents.[3]

In the opening paragraph of the initial column, Houston borrowed the style of Patrick Henry and wrote that he was compelled to act because of intolerable abuses against the Indian. "There is a point of endurance in human suffering, beyond which submission is meanness and silence . . . worse than base slavishness." Houston hoped that President Jackson would assist him in reforming the Indian administration. The series was specifically "directed to the genius, integrity, and intelligence, of the President of the United States . . . which will secure to the Indians justice and stay the hand of their . . . cruel oppressors."[4]

[1] SH to JE, June 13, 1830, Sam Houston, *The Writings of Sam Houston,* Amelia W. Williams and Eugene C. Barker (eds.), I, 152–153.

[2] Thomas Paine, *Rights of Man,* XV.

[3] For a picture of abuses see Flora Warren Seymour, *Indian Agents of the Old Frontier,* pp. 12–13.

[4] SH, "The Indians—Chapter First," *Arkansas Gazette,* June 22, 1830, complete text in Houston, *Writings,* I, 155–157.

Five of Houston's articles appeared. Three were signed by Tah-lohn-tus-ky.[5] One was written under the name "Standing Bear."[6] And the final was a letter in defense of Houston's actions and appeared in a special supplement entitled simply "To the Editor of the Arkansas Gazette."[7] These articles and the answers to them were also published as broadsides and pamphlets.[8]

Houston selected an important paper to publish his articles. The *Arkansas Gazette*, known as "the Old Lady of Arkansas Journalism," was a "great Power" in the Arkansas Territory and the most influential newspaper in the Southwest. The founder, William E. Woodruff, had brought the *Gazette* press down river in a "piroque" made by roping together two hollow logs. This was the only newspaper in the area from its first issue in November of 1819 until 1830. While Houston lived near Cantonment Gibson the paper was enjoying a period of rapid expansion in circulation and influence. Circulation had remained relatively stable with about three hundred subscribers in 1821, expanding to only about five hundred by 1829, however, by 1836 the subscription was over two thousand.[9]

Journals and letters written from Cantonment Gibson show that the *Gazette* was read throughout the Indian country. Sutler Nicks, the subscription agent for the post, distributed issues from his store.[10] Newspapers were the only reliable source of news which reached eastern cities, and papers such as the *Niles' Weekly Register* in Baltimore

[5] SH, "The Indians—Chapter First," *Arkansas Gazette*, June 22, 1830; SH, "The Creek Indians—Chapter Second," *Arkansas Gazette*, July 7, 1830; SH, "The Indians—Chapter Third," *Arkansas Gazette*, September 8, 1830; for the full columns see Houston, *Writings*, I, 155–157, 157–163, 170–177.

[6] SH, "In Defense of the Indians," *Arkansas Gazette*, August 14, 1830; Houston, *Writings*, I, 164–170.

[7] SH, "To the Editor of the Arkansas Gazette," *Arkansas Gazette* (*Supplement*), December 8, 1830; Houston, *Writings*, I, 177–185.

[8] Albert H. Allen (ed.), *Arkansas Imprints 1821–1876*, p. 6, Item 21. The Thomas Gilcrease Institute has an excellent example of one of these broadsides, GSHBF, GRL.

[9] Fred W. Allsopp, *History of the Arkansas Press*, pp. 41–48; 309–338; Jessie R. Lucke, "Correspondence concerning the Establishment of the First Arkansas Press," *The Arkansas Historical Quarterly*, XIV (Summer, 1955), 161–171; Carolyn Thomas Foreman, *Oklahoma Imprints*, pp. xiii, 55.

[10] Sutler's Papers, GFT, GRL.

often reprinted entire items directly from the *Gazette*.[11] Thus the influence of an article written by Houston was felt far beyond the immediate circulation area of the *Gazette*.

Colonel Matthew Arbuckle thought the influence of the series in the *Gazette* was so strong that he requested a special ruling on Houston's rights as a Cherokee citizen. As commandant of Cantonment Gibson, Arbuckle wrote Secretary of War Randolph that he would have decided the question "had the General been free from a newspaper controversy which possibly may bring all he has said and done in this country . . . before the public."[12]

The reactions to the series show that the political power of Tah-lohn-tus-ky and Standing Bear was greater than the power and influence of Sam Houston as an individual. The first column, "The Indians—Chapter First" appeared in the twenty-second of June, 1830, issue of the *Gazette*. In the next issue a sharp reply appeared. Other answers continued through the summer and fall.[13] These attacks were often so vicious that the *Gazette* would not print them in the body of the paper, but used a special dueling supplement for them.

The replies generally were slanders against Houston ("the turbanded Governor"), his Indian wife ("in his matrimonial alliance"), and his associates in the Indian country ("crooks and thieves"). The most vicious attack was signed by Tekatoka.[14] Houston concluded,

[11] Eastern papers were especially dependent upon the *Arkansas Gazette* for news of the Indians and Texas. For example, an article which appeared in the *Arkansas Gazette* for April 17, 1827, was reproduced in *Niles' Weekly Register* for June 2, 1827.

[12] MA to Randolph, July 23, 1830, Matthew Arbuckle Papers (Photostats), GSHBF, GRL.

[13] Answers to Houston's articles appeared as follows: *Arkansas Gazette,* June 29, July 7, July 21, August 4, and October 6, 1830.

[14] "Tekatoka to Standing Bear, alias General Houston," *Arkansas Gazette* (*Supplement*), October 20, 1830. This Tekatoka was a real mystery. At first, it was thought that the name was selected because both Tekatoka and Tah-lohn-tus-ky (the name under which Houston wrote) were chiefs who represented conflicting views of tribal politics. A Tekatoka was a "conjurer," Chief of the Western Cherokees from 1813–1818, and a war chief who was considered a powerful leader of the Western Cherokees. This Tekatoka signed the treaty for removal of the Cherokees from the Hiawassee country of Tennessee in 1817, waged relentless war against the Osages in Arkansas, and invited

". . . it seems from the character of the publication, that it had been composed by the late Ex-Agent . . . and transposed to suit 'Te-Ka-To-Ka'." Houston may have known who this "Te-Ka-To-Ka" was, but refused to reveal "whether Tekatoka has had an agency or not" or to "assail private character."[15]

Houston thought that the columns created such violent reactions because they told of the degradation of the American Indian. The opening Tah-lohn-tus-ky article clearly sets the mood of the entire newspaper campaign. Houston began:

Where stood the Indian of other days? He stood on the shore of the Atlantic, and beheld, each morning, the sun rolling from the bosom of its green waves. In that sun he beheld *his* God, and bowed in homage to the shrine. He felt that no intermediate creature, could usurp the favor of his Divinity. He was monarch of the wilds, and his buoyant steps proclaimed him, "every inch a king." That age has long gone by—the aboriginal character is almost lost in the views of the white man. . . . A succession of injuries has broken his proud spirit, and taught him to kiss the hand which inflicts upon him stripes—to cringe, and ask favors of the wretch, who violates his oath, by defrauding him money promised by treaties—basely retaining it, for purposes of speculation—by becoming a partner in trade, with creatures selected for the purpose—or a secret partner, in all contracts for which the Government has selected him as its agent.

If this were the limit of injustice to, and fraud upon, the Indians . . . it would be tolerable—but when, added to this, the introduction of ardent spirits, in vast quantities, by the *agents*—the quantity sold by their knowl-

---

Sequoyah to his village, where he taught the first class in his new written Cherokee language. He died, however, while accompanying a delegation to Washington to pursue his plan of a confederation of Western emigrant Indians. He was dead when this letter was written. The authors did not determine if Tekatoka was a son of the old chief. Mrs. Carolyn Thomas Foreman has written of the murder of a Tekatoka in March of 1846. Another consideration which reflects upon the authorship is the extensive use of Latin throughout the attack. Houston noted "that the author [was] willing to give publicity to *his* learning and *his* numerous Latin *quotations*." See SH, "To the Editor of the Arkansas Gazette," *Arkansas Gazette* (*Supplement*); Houston, *Writings*, I, 177–178; Emmett Starr, *Cherokee "West" 1794–1839*, pp. 75–83; Carolyn Thomas Foreman, "The Lighthorse in the Indian Territory," *The Chronicles of Oklahoma*, XXXIV (Spring, 1956), 23.

[15] SH, "To the Editor of the Arkansas Gazette," *Arkansas Gazette* (*Supplement*), December 8, 1830; Houston, *Writings*, I, 177–185.

edge and with *their* connivance, ensures the Indians, a *certain,* if not a *speedy* destruction.[16]

Houston was the first major political leader of a Western state to speak so strongly in defense of the Indians. This was a period when it was not popular to champion the cause of Indians, especially Indians such as the Creeks and Cherokees who occupied very desirable lands in the Southern and Western states.[17] In addition, the Indian trade was considered the fastest way to a fortune, and Houston made a special point to attack these traders. It would be difficult to be more direct than Houston, when he wrote:

Will a people, brave and generous as the Americans, countenance such *inhuman robberies*; and can their President who is so great and good, tolerate such panders [*sic*] in office? who have no claims, only upon his magnanimity, and that is *defied by every act of fraud* which is perpetrated by the "lilly livered" crew upon the poor and half naked Indians![18]

Such chapters were Houston's notice to the world that he was not politically dead. They were concrete evidence that he was more than "The Big Drunk." Once more attention was called to Houston and he was the center of controversy. The pride which Houston felt over these columns is evidenced in a letter which he sent to one of his business associates: "[Y]ou will perhaps see in some of the northern papers, 'chapters' signed 'Ta-lou[lon]-tusky,' and every fact contained you may rely upon as true! The author you may guess at." He concluded, "They were written in great haste."[19]

Arkansas was a center for plans to revolutionize Texas. Speculation, even at the time, associated these columns with an alleged plan of Houston's to revolutionize Texas and make himself the Cherokee emperor of a Mexican state. An excuse to come to Little Rock or a ready

[16] SH, "The Indians—Chapter First," *Arkansas Gazette,* June 22, 1830; Houston, *Writings,* I, 155–157.

[17] The best analysis of the popular feelings toward the Southern Indians and the definitive history of the problems of driving the Five Civilized Tribes from their native homes is Grant Foreman's *Indian Removal, the Emigration of the Five Civilized Tribes of Indians,* pp. 229–313.

[18] SH, "In Defense of the Indians," *Arkansas Gazette,* September 8, 1830; Houston, *Writings,* I, 177.

[19] SH to John Van Fossen, August 22, 1830, Houston, *Writings,* I, 187.

explanation for his long stays away from the Cantonment Gibson area was certainly given by the column. Tradition says that Houston met conspirators in Arkansas and there plotted the overthrow of the Mexican government. The only record of a meeting, however, is of one held almost two years after Houston left the Cherokee nation and four years after the last "Chapter" appeared.[20]

The *Arkansas Gazette* columns of Tah-lohn-tus-ky and Standing Bear are still an eloquent statement of the struggles, and "form a definite part of the 'reliable' story of what happened to the Indian."[21] Houston's detailed analysis is a biting indictment of the agency system, exposing the schemes of taking Indian lands, the false promises made to Creek leaders such as Chief McIntosh, the ration-purchase and merchandizing scandals, the theft of specie certificates, the sale of whiskey to the Indians by their agents, and the open bribery in the War Department.

Measuring the influence of Tah-lohn-tus-ky and Standing Bear is impossible. As a private citizen, Houston was without a platform from which to speak. These fictitious Indians gave him this platform. Although the power of one part of a campaign, such as this waged against the Indian Agency System, cannot be estimated, the success of the entire campaign can be evaluated. The Agency organization was revised, corrupt agents were replaced, and the Indians in the West were given more attention and power, at least temporarily. In achieving this result Tah-lohn-tus-ky and Standing Bear were a vital part.

[20] Mrs. Granville Norris of Muskogee, Oklahoma, was the first to call these meetings to the author's attention. See also Richard Stenbery, "Jackson's Neches Claim, 1829–1836," *The Southwestern Historical Quarterly*, XXXIX (April, 1936), 262, 266–270. There were also a number of letters written by Houston from Arkansas during these years. See generally Sue Flanagan, *Sam Houston's Texas*, p. 15, G. W. Featherstonhaugh, *Excursion through the Slave States, from Washington on the Potomac to the Frontier of Mexico,* II, 161.

[21] Sam Houston, *The Autobiography of Sam Houston,* Donald Day and Harry Herbert Ullom (eds.), pp. 61–62.

7. Indian Peacemaker

I will be proud and happy . . . If I can keep peace among the Indians, and between them and the whites.

Sam Houston to Andrew Jackson, May 11, 1829, *Writings,* I, 132–133

The first letter written by Houston after his resignation as governor of Tennessee offered his services to President Jackson as an unofficial peacemaker with the Indian tribes. He wrote that acting "in my individual capacity . . . if I find your favors abused, and injustice done to the Indians . . . I will feel bound, to let you know facts."[1]

Houston pictured himself as an emissary from the white race, adopted by his Indian brothers and especially qualified to act as a peacemaker; and all of his past associations did combine to uniquely qualify him for such a role. From his childhood associations, he had an insight into Indian thinking which few white men ever achieve. From his service as a Cherokee subagent, he had a close and personal knowledge of the problems of the Indian Bureau and the agency administrators. From the days he spent in the United States House of Representatives and as governor of Tennessee, he had learned the considerations which plague elected governmental officials. This was an unusually qualified peacemaker who chose to act in an unofficial capacity by refusing an offer of the Cherokee subagency position.

Another white man who resided in the Indian nation was August Pierre Chouteau, who operated a part of the Chouteau family Indian trading empire. Chouteau was the most influential white man in the Osage country, so influential that when Manuel Lisa was given a trading monopoly over the Osages in Missouri an entire band of the Osage tribe followed Chouteau to a location in Oklahoma.[2]

[1] SH to AJ, May 11, 1829, Sam Houston, *The Writings of Sam Houston,* Amelia W. Williams and Eugene C. Barker (eds.), I, 132.

[2] Herbert E. Bolton, "New Light on Manuel Lisa and the Spanish Fur

Chouteau, a member of the founding family of St. Louis, lived in a frontier splendor which eventually bankrupted him. Washington Irving visited at the Chouteau residence near the Grand Saline and vividly described it in *A Tour on the Prairies* as a "frontier shamble."

Having crossed the ford, we soon reached the Osage Agency, where Col. Chouteau has his offices and magazines, for the despatch of Indian affairs, and the distribution of presents and supplies. It consisted of a few log houses on the banks of the river, and presented a motley frontier scene.

. . . .

The little hamlet of the Agency was in a complete bustle; the blacksmith's shed, in particular, was a scene of preparation; a strapping negro was shoeing a horse; two half-breeds were fabricating iron spoons in which to melt lead for bullets. An old trapper, in leathern hunting frock and moccasons [*sic*], had placed his rifle against a work-bench, while he superintended the operation, and gossiped about his hunting exploits; several large dogs were lounging in and out of the shop, or sleeping in the sunshine, while a little cur, with head cocked on one side, and one ear erect, was watching, with that curiosity common to little dogs, the process of shoeing the horse, as if studying the art or waiting for his turn to be shod.[3]

Houston and Chouteau frequently combined their talents in peace negotiations. The talents of Chouteau and Houston are said to have complemented each other. Houston was the most influential white man among the Cherokees and Chouteau was the most influential white man among the Osages. Although the Osages were a more savage tribe, Chouteau was able to completely dominate all their activities. Houston did not have absolute control over the Cherokees, but his "remarkable hold" on President Andrew Jackson furthered Chouteau's interests.[4]

Warfare between the Osages and Cherokees was continuous from the time of the Cherokee arrival in Arkansas, with the battles more

---

Trade," *The Southwestern Historical Quarterly,* XVII (June, 1913), 61–66; Richard E. Oglesby, *Manuel Lisa and the Opening of the Missouri Fur Trade,* pp. 22, 24–28, 152.

[3] Washington Irving, *A Tour on the Prairies*, pp. 21–22.

[4] Vinson Lackey, *The Chouteaus and the Founding of Salina, Oklahoma's First White Settlement—1796,* p. 21.

than occasional skirmishes.[5] The Cherokee leader "Dutch" openly raided Osage villages in retaliation for their attacks. John McLemore loaded full boats of Cherokee warriors from the East and brought them into the Arkansas Territory to assist in the battles.[6] One of the most interesting of the stories of Indian captivities, *Our Osage Captives*, was written about the little children taken by the Cherokees from an Osage raiding party and sent to the Cherokee mission at Brainerd.[7] The seriousness of this warfare is reflected in a news item which appeared in the *Niles' Weekly Register*: "[There is] . . . news of . . . war by Cherokee against Osages, three or four hundred to start. The Cherokees use the rifle in war, and the Osages the bow and arrow almost entirely, and always fight on horseback."[8]

Knowing the cost of such warfare to their nation, the Cherokees had attempted to make peace. In 1827 a group of Cherokees headed by John Rogers and Walter Webber had carried a message from Chief Jolly and the council to the Indian Superintendent in St. Louis. The message conveyed a "desire [for] a . . . meeting to adjust and settle our differences and to enjoy peace . . . bury the tomahawk, shake hands, be friends."[9] Until Houston's arrival the Osages refused the Cherokee terms for any meeting. They generally looked upon the Cherokees "with a suspicious eye" because "once they became slaughtered victims by a message similar to that sent by Mr. Jolly."[10]

Houston knew that a constant series of treaties had been concluded or negotiated between the Osages and Cherokees, however, none had settled the conflict. There was a constant danger that one tribe would enlist the support of a neighboring tribe and that the conflict would

[5] The scope of the warfare can be seen in the correspondence from agents, tribal leaders, and War Department officials. See generally, Osage Records, OIA, and Osage Letters, GFT, GRL.

[6] See generally John P. Brown, *Old Frontiers: The Story of the Cherokee Indians from Earliest Times to the Date of Their Removal to the West, 1838*, pp. 463–477.

[7] Elias Cornelius, *The Little Osage Captives, An Authentic Narrative.*

[8] *Niles' Weekly Register,* July 20, 1827.

[9] Letter, "Chiefs and Warriors of the Osage Nation from the Chiefs and Warriors of Cherokee Nation by John Rogers, Walter Webber, and George DuVal," February 9, 1827, Captain John Rogers Papers, GFT, GRL.

[10] Major Hamtramack to William Clark, November 1, 1827, GFT, GRL.

rupture into a general Indian war, with the tribes south of the Red River, those from the Plains, and other tribes involved.[11]

A temporary cooperation and friendship between the Osages and Cherokees came soon after Houston and Chouteau began their personal associations. The borderline disputes were submitted to arbitration.[12] Soon Captain John Rogers began operation of the Grand Saline in an area bordering on the Osage Nation. A strong peace came between these tribes and they looked elsewhere for battle.

One of the most interesting and farsighted of the treaties which Houston assisted in negotiating provided for an intertribal council of Osages and Creeks to guarantee "peace forever between the tribes." The Creek-Osage Treaty signed on May 10, 1831, provided that any tribal member who broke the peace would be tried by a joint council composed of ten Creeks and ten Osages. Theft was punished by twenty to thirty-nine lashes, with the exact number determined by the chief of the offender's nation. There were also provisions for the arbitration of other disputes.[13]

The most conspicious example of Houston's failure as a peacemaker was the Maynard Bayou council held in June of 1829. This occurred early in the first summer that Houston spent among the Cherokees and is the only recorded clash of power between Houston and the younger war leaders of the Cherokees. The frenzy of the young Cherokee braves, excited by another white man, B. H. Smith, was too much for Houston to overcome.

In 1828 the savage Tawakoni Indians of Texas had scalped a band of Cherokees traveling in their country, and then danced around their scalps while the remaining Cherokees watched. This was considered a "triumph of our enemies over the scalps of our people" and the young men were determined to revenge the triumph.[14]

The resolution admitting Houston to citizenship had not yet been passed when he went to the Maynard Bayou council as Chief Jolly's

[11] MA to General West, January 10, 1827, Matthew Arbuckle Papers, GFT, GRL.

[12] SH to JE, June 24, 1829, Houston, *Writings,* I, 134–136.

[13] Grant Foreman, *Advancing the Frontier, 1830–1860,* p. 109.

[14] James T. DeShields, *Border Wars of Texas,* pp. 66–76; John Ridge, "The Cherokee War Path," *The Chronicles of Oklahoma,* IX (September, 1931), 236.

official representative. Despite the prestige of Jolly's name, Houston was unable to persuade the young men against warfare. Jolly was not a war chief and the warlike spirit of Smith excited them into "the raising of the Tomahawk of war." Houston wrote to Colonel Arbuckle about this conference:

I attended the Dance and Talk of the Cherokees, and Creeks, and had the mortification to witness (in despite of all my efforts) the raising of the Tomahawk of war. . . . The Creeks did not join and I trust that you may by attending their council prevent them at any future day. . . . It is the project of a few restless and turbulent young men, who will not yield, or listen to the Talk of their Chiefs. . . . I have been informed (but vaguely) that some Osages, Choctaws, Shawanees, and Delawares are to join the Party, and in all make it some 250 or 300 warriors.[15]

The Cherokees were anxious to form a confederation to revenge this triumph and had invited the Creeks to attend the conference. Houston was more persuasive with the Creeks, who had no personal interest in the scalping, and convinced them not to follow the Cherokees to the Red River where the Tawakoni lived. The Cherokees, however, went to the camp of the Tawakonis and quite successfully avenged the death of their brothers.

Soon after his arrival at Jolly's, Houston was summoned to the home of Colonel Chouteau. H. Haralson accompanied him and reported the entire transaction to the secretary of war, Major John H. Eaton. A panel of Osages at Chouteau's requested that Houston, accompanied by Haralson and Doctor Neil, go with them to see how they were cheated and defrauded by Major Hamtramack, their agent.[16]

Houston, Haralson, and Neil each wrote to the Secretary of War outlining the abuses and recommending that Chouteau be appointed agent to the Osages. The Osages, who were locating at Clermont's Town, had been defrauded by every agent since Old Colonel Chouteau and were determined not to accept their annuity until "justice was done." Each concluded that the interest of peace and justice could be saved by appointing Chouteau, who "has resided among them for

[15] SH to MA, July 8, 1829, Houston, *Writings,* I, 136–139.
[16] H. Haralson to JE, June 22, 1829, GFT, GRL.

the last 20 years and who has more absolute control among those Indians than any other man ever among them," as the agent.[17]

During 1829 and 1830 the Delawares and other nomadic tribes attacked the Osages, who were hunting near the Red River, killing eight of their warriors. When war between the Osages and Delawares became almost inevitable John Eaton, secretary of war, appointed a commission "to adjust the differences with the Osages and other tribes of Indians."[18] Commandant Matthew Arbuckle, A. P. Chouteau, and Sam Houston met with Nathaniel Pryor, Osage subagent, and Clermont, the Osage principal chief, in a conference held at the mouth of the Veridgris River.

The Osages agreed to accept one hundred dollars' worth of goods for each of their hunters who had been killed. On May 27, 1830, Chouteau provided from his trading post eight hundred dollars' worth of goods, which Clermont accepted in satisfaction of the eight warriors' lives. The stock included "stranding blankets, butcher knives, and vermilion." This succeeded "in adjusting all difficulties with the Osages and other tribes . . . for the present."[19]

This entire period of Houston's life with the Indians was one of remarkable tranquility among even the most warlike tribes in the region. The peacemaking activities of Houston, Chouteau, and Arbuckle were so successful that Houston wrote Andrew Jackson sometime in 1830 that:

> If the President deems it fit to appoint Colonel Arbuckle, Col. Chouteau, and myself (without fee or reward) to treat with the Pawnees; and to make peace . . . tranquility will reign. . . . The whole western tribes will be at Peace . . . and harmony established between the Indian Tribes, and an acquiescence in the wishes of the Government and the Executive insured.[20]

Houston's understanding of the Indian is reflected in his ideas concerning peace negotiations. The Osages were the only Western tribe in the area to which Peace Medals had been distributed, and Houston suggested that "treaties between the several tribes, and between them

[17] SH to JE, June 22, 1829, GFT, GRL.

[18] JE to Colonel Chouteau, May 29, 1830, Osage Records, OIA.

[19] Grant Foreman, *Muskogee and Eastern Oklahoma,* pp. 28–29.

[20] SH to AJ, date uncertain but sometime in 1830, Houston, *Writings,* I, 146. The remaining direct quotes are from this letter, unless otherwise noted.

and the United States, could be easily effected, by the distribution of some trifling presents, and medals of the President given to the Chiefs by some man who understands the character of the Indians."

Another of his suggestions removed the major impediments to negotiations among many of the tribes. The custom among all of the Indians was to take prisoners. Among tribes such as the Osages and Pawnees, which had "been engaged in war since time immemorial," the number of prisoners had become considerable. An exchange of these prisoners would leave "little difficulty in making peace."

Houston seemed always as ready to negotiate for the government as for an Indian tribe. He frequently offered to travel with the tribes or to visit the tribes in the interest of peace. The first of these offers is typical. Four companies of infantry were assigned by the President to escort and guard the companies trading from St. Louis to Santa Fe. The trains had to pass through the grounds of "Osages, Kansas, Pawnees, Komanches, Arapahoes, and Kowahs . . . at war with each other." Chouteau is suggested as an agent to visit these tribes and promote peace because of the danger of infantry action. If Chouteau was appointed, Houston would "with great pleasure accompany him on the mission."

Houston's most famous expedition into the Indian country left Fort Gibson in November of 1832. From this expedition he never permanently returned to Gibson. Heading toward the south and west, Houston intended to visit the "Pawnee, Kimanchie, Wacoes, Keechi, Tawahconee, Comances," and other tribes in Texas.[21]

Little seems to have been accomplished on this trip, especially with regard to the Comanches, with whom the government was most anxious to make a treaty. Albert Pike, who was a frequent visitor among the Indian tribes, wrote the War Department that Houston would accomplish nothing because he went to the Southern Comanches, who were already friendly. "He will never meet one of the Northern portion from whom is our only danger and should he do so he would be immediately scalped."[22]

Perhaps Houston's most important contribution to peace was his work in the organization of the Indian peace conference. Held at

[21] SH to Ellsworth, December 1, 1832, Houston, *Writings,* I, 267–271.

[22] Albert Pike Letter, in GSHBF, GRL; Robert L. Duncan, *Reluctant General: The Life and Times of Albert Pike,* pp. 57–58.

Cantonment Gibson after Houston had left for Texas, this conference, which is known as the Stokes Conference, was the largest peace negotiation ever held in the Indian Territory. Montfort Stokes presided over representatives from the major tribes throughout the Southwestern United States.[23]

While Houston did visit these tribes and arrange for them to come to Gibson for peace negotiations, this purpose was only secondary. He had corresponded with New York financier James Prentiss in May of 1832 of his intention to visit Texas to arrange for the purchase and extension of land grants.[24] Houston's intention to visit Texas was the compelling factor in the War Department's requesting him to visit the tribes. Since he had already planned to make this trip, the War Department refused to pay all the expenses which Houston submitted.

Houston was the greatest "peacemaker" in American Indian relations. He conducted more peace negotiations and signed treaties with more tribes than any agent, War Department official, or President in the history of the United States. It was not a false modesty but the truth of his nature which led Houston to write President Jackson of his purpose among the Indians:

> To become a missionary among the Indians, is rendered impossible, for a want of that Evangelical change of heart, so absolutely necessary. . . . To ameliorate the condition of the Indians . . . and to direct the feelings of the Indians in kindness to the Government, and inspire them with confidence in its justice, and magnanimity towards the Red People; have been objects of my constant solace, and attention, since I have been among them![25]

To those who argue that Houston was planning a "grand scheme" to capture Texas with the aid of the Indians, these peacemaking activities are of considerable importance.[26] Any hope of an effective force or an Indian confederation depended upon peace not only between the Northern tribes such as the Creeks, Osages, and Cherokees, but also among the tribes located in Texas, Moreover, peace had to be maintained between these Northern Tribes and the Pawnees, Comanches,

[23] For an interesting account of the Stokes's plans examine Grant Foreman, *Pioneer Days in the Early Southwest,* pp. 255–268.

[24] SH to JP, May 24, 1832, Houston, *Writings,* I, 226–227.

[25] SH to AJ, September 19, 1829, Houston, *Writings,* I, 140–143.

[26] Owen P. White, *Texas: An Informal Biography*, pp. 70–75.

and the smaller tribes of Texas. They needed to be at peace not only among themselves but also with the white man, and particularly the white Texans.

Absolute peace was a necessity for the type of Indian confederation which Houston almost succeeded in establishing in Texas. A short-lived Texas Indian confederation came into existence a little more than three years after Houston's last peacemaking trip left Fort Gibson. On the twenty-third day of February, 1836, a treaty was made:

> . . . between Sam Houston and John Forbes, Commissioners on the Part of the Provisional Government of Texas . . . and the Cherokees, and their associate bands now residing in Texas . . . to wit, Shawnees, Delawares, Kickapoos, Quapaws, Choctaws, Bouluxies, Iorwanies, Alabamas, Chochetties, Caddos of Naches, Tahoocattakes, and Unatoquous.[27]

The treaty provided that "It is agreed and declared that the before named Tribes or Bands shall form one community." The treaty was never ratified by the legislature of Texas and the durability of the peace which Houston had negotiated between these tribes was never tested.[28]

[27] "Treaty between Texas and the Cherokee Indians," in Emmett Starr, *History of the Cherokee Indians,* pp. 204–207.

[28] W. W. Newcomb, Jr., *The Indians of Texas: From Prehistoric to Modern Times,* pp. 346–348.

8. The Big Drunk

In his own words he "buried his sorrows in the flowing bowl . . . gave himself up to the fatal enchantress alcohol." . . . A new name [was conferred] on the white counselor—Oo-tse-tee Ar-dee-tah-skee, which means Big Drunk.

Marquis James, *The Raven: A Biography of Sam Houston,* p. 157

The greatest . . . difficulty in Indian trade was whiskey. The "ardent spirits" . . . made madmen of the Indians, yet the flow could not easily be staunched. It was an elemental problem, rooted in uncontrollable human drives —the Indians' fondness for strong drink and the heartless avarice of the whites.

Francis Paul Prucha, *American Indian Policy in the Formative Years,* p. 102

A sprawling giant, drunk in the streets of Gibson, is the only picture normally drawn of Sam Houston during his years with the Cherokees. Houston, according to these accounts, was "not far removed from the wretched outcast who hangs about the dram shops of the frontier."[1] He "buried his sorrows in the flowing bowl . . . and gave himself up to the fatal enchantress alcohol."[2] A tradition persists that Houston was drunk so often that he was renamed Oo-tse-tee Ar-dee-tah-skee or "The Big Drunk." The name appears never to have been in wide use and may have been only a taunt by those surprised to see Houston drunk along the trails.[3]

[1] Alfred M. Williams, "Houston's Life among the Indians," *Magazine of American History,* X (November, 1883), 406.

[2] Marquis James, *The Raven, A Biography of Sam Houston,* p. 157.

[3] The name seems to have been used, if at all, by the Osages. It is not a Cherokee word or a combination of Cherokee words. Although the title is generally thought to be Osage, James suggests that it was used by the Cherokees. James,

But drinking was almost a way of life at frontier posts in the early Southwest. Drunkenness was common, soldiers frequented the disorderly houses kept by the Cherokees on tribal lands just beyond the garrisons, and the open gambling often exploded into drunken brawls. Cantonment Gibson was no exception among these places, for there was little else for the soldier to do except join in the drinking, fighting, and gambling around the post.[4]

General Arbuckle was an indulgent man and at Christmas of Houston's last year in the Cherokee Nation directed that the soldiers' allowance of a gill of whiskey be doubled. On this occasion the officers of the Fort, along with Sutler Nicks and perhaps Houston, joined in a toast which lasted through eleven tankards of rum. Private soldiers at the Fort had to gather at one of the public houses to escape the cold of their quarters, which had been built of green oak and cotton-wood logs without stone foundations. Even large fires did not offset the chill created when the cabins settled into the ground so that the windows and doors could not be tightly closed.[5]

This "intemperate use of intoxicants" was not limited to soldiers at the Fort, but was so widespread that Dr. John Thornton, a member of the Cherokee tribe, who was the surgeon at Gibson and the only physician in the area, reported that "there is considerable sickness in his tribe" and "many deaths have occurred . . . from the intemperate use of intoxicants."[6] Houston estimated that one group of traders "in the short space of six weeks . . . did actually sell to the Indians no less than 250 *barrels of whiskey*, making in all about 8,250 gallons" and concluded that "to say about 40,000 gallons had been introduced and sold to the Indians, would not enlarge upon the truth."[7] One of the most entertaining letters from Cantonment Gibson was written about Hous-

---

The Raven, p. 157; Marion Karl Wisehart, *Sam Houston: American Giant*, p. 62.

[4] Grant Foreman, *Pioneer Days in the Early Southwest*, p. 174.

[5] Henry Leavitt Ellsworth, *Washington Irving on the Prairie, or a Narrative of a Tour of the Southwest in the Year 1832*, p. 4; *Muskogee Daily Phoenix*, January 31, 1932.

[6] *Muskogee Daily Phoenix*, February 7, 1932.

[7] SH, "In Defense of the Indians," *Arkansas Gazette*, August 14, 1830; Sam Houston, *The Writings of Sam Houston*, Amelia W. Williams and Eugene C. Barker (eds.), I, 167.

ton's Cherokee brother-in-law, Captain John Rogers, Cherokee interpreter. Rogers wrote a promissory note to a Mr. Drape which Agent DuVal refused to pay because it was "a gambling debt made by . . . my interpreter . . . having been won from him under the influence of liquor."[8]

Houston quickly joined in this frontier drinking and gambling, for temperance was not one of his virtues. It is reasonable to assume that Houston had joined his Cherokee brothers in their celebrations in Tennessee and it is known that he drank heavily during his days as a soldier. It is recorded that young Houston was one of the heavy drinkers who hoped to impress his older comrades with his manliness. Drink was his solace from the agony of an open wound which caused him constant pain. His love of whiskey was well known in Tennessee, and friends of Eliza Allen speculated that their separation stemmed from this.[9]

Accounts of Houston's drunken performances are so frequent that they must have been more than an occasional drunken card game or celebration. There are letters from Houston which, according to astute observers, were written in a drunken rage.[10] Conduct toward men such as John Jolly, whom Houston respected, can be explained only by drunken abandonment. Houston argued so violently with Jolly that in a drunken temper he struck his adopted father. The screaming Houston was finally overcome by a body of Cherokee warriors; later, struck by remorse and humiliation, he apologized to the National Council and publicly requested Jolly's forgiveness.[11]

The picture of Houston as "The Big Drunk" is particularly appropriate for about six months of his three years among the Cherokees. Unquestionably he was drunk for most of the time from his resignation until his arrival at Jolly's. Observers of Houston on the boat from Nashville record that he was rarely sober, and it was during this time that Houston often drunkenly boasted of building a "Rocky Mountain"

[8] DuVal to McKenney, July 28, 1828, GSHBF, GFT, GRL.

[9] Houston, after his third marriage, gave up drink. See F. N. Boney, "The Raven Tamed," *The Southwestern Historical Quarterly,* LXVIII (July, 1964), 90–92.

[10] Grant Foreman Notes, OFN, OIA.

[11] James, *The Raven,* p. 157; Jennings Wise, *The Red Man in the New World Drama,* p. 369.

Alliance and becoming emperor of the West.[12] According to tradition, James Bowie refused to believe that the drunken, unshaven passenger was Sam Houston.[13] The story of Houston's drunken sacrifice of clothing to the god of wine, Bacchus, illustrates his conduct as "The Big Drunk."[14]

The self-pity which inspired this drunken spirit is reflected in letters to friends in Tennessee. "[I] drank the cup and the *dregs* only remain for me to consume."[15] Just as quickly as the early self-pity came over him, a new feeling of renewed interest in life seems to have come. "When I left the world I had persuaded myself that I would lose all care . . . but it is not so, for as often as I visit Cant. Gibson, where I can obtain News Papers, I find that my interest is rather increased than diminished. It is hard for an old Trooper, to forget the *note* of the *Bugle*!"[16] It has been suggested that the picture of a fallen governor drunk in the gutter was convenient for any political schemes. As long as his associates in Tennessee and his national followers, including the President, pictured him as "The Big Drunk" or a "Squaw Man" his activities might be subject to less scrutiny.

Typical of the conflicting mythology surrounding "The Big Drunk" are the stories of his miraculous recovery from this "drunken exile." Following the shock of a drunken attack on John Jolly, Houston is said to have renounced his drunken ways and become a sober citizen of the Cherokee Nation. Diana, his Indian wife, nursed him back to health, and her devotion to him returned to him the meaning of life. Another story credits the shock of Diana's death as inspiring him to reform himself and go to Texas to establish the new republic as a monument to her. Yet another places the moment of recovery just before he enters the House chambers to defend himself from the charges brought against him for the attacks on Congressman Stanbery. Typical of yet another group of stories is that his mother's death caused him to see the damage he was doing to those he loved.[17]

[12] Wisehart, *Sam Houston,* p. 52.

[13] Paul I. Wellman, *Magnificent Destiny*, p. 298.

[14] James, *The Raven,* pp. 90–91.

[15] SH to AJ, May 18, 1830, Houston, *Writings,* I, 149–150.

[16] SH to AJ, September 19, 1829, Houston, *Writings,* I, 142.

[17] A sampling of these stories can be seen by examining Owen P. White,

The arrival of a shipment of whiskey for General Houston faced Colonel Matthew Arbuckle with the question of "how much whiskey can one man drink?" or more specifically whether five barrels of whiskey was too much for Sam Houston's own use. The "five barrels of whiskey, four of mongahala, and one of corn, one Barrel of Cognac, one Gin, one rum and two wine"[18] were seized by Arbuckle and held at the sutler's store. Houston's right as a trader to keep these for his own use and for sale to army officers and men was placed directly at issue when Arbuckle formally requested the government to "declare the greatest quantity a single trader should be permitted to introduce for private use within one year."[19]

Secretary of War G. C. Randolph would not make a ruling on how much whiskey Houston should be permitted to introduce for his own use, but simply ordered the confiscated liquor returned because of Houston's residence and Cherokee citizenship. Randolph further directed that if the liquor was for the private use of a resident such as Houston it could be brought into the Cherokee Nation.[20] The quantity of whiskey which Houston could use was left for Arbuckle and the local Cherokee agent to decide. Commandant Arbuckle, who was at times a "meddlesome figure in Indian Affairs,"[21] returned the whiskey to Houston, either because he decided that "five barrels" was not too much for "The Big Drunk" or because he did not want to intensify the whiskey controversy.

Five barrels of whiskey for a man with Houston's propensity for drink and for the Wigwam Neosho do not seem like a large quantity, however, when in one evening as many as thirteen toasts with a frontier

Texas: An Informal Biography, p. 76; Wellman, *Magnificent Destiny*, pp. 320–321, Wise, *The Red Man in the New World Drama*, p. 369.

[18] SH to MA, July 21, 1830, Houston, *Writings*, I, 185–186.

[19] MA to Randolph, July 23, 1830, Matthew Arbuckle Papers, GSHBF, GRL.

[20] Randolph to JE, September 11, 1830, Matthew Arbuckle Papers, GSHBF, GRL. See also Benjamin F. Hall (comp.), *Official Opinions of the Attorneys General of the United States Advising the President and Heads of Departments in Relation to Their Official Duties; and Expounding the Constitution, Subsisting Treaties with Foreign Governments and with Indian Tribes, and the Public Laws of the Country*, II, 402–405.

[21] Carolyn Thomas Foreman, Letter dated September 26, 1949, "Arkansas File Box," OIA.

tankard were lifted.[22] A barrel could be considerably drained by the visitors who frequently came to Houston's home, which was located along the Texas Road and at the half-way point between Cantonment Gibson and the trading establishment at Three Forks. The Wigwam Neosho was an ideal place for the traveler to rest, with fellowship warmed from the five barrels.

But less than a month earlier, on June 26, 1830, Arbuckle had made a solemn declaration to Secretary of War Eaton of his intention to restrict traffic on "the damnable ardent spirits" and indicated that he was fearful Houston's supply would reach the Cherokees.[23] Because the Cherokees were located directly on the border of Arkansas Territory and because of the extensive steamboat trade into their own territory, all efforts to prevent the whiskey traffic had failed. George Vashon, in desperation, had written from the Cherokee Agency that:

> The exact number of Persons engaged in the traffic of Ardent Spirits in this nation cannot be correctly ascertained but may be safely computed at about one hundred. A large portion of the whites who have intermarried with the Cherokees, are generally engaged in the traffic, and most of that portion of the Cherokees, of least Indian blood, such as you may have seen at the Dept. of genteel [nature] are also generally engaged in this traffic, and their zealous co-operation with their white associates is the principal obstacle to an effectual enforcement of the system of entire exclusion of Ardent Spirits from this part of the Indian Country.[24]

One of the most hotly debated questions concerning Houston's stay with the Cherokee is, "Did Houston sell whiskey to the Indians?" Houston denied any such intention by a letter to Arbuckle in which he declared "[n]or shall one drop of whiskey be sold to . . . [the] Indian . . . or the agents of the respective tribes. . . . I entertain too much respect for the wishes of the Government—too much friendship for the Indians; and too much respect for myself to make traffic of the baleful

[22] Carolyn Thomas Foreman, "General John Nicks and His Wife, Sarah Perkins Nicks," *The Chronicles of Oklahoma,* VIII (December, 1930) 400.

[23] MA to JE, June 26, 1830, Clarence E. Carter (comp. and ed.), *The Territorial Papers of the United States,* XXI, 242–246.

[24] Vashon to Herring, October 12, 1833, "Cherokee Agency, West," Letters Received by the Office of Indian Affairs, Microfilm Publications, Copy No. 234, Roll No. 78, The National Archives of the United States.

curse!"[25] There is no evidence that Houston made whiskey sales to the Indians, but it would be naive to assume that drinks from these "five barrels" were never enjoyed by his Cherokee guests. Even his political enemies rarely made charges that Houston trafficked in illegal whiskey. The biting attacks of Tekatoka which appeared in the *Arkansas Gazette* alluded to Houston's matrimonial alliance but contained no hint of illegal sale of whiskey.[26] Lester in his *The Life of Sam Houston: The Only Authentic Memoir of Him Ever Published* answered charges that Houston was a "Whiskey Runner."

> During the entire period he resided in that region, he was unceasing in his efforts to prevent the introduction of ardent spirits among the Indians; and though, for more than a year, he had a trading establishment between the Grand River and the Verdigries, he never introduced or trafficked in those destructive drinks. This, too, was at a period when he was far from being a temperate man himself. But, whatever might be his own occasional indulgence during his visits to Fort Gibson and other white settlements, he had too much humanity and love for the Red men, ever to contribute to their crimes or their misfortunes by introducing or trafficking in those damnable poisons.[27]

The peddler, "whiskey runner," or "bootlegger" was subject to open scorn at Gibson and soldiers who were caught were made to "walk sign." During the period that Houston lived in the area, a Private Wilson was found guilty of bringing whiskey into Cantonment Gibson and was sentenced to stand from sunrise to sunset for ten days on a barrel in front of the guard house with a board labeled "whiskey seller" on his back and a bottle in each outstretched arm. Other offenders were forced to carry these signs and empty bottles down the streets while the soldiers and traders ridiculed and scoffed at them.[28]

Much of the controversy over whiskey sales stemmed from a misunderstanding of the nature of the Cherokee, his culture, and his civilization.[29] These were Indians unlike the Osages, who, despite their sav-

[25] SH to MA, July 21, 1830, Houston, *Writings,* I, 185–187.

[26] *Arkansas Gazette* (*Supplement*), October 20, 1830.

[27] C. Edwards Lester, *The Life of Sam Houston: The Only Authentic Memoir of Him Ever Published,* p. 55.

[28] Carolyn Thomas Foreman, "Military Discipline in Early Oklahoma," *The Chronicles of Oklahoma,* VI (June, 1928), 140.

[29] See Chapter 2, "Houston's Indian Brothers."

1. While visiting in Washington, Houston had this miniature painted of himself in his formal Cherokee Indian attire. Courtesy Oklahoma Historical Society.

2. A nineteenth-century illustrator depicted the reunion of Sam Houston and Chief Jolly. From Charles Edward Lester's *Authentic Memoir*.

3. Colonel A. P. Chouteau, a member of the founding family of St. Louis, was the most influential white man in the Osage country. Sketch by Vincent Lackey. Courtesy Oklahoma Historical Society.

4. Andrew Jackson was Sam Houston's mentor. Some historians have seen Houston's retreat to the Cherokee Nation as a plot engineered by Jackson to free Texas from Mexico. Portrait by Thomas Sully. Courtesy Library of Congress.

5. While visiting in Nashville, Houston had himself painted as Caius Marius, a gesture interpreted as an announcement to the world of his intention to return to power. Courtesy Texas State Archives.

6. John Jolly, Chief of the Western Cherokees, adopted the young Sam Houston as his son. Painting by George Catlin. Courtesy National Collection of Fine Arts, Smithsonian Institution.

7. As early as 1818 Cherokee Chief Bowles, who claimed to have given his daughter in marriage to Houston, located a branch of his tribe in Texas. Sketch by William A. Berry. Courtesy Texas State Library.

8. Mellissa Houston, a Kiowa Indian, claimed to be the Indian wife of Sam Houston. This picture, taken when "Granny" was 120 years old, was made at the request of the superintendent of the Kiowa Agency near Anadarko, Oklahoma. Courtesy Oklahoma Historical Society.

9. John Drew, a prominent Cherokee merchant, with whom some historians suggest Houston operated his Wigwam Neosho. Drew also accompanied Houston to Washington as a member of the Cherokee delegation. Courtesy Oklahoma Historical Society.

10. Sequoyah, a citizen of Cherokee Nation West, invented the syllabary which brought literacy to the Cherokee tribe. Courtesy Office of Anthropology, Bureau of American Ethnology Collection, Smithsonian Institution.

11. Dutch, a Western Cherokee leader, was associated with the movement to locate a branch of the Cherokees in the Republic of Texas. Sketch by George Catlin. Courtesy Newberry Library.

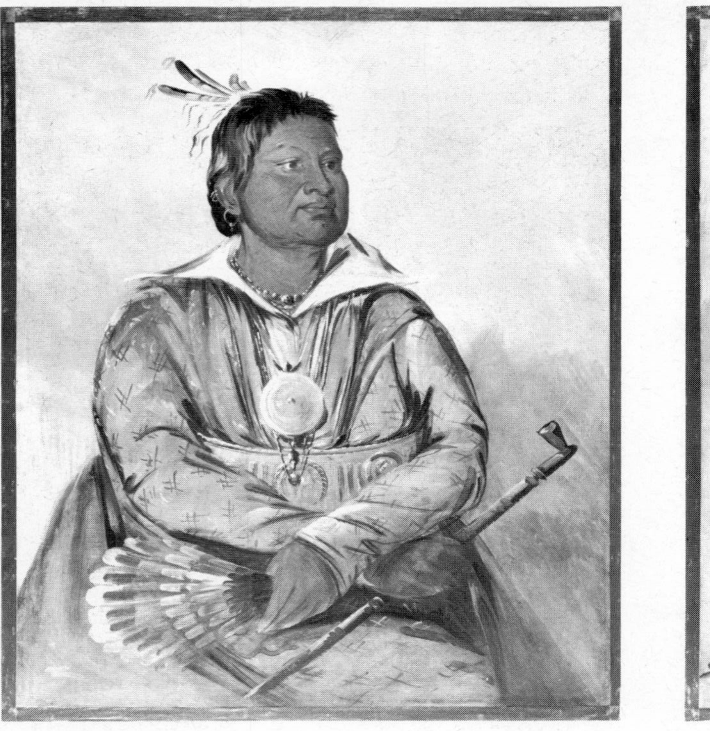

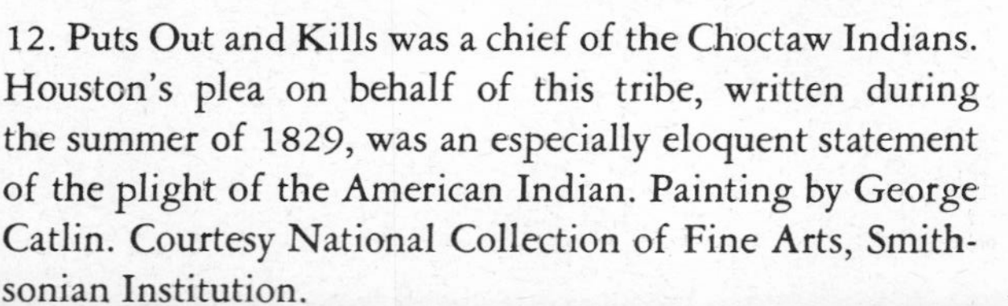

12. Puts Out and Kills was a chief of the Choctaw Indians. Houston's plea on behalf of this tribe, written during the summer of 1829, was an especially eloquent statement of the plight of the American Indian. Painting by George Catlin. Courtesy National Collection of Fine Arts, Smithsonian Institution.

13. Black Coat, second chief of the Western Cherokees, was the delegate in charge of the Cherokees who accompanied Houston to Washington in December of 1831. Painting by George Catlin. Courtesy National Collection of Fine Arts, Smithsonian Institution.

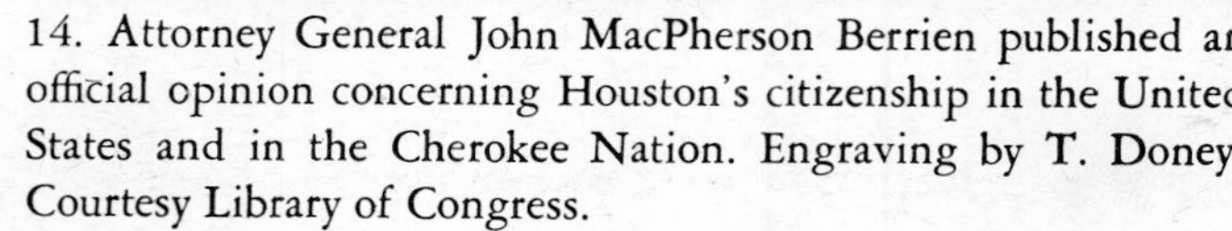

14. Attorney General John MacPherson Berrien published an official opinion concerning Houston's citizenship in the United States and in the Cherokee Nation. Engraving by T. Doney. Courtesy Library of Congress.

15. John Nicks, sutler of Fort Gibson, operated a trading establishment at Gibson and at Fort Smith. Nicks was also agent for the *Arkansas Gazette*, in which Houston's "Indian Chapters" appeared. Courtesy Oklahoma Historical Society.

16. The "Wigwam Neosho." The Historic American Buildings Survey of the WPA photographed this house, which was believed by many to be the site of the Wigwam. Courtesy Oklahoma Historical Society.

17. Houston and the Cherokee delegation which he accompanied to Washington stayed at Brown's Indian Queen Hotel, located on Pennsylvania Avenue. Lithograph by Endicott & Co., ca. 1834. Courtesy Library of Congress.

18. In 1904, with the permission of the War Department, the body of an Indian woman believed to be the wife of Sam Houston was reburied in the Officers' Circle of the United States National Cemetery at Fort Gibson, Oklahoma. Photo by Katherine Cook.

agery, maintained a surprising temperance, or the Pawnees and Quapaws, who were constantly victimized by traders importing large kegs of whiskey and rum. The Cherokees were in much the same position as the white man; in fact, the Indians with whom Houston was intimately associated are said to have made a "genteel" use of spirits, serving wine with meals and brandy to warm the after-dinner conversation.

In 1833 Captain John Stuart wrote to the secretary of war to explain that the rules for the sale of whiskey which applied to most Indian tribes should not be enforced against the Cherokees.

> The Cherokees are so far advanced in civilization and their habits, custom, manner of living so much resembles those of the whites that spiritous liquors are sometimes as necessary with them as with the whites for instance in cases of sickness and neighborhood assemblages—such as House raising, log rolling, and Corn husking. One fact with regard to the Cherokees which may not be generally known is that they in a general way drink much less spirits than the Indians of other nations . . . and from their civilized condition do not when drunk show one half the savage ferocity of other Indians . . . and many of them never do drink spirits to any excess, and some of them do not now, nor ever did drink any.[30]

The Cherokees were themselves engaged in the commercial distillation of whiskey, an enterprise to which members of the merchant class of Cherokees were very early drawn by the high profits. The Rogers family had operated a distillery in Tennessee and had at this time begun operations in the Cherokee Nation West, where Charles Rogers conducted a profitable distillery. Agent Vashon had requested that the War Department purchase Charles Rogers' improvements, because as long as the Cherokees operated their own distilleries the sale of whiskey could never be prohibited.[31]

Attempts to prevent the sale of "ardent spirits" among the Indians were intensified in 1828 and 1829 through the combined efforts of

[30] Captain John Stuart to Lewis Cass, August 12, 1833, "Cherokee Agency, West," Letters Received by the Office of Indian Affairs, Microfilm Publications, Copy No. 234, Roll No. 78, The National Archives of the United States.

[31] The Charles Rogers Distillery is described in considerable detail in Grant Foreman, *A History of Oklahoma,* p. 43; Vashon to Cass, November 20, 1832, "Cherokee Agency West," Letters Received by the Office of Indian Affairs, Microfilm Publications, Copy No. 234, Roll No. 78, The National Archives of the United States.

missionaries, the War Department, and temperance chapters which had been organized among the Indians with a membership limited to the Indians themselves.[32] In May of 1829 Colonel Arbuckle seized the goods of the trading firm of William DuVal and Peter A. Carnes in accordance with the provisions of the acts of 1802 and 1822. Arbuckle and the temperance societies were shocked when neither Samuel C. Roane, the United States district attorney for the Territory of Arkansas, nor the marshall for Arkansas Territory could see a way to bring the traders to trial, and Secretary of War Eaton ordered the return of the illegally seized whiskey.[33]

Houston is associated with the renewed efforts to prevent the sale of whiskey, which came in 1832 under a general directive of the War Department that all stores of whiskey in the Indian country be seized. Under this directive goods held by both native and licensed traders became subject to confiscation and destruction. There is no report that under this directive any whiskey was seized from Houston personally, but Houston was involved by the seizure of large stocks of his business associates—Benjamin Hawkins, Peter Harper, and John Drew.[34]

This seizure was so clearly a violation of the law that Cherokee Agent Vashon demanded payment for the goods taken. In defense of this position he argued:

I do not consider the introduction of said whiskey by the Cherokees a violation of any law . . . and therefore said to the Cherokee owners when making the seizures that I had no doubt they would be paid a fair [price] for it by the government. They knew that their introduction to said whiskey had not been a violation of any former law and that it could not be legally

[32] An excellent detailed discussion of the enforcement of the early laws is found in Francis Paul Prucha, *American Indian Policy in the Formative Years,* Chap. VI, "The Crusade against Whiskey," pp. 102–138.

[33] DuVal & Carnes to MA, September 24, 1829, Matthew Arbuckle Papers, GFT, GRL. Papers dealing with the DuVal and Carnes Case are printed in Carter, *Territorial Papers,* XXI, 32–35, 36–39, 53–55, 58–60, 70–72, 102–104, 120–127, 181, 285, 286, 292–295, 300, 333–336, 346–348, 349–350, 371–375, 381, 385–386, 390–395.

[34] "Muskogee and Environs," Map drawn by Winnifred Clark and Grant Foreman, Item I of the maps, notes, and explanations located in the Foreman Room of the Muskogee, Oklahoma, Public Library.

seized, but . . . they yielded a respectful acquiescence under an impression that they are justifiably entitled to remuneration from the Government.[35]

Included with this letter was an abstract of the seized whiskey of Peter Harper, John Coy, and Colonel Walter Webber.[36]

Abstract of Seizure of Whiskey (November 19, 1832)

Date of Seizure	*Of Whom Seized*	*No. of Barrels*	*Gallons*	*Remarks*
Nov. 1, 1932	Peter Harper, white man with Cherokee family	8	273	Son-in-law of Jas. Rogers
Nov. 2, 1832	James Coy, a Cherokee	3	97	Quantity not correctly ascertained
Nov. 7, 1832	Col. Walter Webber, Cherokee Merchant	29	1072	One of Principal Chiefs
TOTAL		40	1442	

John Drew, with whom Houston operated his Wigwam, refused to deliver his sixty gallons and threatened the use of force to preserve his right of private property. Vashon reported:

I had attempted a seizure of some whiskey held by John Drew, a Cherokee merchant, but he resisted by denying the right of government to such seizure, and declared that it should not be seized until he was overpowered and that he would protect his rights as long as he was able; and therefore I deemed it advisable to decline enforcing a seizure . . . believing it in the best interest of the Service . . . to avoid producing an unfavorable excitement.[37]

However, Drew's supply was finally delivered to the Agents.

[35] Vashon to Cass, November 20, 1832, "Cherokee Agency, West," Letters Received by the Office of Indian Affairs, Microfilm Publications, Copy No. 234, Roll No. 78, The National Archives of the United States.

[36] "Abstract of Seizure of Whiskey," November 19, 1832, "Cherokee Agency, West," Letters Received by the Office of Indian Affairs, Microfilm Publications, Copy No. 234, Roll No. 78, The National Archives of the United States.

[37] Vashon to Cass, November 20, 1832, "Cherokee Agency, West," Letters Received by the Office of Indian Affairs, Microfilm Publications, Copy No. 234, Roll No. 78, The National Archives of the United States.

The Cherokee National Committee and Council, governing bodies of the nation, issued a joint resolution in which they demanded that the Department "be restrained until such times as the Nation can have the opportunity of consulting the Department." The Committee and Council "acknowledge[d] the prohibited article to be very injurious to our people, but think is a question to which the Cherokees ought to have the right of arguing."[38] In addition to this resolution, Drew prepared "A Memorial" of six pages, in which he set out the rights of Cherokee merchants and demanded compensation for the goods "illegally seized."[39]

Whether Houston participated in the Committee and Council meeting or in drafting Drew's memorial is uncertain. He had, however, returned from Washington when the resolution was passed, and this resolution plus the letter of protest are very much in the style of the earlier memorials written by Houston. Houston seems to have had a financial interest in the outcome, and his associates Webber and Rogers both signed the letter containing the resolution.

As in the cases of 1829, ". . . the whiskey which had been previously introduced by the Cherokees, was not legally liable to seizure." Vashon in another letter to Elbert Herring emphasized that:

> In my conference upon this subject with Sam C. Roane, Esq. U.S. District Attorney for Arkansas Territory, he distinctly stated that in this case he is clearly of opinion that the seizure was made without sufficient warrant of law, and hence an attempt to prosecute . . . would fail . . . as the whiskey introduced by an Indian into the Indian Country, previous to the Prohibitory Act of 1832 . . . could not be condemned . . . there being no law to operate on cases of this class.[40]

[38] Resolution of National Committee and Council contained in a letter to Vashon, October 10, 1832, signed at Tahlontuskee by John Rogers, The Glass, William Thornton, and Colonel Walter Webber, "Cherokee Agency, West," Letters Received by the Office of Indian Affairs, Microfilm Publications, Copy No. 234, Roll No. 78, The National Archives of the United States.

[39] John Drew, "A Memorial to Lewis Cass," March 6, 1833, "Cherokee Agency, West," Letters Received by the Office of Indian Affairs, Microfilm Publications, Copy No. 234, Roll No. 78, The National Archives of the United States.

[40] Samuel Roane, U. S. District Attorney for Arkansas Territory, quoted in a letter from Vashon to Herring, October 15, 1833, "Cherokee Agency, West,"

However, a Grand Jury was called in Little Rock to investigate the whiskey seizure and the traffic in the Indian country. With the precedents of the 1828 and 1829 seizure the position of the traders was strong. The Grand Jury returned a petition, which strongly condemned sale of "ardent spirits" to the Indians, but brought no indictments. In accordance with the opinion of the District Attorney, the seized whiskey was ordered returned.[41] Benjamin Hawkins, Peter Harper, and John Drew considered themselves vindicated of any charges against them. Sam Houston, their partner, should have felt equally free from the stigma of corruption and violation of Indian rights.

The popular tale is that Houston lay in the gutter of life suffering from the wounds of his marriage failure and drank himself through a period of three years. Nothing could be farther from the truth, for this was one of the most productive periods in Houston's life. If Houston were "The Big Drunk" this is a perfect application of Lincoln's purported request to know the brand name of the whiskey which General Grant drank so that he could issue it to his other generals.

Sam Houston accomplished more during these three years than many men do in a lifetime. During his years with the Cherokees, Houston made two trips to Washington to assist in negotiation with Jackson and the War Department, and his negotiation to end the warfare between the Osages and the Creeks and the Cherokees was the most successful in thirty years of attempted settlements. A long-range reform program in the Indian Agency system as well as removal of agents of questionable ability and honesty resulted from his intervention; through his political column in the *Arkansas Gazette* and the pamphlets of Tah-lohn-tus-ky and Standing Bear, Houston spearheaded the Indian Bureau reform programs.

Letters Received by the Office of Indian Affairs, Microfilm Publications, Copy No. 234, Roll No. 78, The National Archives of the United States.

[41] Grand Jury Presentment, Little Rock, Grand Jury of the United States for the Territory of Arkansas, July 12, 1832, conclusions in Carter, *Territorial Papers,* XXI, 517–519. No actual records of the Grand Jury were kept, since the proceedings were secret. See Roane's letter to Secretary of War, September 19, 1832, Carter, *Territorial Papers,* XXI, 543, also see pages 530–531 and 887–888.

9. Indian Wives and Children

> Some of the most adventurous spirits have . . . mingled their blood with the Cherokees . . . among them . . . Sam Houston.
>
> Alfred M. Williams, "Life among the Cherokees," *Lippincotts Magazine*, XXVII (February, 1881), 200

Houston is said to have "loved the Indian woman."[1] The legends of Indian wives and children of Sam Houston are widespread in both Oklahoma and Tennessee. The truth of most of these stories is as uncertain as their origin. The story of Talihina, or Diana Rogers, is documented, but the others depend upon the statements of the alleged wives and children.

A wound which Houston received in the Battle of Horseshoe Bend remained a "running sore in his groin" and is said to have repulsed his first wife, Eliza Allen.[2] Many of these legends grow from this wound and the rejection by Eliza. Indian women are said to be more sympathetic and many are supposed to have nursed him back to health, while others came to love him because he had been rejected.

Mellisa Houston is perhaps the most interesting of these wives.[3]

[1] The frequency of stories of Indian wives and loves can be observed from the historical surveys and interviews in the "Indian-Pioneer Papers," Typescripts of Interviews of the Works Progress Administration, OIA, PC, UOL. See especially Vol. 57, p. 507; Vol. 76, p. 501; Vol. 79, pp. 108–110.

[2] Louise Davis, "The Mystery of the Raven," *The Nashville Tennessean,* August 5, 12, 19, 1962.

[3] Although references to an Indian wife of the Plains tribes are often made, "Granny Houston" is discussed in detail in only a few places. For a complete picture of "Granny" see W. P. Campbell, "Sam Houston in Indian Territory," *Historia Quarterly,* VIII (July, 1919), 3–4, and "More about Houston in Oklahoma," *Historia Quarterly,* VIII (October, 1919), 6–8; H. F. O'Beirne, *Leaders and Leading Men of the Indian Territory,* p. 319; "Melissa Houston, full blood Kiowa and one time wife of Sam Houston, is dying of neglect and starvation in her tepee near Anadarko, Oklahoma. Pathetic Story of Old Woman" in *Mus-*

Referred to as "Granny" Houston, or the Kiowa wife of Sam Houston, she insisted until her death that she had been married to him. Her presence was reported by the superintendent of the Kiowa Agency, after which she became a popular figure in the press. Once a handsome woman, at the time she was discovered near Anadarko, Oklahoma, she had been abandoned by her tribesmen to die. Even at this time, she was living in a large tepee within three miles of the Kiowa agency and owned many head of horses and cattle. The question of where she got this wealth is often answered by saying that Houston gave his possessions to her when he went to Texas.

Granny Houston, according to one account, was a full-blood Wichita who came from Texas in 1859 to make her home near Anadarko. She was considered a stoic even among her own people. Texas was a name which she seemed to detest, "and no one knew why." She would not tell about her life with Houston. When asked she would react with a "drawling 'sa-am,' with an ominous fling of the hand as though Texas, Sam and everything connected with either word was the acme of repulsion."

According to other accounts Granny Houston freely told the story of her marriage to Houston. They were associated, she claimed, in the vicinity of the Canadian River at the eastern portion of the Choctaw Nation. Granny stated they "lived . . . on the Canadian and close to Caddo, now on the M. K. & T. Railroad" and that "he was a kind and gentle husband, and a good hunter, always keeping the wigwam well supplied with game and fish."

Little is known about Granny Houston. She lived with the Kiowas near Anadarko until her death. Although she claimed to be a Kiowa she was considered by some to be a Wichita. If she were a Kiowa or Wichita then she could not likely have been married to Houston. At the time of her "marriage to General Houston," neither the Kiowas nor the Wichitas had been removed to Oklahoma, but were still inhabiting Southern Colorado, New Mexico, and Western Texas. They would not have been "at all disposed to intermarriage or cohabitation with white men settled so far east of their hunting grounds." There

---

kogee Times Democrat, January 1, 1909, p. 5, col. 2. All information about "Granny" comes from these articles.

was much speculation that Granny was a Cherokee of the old settlers or Western band; however, she was held in high esteem by the Kiowas and Wichitas.

The classic response to Granny's picture is the remark that "Houston would not have married such a woman."[4] By her own calculations, Granny was older than Houston. She was born in 1781 and would have been 48 years old when 36-year-old Houston came to live with the Cherokees. She was reported in excellent health as late as 1909, at which time Granny would have been 128 years old.

Another of Houston's supposed Indian brides provides quite a contrast to "Granny." "Caroline" is described as a beautiful and intelligent young woman who had a college education in an age when few men graduated from high school. Houston is said to have married her near Fort Smith, Arkansas. He lived with Caroline on a large farm in the Arkansas River bottom. When Caroline died a short time after they were married, Houston erected a monument over her grave and went to Texas.[5]

Chief Bowles, or "The Bowl," leader of the Texas Cherokees, gave his daughter to Houston in marriage, according to statements made by the Bowl himself. Since the Bowl was leader of the entire confederation of Indian tribes in Texas, an alliance with his daughter would have been in the political tradition of Houston's marriages. Houston did correspond with Bowles and spoke of Bowles' family as his own. The story of this marriage was recorded by Samuel Maverick in 1838. Bowles returned from the city of Houston by way of the Maverick house with ten or twelve of his tribe. It was here that Bowl acknowledged the marriage.

Maverick noted that:

> . . . after tea, we were dancing when "Bowles" came in dressed in a breech-cloth, anklets, moccasins, feathers and a long white linen shirt. . . . He said the pretty girls in Houston had danced with, kissed him and given him rings. We, however, begged to be excused and requested to retire, when

[4] Granny Houston seems to be a favorite of the librarians at the Oklahoma Historical Society. These ladies have observed responses to her and also provided the authors with much of the source material on her life, as well as the picture which appears in this volume.

[5] "Indian-Pioneer Papers," Vol. 40, p. 507, OIA, PC, UOL.

he in great contempt stalked out and our dance broke up. Bowles told us President Houston had lived in his Nation, that he had given Houston his daughter for his squaw.[6]

The common feature of most of these women is that they are astonishingly beautiful. "Eusbaia," whose existence is doubtful, is typical of the girls in the Cherokee country in Tennessee. She was a red-haired beauty whom he took to dances. They danced "half the night away," and he sought to rouse her quick jealousy by flirting with other girls. He is said to have called her "Sabia" and always kissed her gently.[7]

Houston's youth was by his own admission "wild and impetuous."[8] In the Hiwassee country, he is said to have enlivened the walks of young ladies with his recitations from the *Iliad*. "When the *Iliad* didn't suffice, they used sign language and a few words to convey meaning that needed no words at all." Houston later recalled "wandering along the banks of streams by the side of some Indian maiden, sheltered by the deep woods, conversing in that universal language which finds its sure way to the heart."[9]

An Indian, according to one account, married Houston and came down to live with him in Tennessee. Later she returned to her people. Another version of apparently the same story states that Houston wanted to marry one of the Indian maidens and bring her down to the white settlement, but that he became involved in politics and never returned for her.[10]

An entertaining story of a highly questionable origin based on these days in the Cherokee Nation in Tennessee is told about Houston's sister. She dressed as an Indian, darkened her skin, and came to the door of their home, where Houston was living after his return from the

[6] Rena Maverick Green (ed.), *Samuel Maverick, Texan: 1803–1870,* p. 70; see also Dorman Winfrey, "Chief Bowles of the Texas Cherokees," *The Chronicles of Oklahoma*, XXXII (Spring, 1954), 35.

[7] John M. Oskison, *A Texas Titan*, pp. 25–26.

[8] C. Edwards Lester, *The Life of Sam Houston: The Only Authentic Memoir of Him Ever Published*, p. 259.

[9] Marion Karl Wisehart, *Sam Houston: American Giant,* p. 12; Lester, *Authentic Memoir*, p. 259.

[10] Margaret West to Grant Foreman, October 26, 1937, Grant Foreman Letters, "Arkansas File Box," OIA.

Cherokee country. A brother announced to Houston that one of his "Indian Sweethearts" had come to see him. When Sam saw his sister, he stormed from the house in disappointed rage.[11]

Houston often returned from the Cherokees to visit with his mother and to borrow money from her to buy trinkets for the Cherokee girls. He loved to make presents and is said to have gotten so deeply into debt from buying his extravagant presents that he was forced to teach school to pay his bills.[12]

Frequently the story is told of Houston's love for one of Chouteau's Indian daughters or wards. Houston was often a guest in the Chouteau home. Chouteau, himself, had at least two Indian wives and many Indian children. Such an alliance with Houston cemented by the love or perhaps marriage of one of his daughters would certainly have pleased Chouteau.[13]

With stories of so many Indian wives, there would naturally be stories of Indian children. A *Lippincott's Magazine* story makes a sly aside to the questionable paternity of some Cherokee children.

> Some of the most adventurous spirits have found homes and mingled their blood with the Cherokees, from the days of the early colonists to the present time, and more than one name indicating such lineage is to be found among them, from Alexander Ross to Sam Houston.[14]

Another magazine was neither as sly nor as clever as *Lippincott's*. Mrs. Temple Houston collected a judgment in a libel suit for a statement that Temple Houston, son of Margaret Moffatt Lea Houston and

[11] Oskison, *A Texan Titan*, pp. 22–23.

[12] Marquis James, *The Raven: A Biography of Sam Houston*, p. 24.

[13] While there is absolutely no documentation of such a relationship, the Salina–Chouteau–Northeast–Oklahoma area continually produces legends of such a relationship. Whether this results from confusion with Diana Rogers or from Colonel Chouteau's practice of providing Osage wives for distinguished visitors is uncertain. Of this practice Henry Leavitt Ellsworth observed, "Mr. Pourteles [a companion] had become so completely beguiled by the stories of Osage customs and privileges, that notwithstanding all objections as to his course, he determined to part with us—Mr. Chouteau had assured him of the facility of getting an Osage wife during his residence. That this object blinded his eyes to all danger—." *Washington Irving on the Prairie, or a Narrative of a Tour of the Southwest in the Year 1832*, p. 5.

[14] Alfred M. Williams, "Life among the Cherokees," *Lippincott's Magazine*, XXVII (February, 1881), 200.

Samuel Houston was, in fact, the son of Sam Houston and an Indian wife.[15]

An old chief of the Yuchi claimed that he was the Indian son of Sam Houston. His son, Billy Brown, who was also a Yuchi chief, always said that his father was Houston's son. As late as 1938, Billy Brown, who was fifty-five at that time, strongly insisted that his grandfather was Sam Houston. Those who knew the old Yuchi chief said that he had "no facial characteristics of Sam Houston."[16]

One of the most interesting and mysterious manuscripts bearing Houston's name is a poem composed in Washington during 1831. Entitled simply "Poem to a Lady," these short verses which appeared in C. W. Raines' *Year Book* might have been inspired by Houston's separation from his Indian wife, Diana Rogers, or perhaps another lady.[17]

Oh, where's the step that once was light,
The Heart that felt no throb of sorrow,
When every morning's rays were bright,
And Hope could gild the coming morrow?

That Heart has ceased to beat with joy,
Has ceased to hope for coming pleasure;
It smiles on Glory as a toy
And Virtue as the only treasure.

Farewell! I wish it were not so,
That we must part and part forever,
But let the wandering exile go,
My heart from thee no change can sever.

—SAM HOUSTON

[15] Temple Houston Vertical File, OBF, ORL.
[16] "Indian-Pioneer Papers," Vol. 33, p. 236, OIA, PC, UOL.
[17] SH, "Poem to a Lady," Washington City, 1831, in Houston, *Writings*, I, 195.

10. The Campaign against Houston

> We regard the residence of . . . Governor Houston among the Indians, as a most injurious circumstance. He is vicious to a fearful extent, and hostile to Christians and Christianity. . . . he has very considerable influence.
>
> The Reverend Cephas Washburn, Missionary to the Cherokees, September 1, 1830, in Thomas Benton Williams, *The Soul of the Red Man,* p. 85

Houston came to the Cherokees to escape the scathing attacks which he was suffering as governor of Tennessee. Leaving Nashville just ahead of a vicious mob, Houston looked forward to peaceful days spent hunting in the forest and resting in the home of his old friend, John Jolly. Houston expressed a feeling of relief as he embraced Jolly, his foster father and Cherokee chieftain. According to his *Authentic Memoir,* "Houston has often been heard to say, that when he laid himself down to sleep that night, after the gloom and sorrow of the past weeks, he felt like a weary wanderer, returned at last to his father's house."[1]

Houston's life with the Indian brothers was not to be so peaceful as he had dreamed, for during these years Houston was constantly under attack. "Seldom, if ever, in the history of this county, has so malignant a persecution been waged against a public man."[2] Attack came from all sides: from the Church because of his intemperance and influence over the Indians; from other traders because of his alleged influence and favoritism among the Cherokee leaders; from the commandant of Cantonment Gibson because Houston would not purchase a trader's license and because the commandant feared Houston sold whiskey to the Indians; from Eliza Allen's family because of the rumors resulting from his

[1] C. Edwards Lester, *The Life of Sam Houston: The Only Authentic Memoir of Him Ever Published*, pp. 51–52.

[2] Lester, *Authentic Memoir*, p. 62.

separation and resignation; from his political enemies in Tennessee, who feared his return; from the readers of the *Arkansas Gazette* because of his column; from Congressman Stanbery and the "Indian Ring," which he attacked; from the enemies of President Jackson, who had hoped to injure "Old Hickory" through Houston; and from the gossip mongers, who love to tell a new tale.

Public attacks for his aid to the Cherokees were not new to Houston, who, as subagent, incurred the wrath of Secretary of War Calhoun when he accompanied a Cherokee delegation to Washington dressed in his Indian attire. Calhoun never understood Houston's explanation that wearing the native costume helped him deal with Cherokees or that Governor McMinn had asked him to wear his Indian habit. Calhoun developed a strong dislike for Houston and charged him with smuggling slaves and with irregularities in his subagency finances. Even though Houston was exonerated, these charges haunted him through his entire political career and were frequently used against him even during the years he lived with the Cherokees.[3] It should be noted that Houston eloquently refuted all of these charges brought against him.[4]

Rumors circulated against Houston of a "grand design" to make himself emperor of Texas with the assistance of the Cherokee Indians. These rumors opened him to question by his old friend General Jackson. The rumors were designed to end his political career forever and seem almost to have worked.[5]

Perhaps the most vicious attacks appeared as a result of the articles which Houston wrote as Tah-lohn-tus-ky and Standing Bear in the *Arkansas Gazette*. Tekatoka wrote to Standing Bear, alias General Houston:[6]

> . . . Sir, you may rest assured that the mere ridiculous, feeble and contemptible asservations of every *vagabond* and *fugitive* from the just in-

[3] Margaret Coit, *John C. Calhoun*, p. 122; John P. Brown, *Old Frontiers: The Story of the Cherokee Indians from Earliest Times to the Date of Their Removal to the West, 1838*, pp. 476–477; Marion Karl Wisehart, *Sam Houston: American Giant*, p. 22–24; *Arkansas Gazette* (*Supplement*), October 20, 1830.

[4] SH, Speech, September 9, 1850, Sam Houston, *The Writings of Sam Houston*, Amelia W. Williams and Eugene C. Barker (eds.), V, 238–252.

[5] For a more detailed discussion of these rumors and of Houston's reaction see Chapter 17, "Cherokee Emperor of Texas."

[6] *Arkansas Gazette* (*Supplement*), October 20, 1830.

dignation of an offended community . . . will neither be regarded by his friends nor credited by his enemies . . . without wishing, sir, to triumph over *fallen greatness*. . . . I will now bid your turband honor adieu, leaving you in the enjoyment you may find in your matrimonial alliance, hoping your fair bride may induce you to make a prudent husbandry of whatever resources you may have left, awaken you to a sense of your degradation and in the belief "*stat magni nominis umbra.*"

Signed—Tekatoka

Many traders in the area bitterly hated Houston because he was allegedly a favorite among the Cherokees and received contracts and other rights from them. The attacks which he constantly made upon traders and agents provoked criticism so severe that Colonel Hugh Love, who was later associated with Houston, is reported to have said ". . . some things . . . which were so harsh that they could not be repeated."[7]

Sam Houston and certain missionaries were in a constant battle for influence among the Cherokees. Houston wanted to be the center of the entire Indian community and there was no place in his plans for interference from the church or church workers.[8] Houston expressed his distrust for the missionaries among the Indians to the famous French social observor Alexis de Tocqueville, whom he met on a trip down the Mississippi in the winter of 1832. Their dialogue was recorded by Tocqueville, who asked Houston of Christianity among the Indians. Houston replied, "My opinion is that to send Missionaries among them is a very poor way to go about civilizing the Indians . . . Christianity is . . . above the intelligence of the people so little advanced in civilization . . ."[9]

The missionaries seemed even less pleased about Houston's presence among the Cherokees. Yet Miss Nancy Thompson, who devoted her life to bring Christianity to the Indians at mission schools such as Brainerd, Park Hill, and Tullahassee, is said to have "known Sam Houston and . . . listened to his tales" and "'learned to match his skill, and at the same time to satisfy her own rigid Christian scruples, in dealing with the Indians. She knew when patience ceased to be a virtue, and she knew how, when punishment was necessary, to make the punish-

[7] *Muskogee Daily Phoenix,* December 27, 1931.

[8] Carolyn Thomas Foreman, Interview, August 20, 1964.

[9] George W. Pierson, *Tocqueville in America,* p. 388.

ment fit the crime."[10] The conflict between the missionaries and Houston is vividly illustrated by an open attack which Cephas Washburn, long-time missionary among the Western Cherokees, wrote against him:

> We regard the residence of such a man as Governor Houston among the Indians, as a most injurious circumstance. He is vicious to a fearful extent, and hostile to Christians and Christianity. This I would not wish to have known as coming from me, as he has very considerable influence. As an offset to his influence, I am happy to inform you of the recent arrival of Captain Vashon, the new agent.[11]

While Houston was among the Cherokees they began to organize a school system which was independent from the mission schools. John Rogers and John Drew, who were generally recipients of the Cherokee Council contracts for supplies, actively sought an independent school system unassociated with Dwight Mission. Rogers, according to reports of the missionaries, was hostile to their activities and openly attacked them in speeches and private conversations.[12]

These attacks on Houston made by Washburn and the missionaries at Union Mission were not universal. A warm friendship existed between Houston and Dr. Marcus Palmer of the Fairfield Mission, which was located near Tahlontuskee. The relationship was so close that Houston's associates encouraged the expansion of Palmer's Fairfield Mission, and Houston wrote that "Mr. Palmer is a useful and intelligent Gentleman, and worth all the missionaries in the Nation of the Cherokees. If he can be assisted it will be well for the Indians."[13]

At this same time Houston was encouraging the abolishment or removal of Union Mission. The relocation of Union had been a favorite scheme among the Cherokees for many years. When Houston joined in this advocacy, the missionaries, Agent Vashon, and Colonel Arbuckle attacked him as encouraging a plan for the benefit of a few

[10] Althea Bass, *The Story of Tullahassee*, p. 65.

[11] Cephas Washburn Report, September 1, 1830, in Thomas Benton Williams, *The Soul of the Red Man*, p. 85.

[12] Althea Bass, *Cherokee Messenger*, pp. 184–185.

[13] Carolyn Thomas Foreman, "Fairfield Mission," *The Chronicles of Oklahoma*, XXVII (Winter, 1949–1950), 376–377.

greedy men.[14] The missionaries also opposed Houston for his intemperance. Their organized programs to get the Cherokee Committee and Council to prohibit the sale of whiskey obviously suffered from the activities of Houston and his native Cherokee trading partners. The example of "The Big Drunk" was difficult for the missionaries to overcome.

While Houston and Commandant Matthew Arbuckle were generally quite friendly, joining together in many poker games and evenings of drinking at Cantonment Gibson, the relationship was not always free from dispute. As commandant of the Fort, Arbuckle was especially sensitive on the question of sale of whiskey, and upon two occasions the two men openly clashed over this question. First, when Arbuckle seized Houston's whiskey and demanded that a license be purchased, and, again, when the stores of whiskey belonging to merchants Drew and Harper were seized.[15]

During his stay at Cantonment Gibson, Houston was never free from the attacks of his wife's family, the Allens, and their friends. Because of the rumors surrounding his separation from Eliza Allen, the family felt compelled to clear their daughter, and the former governor's political enemies were willing to join them in placing all blame and scandal upon Houston. The fever of accusation against Houston became strong enough to cause the formation of a committee, which issued a formal report, and published a confidential letter that Houston had written to John Allen concerning the separation of Eliza Allen and Houston.[16]

These attacks were so vicious that Houston wrote a satirical "Proclamation," which appeared first as an advertisement in a Nashville Paper and was later copied in newspapers throughout the country.[17] The ad was as follows:

[14] George Vashon to Lewis Cass, January 4, 1832, in *Muskogee Daily Phoenix*, January 17, 1932.

[15] See Chapter 8, "The Big Drunk."

[16] John C. Guild, *Old Times in Tennessee*, p. 272.

[17] *Nashville Banner and Nashville Whig*, July 13, 1831; *Arkansas Gazette*, August 3, 1831; *Niles' Weekly Register*, August 27, 1831; Houston, *Writings*, I, 196.

A PROCLAMATION

. . . I, Sam Houston, "the late Governor of the State of Tennessee,"[18] do hereby declare to all *scoundrels whomsoever,* that they are authorized to accuse, defame, calumniate, slander, vilify, and libel me to any extent . . . and I will in *no wise* hold them responsible to me . . . Be it known for the especial encouragement of all scoundrels hereafter . . . that I do solemnly propose . . . to give to the author of the most *elegant, refined and ingenious lie or calmuny,* a handsome gilt copy (Bound in sheep) of the Kentucky Reporter, or a snug plain copy of the United States Telegraph,[19] (bound in dog) since its commencement.

Given under my hand and private seal (having no seal of office) at Nashville, in the State of Tennessee.

SAM HOUSTON

The most vocal group in attack was the so-called "Indian Ring" —an informal group which Houston suspected contained not only the corrupt Indian agents but also many politically powerful figures, some in the Congress. Five of their "members" had been discharged as agents because of Houston's influence, and the valuable Indian rations contracts almost slipped through their fingers when Houston submitted a bid calling for a higher standard of food and distribution of the supplies to the Indian villages.[20]

A charge of corruption was made directly against Houston and Secretary of War Eaton and, by implication, against President Jackson. Out of these charges comes one of the most amazing stories in the history of the United States Congress, whereby the House of Representatives tried and convicted Sam Houston, a private citizen, of assaulting William Stanbery, a representative from Ohio, on a public street in Washington.[21]

[18] In these attacks Houston was often referred to as "the late Governor of the State of Tennessee" rather than by name.

[19] The reference is made to these publications because many of the most vicious attacks were carried in *The Kentucky Reporter* and *United States Telegraph.*

[20] George Creel, *Sam Houston, Colossus in Buckskin,* pp. 44–46.

[21] The Stanbery caning is generally beyond the scope of this book. However, the reader who is interested in this legal episode should see Lester, *Authentic Memoir,* pp. 56–63; Marquis James, *The Raven: A Biography of Sam Houston,*

Houston wrote William Stanbery following charges made on the floor of Congress and asked Stanbery if the *National Intelligencer* had correctly quoted him saying, "Was the late Secretary of War removed in consequence of his attempt fraudulently to give to Governor Houston the contract for Indian Rations?"[22] The letter was in effect an invitation to a duel, to which Stanbery never replied. When they met on the street Houston called him "a damned rascal" and took after him with a cane. Stanbery drew a gun, which when he pulled the trigger did not fire. Houston then finished the caning.[23]

The attack created a national sensation, which Houston shouted was strengthened by a desire to use the caning against the President. The "Hickory Cane" had been cut from a tree at "The Hermitage" when Houston had stopped there to show the Cherokee delegation which he accompanied to Washington. Many of Jackson's enemies considered this cane to be an appropriate weapon to turn on "Old Hickory."[24]

Houston was brought before the House of Representatives, formally charged with assault of a United States congressman, and interrogated. Francis Scott Key, who had written the "Star Spangled Banner," was

---

pp. 162–173; also Houston, *Writings,* I, 199–257 (where many of the actual documents and speeches are reprinted); Sam Houston, *The Autobiography of Sam Houston,* Donald Day and Harry Herbert Ullom (eds.), pp. 66–71.

[22] *National Intelligencer,* April 2, 1832; SH to Stanbery, April 3, 1832, Houston, *Writings,* I, 199–200. A. W. Terrell gives an interesting account of the caning which conflicts with certain known facts but which is entertaining and illustrative of the way legends grow. "Recollections of General Sam Houston," *The Southwestern Historical Quarterly,* XVI (October, 1912), 123–124.

> Houston having just been elected governor was in a cheerful mood and . . . entertained us until midnight with interesting events of his career. Williams' *Life of Houston* places him in Washington in March of 1832, when Stanbery first made his offensive remark. This is an error. Houston told us that Stanbery went out of the way to assail his conduct, and that a friend sent a newspaper clipping to him in the Indian nation to inform him. This fact did not appear in the trial, nor did Houston refer to it in his speech, for it was not in the record. He told us he wrote at once to Stanbery demanding a public retraction . . . and sent his letter by a Cherokee Indian to be mailed at Ft. Gibson. After waiting a reasonable time . . . he borrowed from a Cherokee friend named Apoth-la-a-hoo-lah his fringed buckskin hunting shirt with a beaver skin collar, and armed with a Bowie knife and hickory cane that General Jackson once gave him, he started for Washington. There were no railroads west of the Alleghanies and the journey was tedious.

[23] Lester, *Authentic Memoir,* pp. 57–62.

[24] Houston, *Autobiography of Sam Houston,* pp. 66–68.

Houston's lawyer. Houston spoke in his own behalf on three occasions.[25] His defense before the House of Representatives was so strong that a motion was made to dismiss the charges against him; the motion failed. He was convicted and fined $500. In symbolic defiance of the House of Representatives, Houston wore his Indian garb on the day he was sentenced. Thereafter, President Jackson entered an official remission of the fine.[26]

Ironically, those members of the "Indian Ring" who sought hardest to destroy Houston gave him the platform he needed to carry out his plans for Texas.[27] Houston's pleas to the public created tremendous sympathy and publicized the wrongs being perpetrated against the Indians. The unprecedented prosecution of doubtful legality against a private citizen for an act committed outside the House chambers caused the public to question their motives.[28] Houston expressed the importance of this caning to his career: "I was dying out and had they then taken me before a justice of peace and fined me ten dollars it would have killed me. But they gave me a national tribunal for a theatre, and that set me up again."[29]

[25] Houston, *Writings*, I, 207, 245, 250.
[26] AJ, Remission of Fine, July 3, 1834, Houston, *Writings*, I, 289.
[27] John A. Wharton to SH, June 2, 1832, Houston, *Writings*, I, 230–231.
[28] Lester, *Authentic Memoir*, 60–61.
[29] George W. Paschal, "Last Years of Sam Houston," *Harper's New Monthly Magazine*, XXXII (April, 1866), 35.

11. Cherokee Ambassador to President Jackson

> My son Gen Houston or the Raven came to me . . . and my heart embraced him. . . . He is now leaving to meet his white father, Genl. Jackson . . . and I hope he will take him by his hand and keep him as near his heart as I [have] done.
>
> John Jolly to Great Father [Andrew Jackson], December 3, 1829, Letters Written for John Jolly, Thomas Gilcrease Institute

The Cherokees knew of the friendship and mutual respect between Andrew Jackson and Sam Houston, who was the President's protégé and who before his departure for the Cherokee country was considered Old Hickory's handpicked successor to the Presidency. Captain John Rogers knew them both and had seen their warm friendship when he served with them in the Battle of Horseshoe Bend.[1] John Jolly saw the importance of "the Raven's" influence with General Jackson and thought of the relationship between Houston and Jackson as a father and his "foster-son." Houston's official biographer expressed this idea:

> He knew that General Jackson, who was then President, felt towards him the affection and confidence of an old and tried friend, and he was resolved to scrutinize the actions of the Indian agents . . . and report the result of his observations to the President.[2]

A man of affairs, such as Houston, who was personally acquainted with the "Great Father" Jackson, made an ideal ambassador for the

[1] Houston's role in the Battle of Horseshoe Bend and the Creek Wars is very clearly and concisely presented in Alexander Hynds, "General Sam Houston," *The Century Magazine*, XXVII (August, 1884), 496–498. See also the list and origin of names of Cherokee chiefs and officers who served under Jackson in the War of 1812 in "Chronicles," *Niles' Weekly Register,* X (1816), 16, 127.

[2] C. Edwards Lester, *The Life of Sam Houston: The Only Authentic Memoir of Him Ever Published,* p. 53.

Cherokees in Washington. It may have been with this in mind that Cherokee citizenship was conferred upon Houston in October of 1829. In December, Houston assumed his duties as unofficial ambassador for the Cherokee Nation.

Houston left Tahlontuskee, the Cherokee capital in the West, and began his journey to Washington.[3] The letter which Houston wrote from the "Steam Boat Amazon" to a friend attempts to hide the purpose of his trip, as outlined in his letters of instruction from Jolly. Houston said to John Overton, "I am on my way to Washington. . . . Many will be the conjectures as to my object . . . it is neither to solicit office or favors . . . of our friend, the President . . . this assurance I will give you."[4] Jolly wrote Jackson that Houston was "leaving to look upon his white father" and sent instructions listing complaints and requests of favors for Jackson to consider.[5]

The instructions for the Cherokee delegation were written by Houston and the official copies are in his handwriting. Captain George Vashon was so fearful of the influence which Houston had over the chiefs of the Western Cherokees that he sent a letter to Lewis Cass, secretary of war, in which he requested that whole sections of the instructions be ignored because "the instructions are in the handwriting of Gen Sam Houston" and "would be a sacrifice of the true interests of the Cherokees to gratify the private views of a few individuals."[6]

Houston knew that provisions of the treaty of 1828 had never been fulfilled and the Cherokees came to Washington to demand their fulfillment. Promised payments for improvements in Arkansas were overdue and the payments which were made had been issued in specie certificates of little value to the Indians. The land had never been surveyed and the Cherokees were unable to make definite claims to por-

[3] The correspondence and instructions of this delegation are found in "Cherokee Agency, West," Letters Received by the Office of Indian Affairs, Microfilm Publications, Microcopy No. 234, Roll No. 78, The National Archives of the United States.

[4] SH to Overton, December 28, 1829, Sam Houston, *The Writings of Sam Houston,* Amelia W. Williams and Eugene C. Barker (eds.), I, 144–145.

[5] John Jolly to Great Father [Andrew Jackson], December 3, 1829, Letters Written for John Jolly, GFT, GRL.

[6] Vashon to Cass, January 4, 1832, in *Muskogee Daily Phoenix,* January 17, 1932.

tions of their land. Jolly's letter to Jackson explains these difficulties quite eloquently:

> Like a father you ask me to let you know what my troubles are . . . that you may take them far from me. . . . More than a year ago, the last Treaty made by the great Father and my Nation was to have been made good . . . and it is not yet done—the lines are not run to show my people where to make their houses and clear their fields. The Osage missionaries yet live on the land given to my people and also a number of Osage families live near to them. I wish them all removed. The Cherokees have missionaries of their own and want no more! . . . [t]he country containing the Reservations granted to Col. Chouteau . . . was ceded to the Cherokees. They are in the midst of our Country and many white people are settled upon them and I now hope my father will have them . . . given to the Cherokees. If it is not done I will have no peace, for troubles will arise with those white men who have no laws . . . and blood may be shed and my people blamed when not in fault.[7]

An equally serious problem facing Houston's delegation was the removal of the Cherokees in the East. Jackson had introduced his first removal bill, and the inevitability of Cherokee removal had become obvious. Fear of the loss of lands to the Eastern Cherokees compelled the Houston delegation and the whole body of Cherokees in the West to demand that additional lands be granted for their brothers as they were removed West. Their concern is expressed in the letter which Houston probably wrote for Jolly.

> I want my father to send my people to me from the old nation, but want him to give them land to settle on when they do come, for I have not more land here than is necessary for my children who are here—if more land is not given for them there will not be room for them, and they will not be happy. If land is given to them here, they will soon come to it and be peacy and happy.[8]

Houston's interest in the Osages and Osage land is reflected in the delegation. This Osage warfare remained a fear of the Cherokees, and the delegation requested help in preventing it. The instructions related that for the killing of a Cherokee "the young men say they

[7] Jolly to AJ, December 18, 1829, Letters Written for John Jolly, GFT, GRL.
[8] Jolly to AJ, December 18, 1829, Letters Written for John Jolly, GFT, GRL.

will have blood for blood," but the chiefs want the "young men to be clean, and unstained with blood."[9]

Vashon, as agent, saw a relationship between Houston's purchase of reserve of Osage land from Colonel A. P. Chouteau, the sale of part of this land, and "a favorite scheme with Houston" to remove the Osage Indian Mission. Houston's instructions asked for the literal compliance with the treaty of 1828, which Vashon reasoned, ". . . stipulates for the removal of all persons unacceptable to the Cherokees" and includes the Union Mission. He argued that "Union Mission [was] most judiciously located, as affording the superior advantage of conferring moral instructions to the children of the Cherokees, Creeks and Osages."[10]

This appeal that Union Mission remain at the location within the Cherokee Nation was followed. Houston's position that the mission was not wisely located proved true, however, and the mission was abandoned in March of 1836, ". . . because the Osages were never too friendly at any time with their new neighbors the Creeks and Cherokees."[11]

Houston's success in Washington depended upon his acceptance by President Jackson, with the strategy of the Cherokees geared to Jackson's open recognition of the exiled governor of Tennessee. Traditionally they were reunited at a formal reception given by the President for the members of the diplomatic corps, where Houston, who considered himself Cherokee ambassador, appeared in the formal attire of the Cherokee Nation—a turban and the bright-colored cloak which is often called a "blanket."[12] A miniature of Houston painted at the Brown Hotel in Washington shows him in this "costume." For dramatic effect Houston chose the native dress of his Cherokee brothers and is said to have been differently costumed for every occasion during his Washington trip.

[9] Jolly to AJ, December 3, 1829, Letters Written for John Jolly, GFT, GRL.

[10] Vashon to Cass, January 4, 1832, "Cherokee Agency, West," Letters Received by the Office of Indian Affairs. Microfilm Publications, Microcopy No. 234, Roll No. 78, The National Archives of the United States.

[11] Morris L. Wardell, "Protestant Missions among the Osages, 1820–1838," *The Chronicles of Oklahoma*, II (September, 1924), 295–296.

[12] The most vivid account of this reunion is found in Paul I. Wellman's novel *Magnificent Destiny*, pp. 325–327.

The brightly clad Cherokee ambassador is said to have stood in the shadows when the negro slave announced the appearance of President Jackson, who spotted Houston at once, yelled across the room, and came to embrace him in a wild bear hug. Quickly, the President took Houston by the arm and introduced the Cherokee ambassador to his diplomatic colleagues.[13]

Jackson's acceptance of Houston is reflected in the results of the Washington conference. After this visit, Lt. Nathan Boone was sent to Cantonment Gibson to complete a survey of the area, and plans were made for further negotiations of the Osage difficulties.[14] The issue of additional land grants in the event of the Cherokee removal was not resolved because of the unwillingness of the Eastern Cherokee to consider the question of removal.

All of the Indians came to look upon Sam Houston as their unofficial ambassador—as a direct approach to President Jackson. Many of the tribal complaints were against the Indian agents, and the chiefs were fearful that these would never reach the President or would be so distorted that they would be ignored. The Indians soon discovered that their letters were of considerably more influence when written and signed by Sam Houston than by a tribal chieftain.

The Osages enlisted his support in their campaign against Agent Hamtramack almost immediately after his arrival. Houston had been in the Indian country less than a month when the chiefs of the Creeks came to him with their complaints. Houston witnessed and endorsed a memorial which was written to the President on June 22. It was accompanied by a short note in which Houston expressed his confidence in the honesty and integrity of the Creeks, but disavowed any personal knowledge of the changes. An additional endorsement was written when Major Anthony, the agent, wrote to Jackson denying the facts in the memorial. In this letter, Houston says that he does not know of

[13] However, the *Cherokee Phoenix,* March 4, 1830, p. 3, col. 2, suggests that Houston abandoned his "Cherokee costume."

[14] Nathan Boone was the son of Daniel Boone and commanded a company of Rangers. "One of his chief duties was to supervise the Delaware and Cherokee land in this section," *Muskogee Daily Phoenix,* February 11, 1932. The Boone surveys of the area may be found in "Cherokee Agency, West," Letters Received by the Office of Indian Affairs. Microfilm Publications, Microcopy No. 234, Roll No. 78, The National Archives of the United States.

the truth of all the charges, but that the truth of facts dealing with the "Beef Contract Scheme" were admitted to him by the agents.[15]

Similar memorials were written on behalf of the Pawnees, Osages, Cherokees, Choctaws, and several Western Indian tribes. One of these written on behalf of the Choctaws to the secretary of war is quite typical.

> An old Choctaw Chief called on me today, and complained that the white People were on their lands and were treating them badly. They take the Choctaws houses, and will not let them go *into* them. Some emigrants have lately arrived and have not houses to go into, and complain that Gen Jackson . . . told them if they would come west that they should be happy, and when they have come that the whites are on their land and they are not happy.[16]

Houston accompanied the Cherokees on a second trip to Washington. On the first day of December in 1831, a delegation consisting of Major Alexander Saunders, Black Coat, Captain Rain Crow, Captain John Rogers, Jr., and Andrew M. Vann was appointed to "visit with our father in Washington City." Edward Hicks was their secretary and Captain Rogers replaced John Drew as the official interpreter.[17] Houston escorted these Cherokees by way of Nashville, where he showed them Andrew Jackson's home, "The Hermitage." Before reaching Washington they stopped and visited with the Cherokees in Tennessee and Georgia.

The purpose of this trip was similar to one which Houston had made while he was a subagent in 1818. The Western Cherokees were becoming more and more concerned with the problems of removal. Houston felt an obligation to the Western Cherokees, since he had encouraged their migration. Jolly hoped that the two factions might be reunited west of the Mississippi, and this trip reflects the Council's

[15] SH, Memorial, June 22, 1829, and SH to AJ, June 25, 1829, GBF, GFP, GRL.

[16] SH to JE, July 22, 1829, Houston, *Writings,* I, 139–140.

[17] The correspondence, records, and reports of this delegation are found in "Cherokee Agency, West," Letters Received by the Office of Indian Affairs. Microfilm Publications, Microcopy No. 234, Rolls No. 77 and 78, The National Archives of the United States.

determination to expand the size of the Cherokee Nation to accommodate the Eastern Cherokees, whom they felt would inevitably be removed.

Jolly addressed the instructions for the trip to their agent and to Chief John Ross of the Eastern Cherokees. He wrote:

> Our Eastern brethren have been induced to think we feel unfriendly towards them. . . . Those who have joined us in the West have been acclaimed our brothers. . . . And whenever you and your people should become disposed to join us in the West, and partake of our exemption from the troubles we left behind, you will find a hearty welcome awaiting your arrival. My Brother chiefs! We have performed the arduous duties of the pioneers of our nation, our troubles are all over—let us as brother-chiefs unite to obtain for our people, whatever may be deemed essential to the promotion of the future prosperity of our nation.[18]

The failure of this delegation can be traced more to the refusal of the Eastern Cherokees to recognize the inevitably of removal than anything else. Houston had always felt that the Indians' only hope was an empire outside and beyond the possible influence of the white man. The Western Cherokees had followed Houston's leadership and removed West. They had "left their troubles behind," but Houston could not persuade the remaining Cherokees to follow him.

The success which Houston had in making claims for the Cherokees is demonstrated in a request made by Cherokee Agent George Vashon to Secretary of War Lewis Cass.

> In further support of my application for the continuance of the former allotment [Vashon pleaded], I would ask permission to state that the rejection of my recommendation of the 30th April 1831 and the subsequent acquiescence in the Chiefs' application made through a private friend, has a strong tendency to strengthen an existing pernicious influence and to offset the usefulness of the government's agent. The Chiefs no doubt felt great merit in obtaining through a private friend, what their agent had failed to procure; and if the Fund for presents is not sent . . . these deluded people will be again told that it is owing to the inefficiency of their agent.[19]

[18] John Jolly to John Ross, December 31, 1831, "Cherokee Agency, West," Letters Received by the Office of Indian Affairs. Microfilm Publications, Microcopy No. 234, Roll No. 78, The National Archives of the United States.

[19] Vashon to Cass, August 19, 1832, "Cherokee Agency, West," Letters Re-

Nevertheless, Indian officials sought Houston's influence with the Cherokees whenever a dispute was especially difficult to negotiate. In reply to Chief Jolly's letter of December 3, 1829, Thomas McKenney answered that the Cherokees should "put away the desire to revenge . . . the Osages" and further expressed a belief that Houston could persuade Jolly "to live in Peace with the Osages." McKenney concluded: "Jolly knows the President and loves him. The President is the Father of the Osages and Cherokees. He wishes them both to be happy and peaceful. Perhaps his wishes, conveyed by the mouth of the Raven, would be respected."[20]

---

ceived by the Office of Indian Affairs. Microfilm Publications, Microcopy No. 234, Roll No. 78, The National Archives of the United States.

[20] Thomas L. McKenney to JE, January 21, 1830, in Clarence E. Carter (comp. and ed.), *The Territorial Papers of the United States,* XXI, 177–178.

12. Sam Houston: International Lawyer, Frontier Style

> The amount of the deduction of $3,330.98 . . . is held . . . for the claimants, subject to the order of Gen. Saml. Houston their attorney . . ."
>
> William Clark to Colonel Thomas L. McKenney, April 16, 1830, William Clark Letters, Thomas Gilcrease Institute

Sam Houston was perhaps the first practicing lawyer in what is today the state of Oklahoma. By profession a lawyer, Houston came to the Cherokee country when the Indians needed legal advice in dealing with their agents, the government, and the white men who had illegally entered their lands.

In 1829 there were no courts in this Indian country. The soldiers were subject to military discipline.[1] Traders and trappers were responsible to both the Indian and the military authority of the United States government, which was centered in the War Department.[2] White men in the territory "had no laws."[3] The Cherokees had only begun to adopt a legal code administering justice under written laws, which were remarkably like their white neighbors.[4] Tribes such as the Osages still retained their primitive tribal customs.[5]

Houston's law practice in the Indian country could be described as international law, frontier style. In fact, the legal relationship between

[1] Carolyn Thomas Foreman, "Military Discipline in Early Oklahoma," *The Chronicles of Oklahoma,* VI (June, 1928), 140.

[2] Matthew Arbuckle Papers, GFT, GRL.

[3] John Jolly to Great Father [Andrew Jackson], December 3, 1829, Letters Written for John Jolly, GFT, GRL.

[4] See generally Cherokee Nation, *Laws of the Cherokee Nation Adopted by the Council at Various Periods,* pp. 149–179; George W. Pierson, *Tocqueville in America,* pp. 388–389; Lester Hargrett, *A Bibliography of the Constitutions and Laws of the American Indians,* p. 18; Rennard Strickland, "From Clan to Court: The Cherokee Legal System Emerges," Typescript, Law School Library, University of Virginia.

[5] "Osages," *The Missionary Herald,* XXV (April, 1829), 123–126.

the Indian tribes and the United States was almost the same as the relationship between the United States and a foreign country. The government still recognized the rights of Indian nations to make treaties, and even the Indian political sovereignty was recognized in many areas. In dealing with each other, tribes were sovereign powers, whose right to sign binding treaties was recognized.[6] Houston was, in effect, the international lawyer for these tribes, acting as their legal representative to a foreign power.

During his entire career Houston was the frontier lawyer who used the simple talk and the logic of the Bible and the almanac, whether dealing with the secretary of war or a Texas jury. Described as "a man so gifted in rare good sense and penetrating genius" that neither "many books, nor much dull plodding could enable" other lawyers "to measure weapons" with him,[7] Houston never owned many law books.[8]

Houston's talent was as an orator—"a talker." His voice was said to have been as clear as a bugle. A Texan who knew Houston recalled:

> . . . his thorough knowledge of the impulses and habits of thought of the fearless men . . . enabled him to exercise a wonderful influence . . . Houston was one of them, and his knowledge of human nature enabled him to impress and move them with consummate skill. He was a product of strange environments in the progress of society, and for that reason we will not see his like again.[9]

He was a frontier lawyer who was well trained for his time. The story of his early legal experience is told in his *Authentic Memoir*:

[6] Francis Paul Prucha, *American Indian Policy in the Formative Years,* pp. 1–4, 188–212; George Dewey Harmon, *Sixty Years of Indian Affairs,* pp. 40–79, 150–152, 182–196. One of the authors is especially indebted to Professor Neil H. Alford, Jr., of the University of Virginia Law School for his interest and assistance in a number of projects on the evaluation of the Cherokee legal system and the lawyer's role in Indian law.

[7] C. Edwards Lester, *The Life of Sam Houston: The Only Authentic Memoir of Him Ever Published,* p. 44.

[8] Oklahoma District Judge Claude Garrett, who is something of a "frontier lawyer" himself, visited the old Houston law office while it was still intact and commented that even this office in Tennessee was almost bare of books. Judge Claude Garrett, Interview, August 26, 1964. See also Lester, *Authentic Memoir,* p. 44.

[9] A. W. Terrell, "Recollections of General Sam Houston," *The Southwestern Historical Quarterly,* XVI (October, 1912), 120–121.

He entered the office of Hon. James Trimble. . . . He began his studies in June. . . . He read a few of the standard works prescribed in a course of law studies, and read them thoroughly. . . . His teacher had prescribed eighteen months' study; in *one-third of the time* he was recommended to apply for license, and he was admitted with *eclat*. . . . He was elected District Attorney of the Davidson District. [Attorney-General for the Nashville Circuit] The labors of District Attorney were unceasing. . . . He resigned his post at the end of twelve months, and resumed the regular practice of his profession in which he rose to great and sudden distinction.[10]

In practicing law Houston "was uniformly successful"; it is said that while he was Tennessee prosecuting attorney he never sent a bill before a grand jury unless he was satisfied from careful investigation that the proof made out the case. The rawness and frontier manner which made him so popular in Texas caused him to be "jeered at by older members of the bar" in Tennessee.[11]

That Houston practiced law in the Cherokee Nation might be pure speculation except that the Osage Records contain the file of one of his cases.[12] Houston represented the Osages in the annuity controversy of 1830. The entire amount of the annual annuity due under the Osage treaty had been paid to their agent Hamtramack. Of this amount, $3,330.98 was to discharge the accounts of A. P. Chouteau, Hugh McDurmed, and Elijah Carter.

William Clark of the St. Louis Superintendency of Indian Affairs visited with Hamtramack and Houston. This amount was held "for the claimants, subject to the order of Gen. Saml. Houston their attorney." Clark wrote to Thomas L. McKenney that "the amount of the deduction of $3,330.98 is this day paid on Genl. Houston's order to W. P. Chouteau, Jr."[13]

A number of powers of attorney were issued to Houston by both the Creeks and the Cherokees during his residency and immediately after he left for Texas. The most interesting of these is written in Hous-

[10] Lester, *Authentic Memoir,* pp. 42–48.

[11] Alexander Hynds, "General Sam Houston," *The Century Magazine,* XXVII (August, 1884), 498–499.

[12] William Clark to Colonel Thomas L. McKenney, April 16, 1830, William Clark Letters, GFT, GRL.

[13] William Clark to Colonel Thomas L. McKenney, April 16, 1830, William Clark Letters, GFT, GRL.

ton's handwriting and was issued by his Indian wife, Diana Rogers, in his favor in 1833.[14] It is said to have been in lieu of a divorce, to have been a statement that they were never man and wife, to have been an assignment of her property interest in preparation of her departure to Texas, and to have been the assignment of rights in Arkansas.[15]

Power of Attorney

Cherokee Agency, West
27th June 1833

Know all men by these presents, that I Diana Gentry, widow of the late David Gentry of Frog bayou; Do by these presents authorize, constitute, and appoint Saml. Houston, late of the Wigwam, my true and lawful attorney, to settle, and adjust all my accounts, for stock destroyed, and property lost within the Territory of Arkansas. And I do further authorize and empower the said Houston, to receive, and receipt for all monies, which may be due and coming to me; and in my name to do, and execute, all manners of things, as tho' I were personally present, and assenting to the same, hereby ratifying and confirming the same, hereby revoking all other powers; Witness my hand at the Cherokee Agency, on Arkansas The day and the date above written.

her
DIANA X GENTRY[16]
mark

Captain John Rogers, Jr., called upon his brother-in-law Sam Houston for legal assistance in 1830. Agent DuVal proposed to dismiss Rogers from his position as official interpreter for the Cherokee Nation. Rogers had been appointed to this position before the removal in 1817 and was still the choice of both the chiefs and the National Committee and Council. DuVal dismissed him because the agent feared that his close relationship with specie-certificate holders such as John Drew, another brother-in-law, would cast doubt upon his actions. Houston represented Rogers. Part of the correspondence is in Houston's handwriting and the resolutions issued by the National Committee and

[14] Grant Foreman, "Some New Light on Houston's Life among the Cherokee Indians," *The Chronicles of Oklahoma,* IX (June, 1931), 149; Marion Karl Wisehart, *Sam Houston: American Giant*, p. 84.

[15] There is no basis for any of these theories in Houston's correspondence.

[16] G. Foreman, "Some New Light," p. 149.

Council reflect Houston's style. Houston was successful and Rogers was officially reinstated as interpreter by an order from the United States War Department.[17]

Houston accompanied the Cherokee delegation to Washington in 1832, not as a member but as an unofficial advisor. No claim was made to the government for his expenses. This, plus the fact that he had often written instructions for the Committee and Council, in addition to letters for the chiefs, suggests that he was filling the position of "legal advisor" to this Cherokee delegation and the Nation as a whole.[18]

During the three and one half years from 1829 to 1833 that Houston spent with the Cherokees their legal system was quickly expanded. The number of tribal laws almost tripled during this period, and their nature and scope were expanded. The Western Cherokees seem to have crossed over from a primitive legal system attempting to adopt the Anglo-Saxon traditions to a working legal system with provisions for criminal as well as civil justice.[19] Though Houston was a counselor of the tribe, it is uncertain whether he participated in the drafting of these new laws. The presence of someone trained in the legal system, however, would have been invaluable to the Cherokee Nation.

Much of Houston's legal activities in the Cherokee Nation were directed toward management of his own affairs. He drew the deeds for the speculation in Osage lands bought from Chouteau, and presented his own arguments before the secretary of war for his rights to trade as a native Cherokee merchant. He was conducting negotiations with the New York land interests represented by James Prentiss to acquire land in Texas, and continued to advise his New York partners on obtaining Indian ration contracts from the War Department.[20]

[17] Documents of the Rogers dismissal controversy including Resolutions by the National Council and Committee, Agent DuVal, John Jolly, and Walter Webber are found in "Cherokee Agency, West," Letters Received by the Office of Indian Affairs, Microfilm Publications, Microcopy No. 234, Rolls 77 and 78, The National Archives of the United States.

[18] Records of the Cherokee Delegation to Washington, "Cherokee Agency, West," Letters Received by the Office of Indian Affairs, Microfilm Publications, Copy No. 234, Roll 78, The National Archives of the United States.

[19] The laws of the Western Cherokees are gathered in Emmett Starr, *An Early History of the Cherokees,* pp. 139–176.

[20] For a more detailed discussion of the Osage land purchase and the Indian

Everywhere he went, Sam Houston was a lawyer. In Texas, less than a month after his arrival he was already practicing law. A brilliant courtroom lawyer, Houston unquestionably influenced the practice of law on the Oklahoma-Texas frontier. His son Temple Houston was described as the most exciting lawyer in the West. As a boy, Houston's biographer Marquis James remembers coming into town to hear Temple speak. And yet, Temple Houston, the man who was the model of the frontier lawyer in Edna Ferber's *Cimarron,* a man whose style was copied by thousands of courtroom "dandies," was always haunted by a dream to be as good an advocate as Sam Houston, the frontier lawyer.[21]

---

ration contracts see Chapter Fifteen, "Speculation in Indian Lands and Rations." The Texas land-purchase agreements are considered in Chapter 17, "Cherokee Emperor of Texas."

[21] Temple Houston File, OBF, ORL; Angie Debo and John M. Oskison (eds.), *Oklahoma: A Guide to the Sooner State,* p. 379; Edna Ferber, *Cimarron*; note Marquis James' childhood remembrances of Temple Houston in Marquis James, "On the Trail of Sam Houston," *The Texas Monthly,* VI (July, 1930), 4.

13. Cherokee Merchant—"Measuring Cloth and Weighing Flour"

> Houston operated on the Texas Road a small trading post called the Wigwam . . . there he sold bright colored cloth and sacks of flour to the Indians.
>
> *Old Fort Gibson,* Indian Archives, Oklahoma Historical Society

To anyone familiar with his character, it is impossible to imagine Sam Houston behind a counter measuring dry goods or weighing sacks of flour. Management of a country-frontier mercantile establishment cannot be reconciled with Houston's spirit and flair for the adventures in life. As a boy, Houston had fled to the Cherokees when his older brother placed him in a Maryville, Tennessee, store to clerk for a Mr. Sheffy. The youth is said to have had "a preference for deer tracks to tape."[1]

It is much more plausible to imagine Houston as a speculator, lawyer, or political advisor, than as a merchant. In truth, Houston's association in the mercantile trade was not as a clerk behind a counter but as a planner and dreamer of a Cherokee "merchant empire," joining the trading establishments of men such as a Colonel Walter Webber, John Drew, Peter Harper, Captain John Rogers, and John Jolly.[2]

The merchant operations of the Cherokees were unique among the Indians because they did not rely upon outside traders. Almost all business transactions were conducted by the natives themselves, who purchased their own goods in the eastern cities and in New Orleans and

[1] A. W. Terrell, "Recollections of General Sam Houston," *The Southwestern Historical Quarterly,* XVI (October, 1912), 113–114; Marquis James, *The Raven: A Biography of Sam Houston,* pp. 16, 22.

[2] For the extent of these merchant activities see "Muskogee and Environs," Map drawn by Winnifred Clark and Grant Foreman, in the Foreman Room, Public Library, Muskogee, Oklahoma. See also Carolyn Thomas Foreman, "A Creek Pioneer," *The Chronicles of Oklahoma,* XXI (September, 1943), 271.

had them transported up river at their own expense. Captain John Stuart wrote the War Department that "there is I think but one licensed trader in the nation, and he is in partnership with a Cherokee." The Indians were such astute merchants that James Rogers was later appointed sutler for Cantonment Gibson.[3]

The Cherokee agents seemed fearful that this "merchant empire" or league was being consolidated and more closely organized among the native kinsmen to whom Houston was closely related by marriage or adoption. Both John Drew and Captain John Rogers were Diana Rogers' kinsmen; Jolly was Houston's adopted father; several of the young traders, such as Peter Harper, were married to Rogers' nieces and nephews. Vashon dismissed John Rogers, who had been the Cherokee interpreter since 1817, because of the family relationship between Rogers, Drew, Harper, and Jolly, which complicated the investigation of payment of specie certificates.[4]

Perhaps Houston exerted influence for the removal of agent DuVal because DuVal maintained a partnership in a Cherokee trading company, which owned a prosperous store that in one month is said to have sold over two hundred gallons of whiskey to the Indians. It was at first rumored, and then openly asserted, that Houston's opposition to DuVal was connected with the "mercantile empire" of the Cherokee natives.[5]

The alliance between Houston and the native merchants was openly affirmed in a letter written to the secretary of war at the request of Colonel Walter Webber. In refutation to rumors alleging that Webber was a man of bad character, Houston said, "He has always maintained a high standing . . . and that this hostility arises . . . from the circumstances of his being a merchant, and DuVal's being also engaged in Mercantile business."[6] At the same time Houston wrote a letter of

[3] Stuart to Cass, August 12, 1833, in "Cherokee Agency, West," Letters Received by the Office of Indian Affairs. Microfilm Publications, Microcopy No. 234, Roll No. 78, The National Archives of the United States.

[4] For a more detailed discussion of the family relationships see Chapter 4, "The Legend of Talihina."

[5] See Chapter 8, "The Big Drunk." For a complete discussion of DuVal's trading activities see Francis Paul Prucha, *American Indian Policy in the Formative Years,* pp. 102–138.

[6] SH to JE, April 1, 1830, Sam Houston Papers, GFT, GRL.

credit for Webber, who was in Baltimore and planning to go to Pittsburgh to purchase goods for his store. The order of hardware which he was contemplating was so large that he did not have funds to cover the purchase.[7]

In addition to this manipulation for the "merchant empire," Houston is often pictured as a trader behind a counter at his "small storeroom" trading "in groceries." While Houston did operate a store, it was a small post operated in partnership for about a year.[8] "Wigwam Neosho" was the name of Houston's home as well as his trading post. The name identified its location on the Neosho River, and it was actually known as "The Wigwam." It is this name which Diana Rogers uses in a power of attorney which she executed in Houston's favor, for this was the wigwam on the Neosho, just as Jolly's home on the Illinois was referred to in his letters as "Wigwam Illinois."[9] The name "Wigwam Neosho" was used by Houston for his home before June of 1830, when he began to make plans to open his trading post.

When he left Tennessee, Houston's friends are said to have "sent a small stock of goods to him suited to the Cherokee trade, and without his previous knowledge, for they knew his indifference to money."[10] But there is no record of Houston's discussing opening a trading post until he had been with the Cherokees for over a year. Even then the opening was delayed by the license controversy, in which he maintained that as a Cherokee citizen he was not subject to the Intercourse Act nor required to obtain a license from the government. Houston seems to have successfully defied the government on the licensing question, since the United States government records of Indian trading show that a license was never issued to Houston. A. P. Chouteau, Co.,

[7] Walter Webber to SH, March 30, 1830, and Letter of Credit, Houston for Webber, April 1, 1830, Walter Webber Papers (Typescripts), OBF, OIA.

[8] "For more than a year he had a trading establishment between the Grand River and the Verdigris," C. Edwards Lester, *The Life of Sam Houston: The Only Authentic Memoir of Him Ever Published,* p. 55. "Houston also traded in groceries, his shop being in a small storeroom attached to his cabin," Sarah Barnwell Elliott, *Sam Houston,* p. 17.

[9] John Jolly to Great Father [Andrew Jackson], December 3, 1829, Letters Written for John Jolly, GFT, GRL.

[10] Terrell, "Recollections," p. 117.

Hugh Love, Thompson and Drennan, James B. Turley, and A. P. Chouteau received the only licenses granted during this period.[11]

In fact, the original shipment of goods which Houston reports having received is the only one that the records of the shipping lines show as arriving for his use. The steamboat accounts and warehouse receipts are filled with shipments to traders, such as Chouteau, Drew, Webber, and Rogers, but only one is mentioned for Sam Houston. This shipment of assorted store supplies and nine barrels of whiskey came up the Arkansas, was loaded on a keel boat, brought to the banks of the Verdigris, and taken three miles overland to the store.[12]

Virtually the only method of payment which the Indians had was the specie certificates issued by the agents. Drew, Webber, Rogers, and Jolly each returned thousands of dollars worth of these certificates. In 1831 Drew had over $30,000 in certificates, for which he demanded payment, but Houston appeared to have made no claims on any specie certificates, although his political enemies accused him of trading in them.[13]

Further proof that Houston's operation was a "partnership" with John Drew is shown by the absence of accounts for Houston with Drew, whose trading activities were so widespread that he was a "wholesaler" for Webber and Rogers. Nor are there accounts of Houston with the sutlers at the post between the years of 1829 and 1833.[14] This absence of record of Houston's trading activities, plus the fact that he was so frequently absent from the Wigwam Neosho, indicates that the operation was run almost entirely by others.

A number of partners in addition to Drew have been suggested as

[11] Abstract of licenses granted to Indian Traders, December 31, 1831, George Vashon, Indian agent for the Western Cherokees, in "Cherokee Agency, West," Letters Received by the Office of the Indian Affairs. Microfilm Publications, Microcopy No. 234, Roll No. 77, The National Archives of the United States.

[12] Grant Foreman, "River Navigation in the Early Southwest," *The Mississippi Valley Historical Review,* XV (June, 1928), 38.

[13] James, *The Raven,* p. 126. The records of demands for repayment of specie certificates show no claims made by Sam Houston. See "Cherokee Agency, West," Letters Received by the Office of Indian Affairs. Microfilm Publications, Microcopy No. 234, Roll No. 78, The National Archives of the United States.

[14] See John Drew Papers and Accounts, GRL.

having operated Houston's business during his stay with the Cherokees. The most frequently mentioned of these are Peter Harper and Benjamin Hawkins, who were in the area at this time and who seem to have been most active in business affairs. Harper, a son-in-law of James Rogers, operated businesses both in connection with Drew and independently.[15]

A very plausible explanation for the one shipment of goods received in Houston's name is that he intended to use these in opening the sutler's store at Cantonment Gibson. Using his political influence, Houston sought the position of sutler for Cantonment Gibson. This was a licensed position, and one of the most profitable available, since the military road between Fort Smith and Cantonment Gibson had been completed in 1827, bringing visitors and traders to the post. The steamboat trade up the river was prospering. John Dillard's boarding house was always full, and the weddings, horse races, theatre performances, and community dinners stimulated business. The large army payroll added to the prosperity, as did the Indian tribes which were brought to Gibson to negotiate, sign treaties, and receive their annuity payments. The whole of this territory was almost totally dependent upon Cantonment Gibson. The post was so profitable that when Sutler Nicks died his wife inherited over $20,000 in cash, the goods of the store, and considerable property, including several slaves and one of the largest homes in the territory.

When rumor reached Houston that Sutler Nicks was to be removed from the post, he wrote to the secretary of war requesting the appointment.[16] Upon his return from Washington, Houston learned that Nicks had been retained and that he, Houston, was the object of considerable scandal in Washington. He quickly wrote to Secretary of War Eaton another letter, in which his application was withdrawn and in which he denied any plots charged against him.[17]

[15] The question of who was Houston's partner has never been answered. Almost every trader in the area, including ones such as Hugh Love with whom Houston was engaged in a violent dispute, has been suggested. See Carolyn Thomas Foreman, "A Creek Pioneer," *The Chronicles of Oklahoma,* XXI (September, 1943), 271; and "Muskogee and Environs," Map drawn by Winnifred Clark and Grant Foreman, Foreman Room, Public Library, Muskogee, Oklahoma, Item One.

[16] SH to Lewis, May 20, 1830, OBF, ORL.

[17] SH to JE, June 13, 1830, and JE to SH, July 28, 1830, in Grant Foreman,

After news reached him that Nicks had been retained, Houston may have remembered the prosperity and activity of Chouteau's trading post and decided to open his own. Houston dreamed that he would make a fortune in the Cherokee trade. And why not? The Chouteau establishments were so prosperous that their owners constantly looked for new places to expand, such as the shipyards where they built from native timber their own boats in which to ship thousands of pelts and tons of cotton and pecans to New Orleans. Prosperity from the Indian trade was not limited to the Chouteaus, and even at the settlement at Three Forks, which was just three miles from Houston's own Wigwam, there was a shipyard. Trade at Three Forks with the Osages and Creeks was so brisk that there was never enough of the bright silk, blankets, beads, and trade pipes which attracted the Indians. Early in the spring of 1828 the ship *Facility* was so packed with hides and pelts that there was barely room for the five hundred barrels of pecans loaded at the Creek Agency.[18]

With his knowledge of the Indians, Houston must have felt he could organize the trains which left the Cherokee country to trade with wilder tribes, such as the Comanches, Tonkawas, and Kiowas. Profits from these expeditions exceeded the normal traders' bartering of pelts for pipes, hatchets, and mackinaws, and competition was never as great as in the Three Forks-Gibson area. A man as popular and respected as Houston could easily have traded furs, yet none were ever shipped in his name. The rich pelts which Chouteau and Drew sent down the Mississippi were quickly sold and the profits returned in goods which made these men wealthy.

Sam Houston seems to have had the same opinion of many of the merchants as did the artist George Catlin, who described a trading company setting out from Fort Gibson in 1834:

There is already in this place a company of eighty men fitted out, who are to start to-morrow, to overtake these Indians a few miles from this place, and accompany them home, with a large stock of goods, with traps for catching beavers, &c., calculating to build a trading-house amongst them, where

"Some New Light on Houston's Life among the Cherokee Indians," *The Chronicles of Oklahoma,* IX (June, 1931), 140–143.

[18] Foreman, "River Navigation," p. 41.

they will amass, at once, an immense fortune, being the first traders and trappers that have ever been in that part of the country.

I have travelled too much among Indian tribes, and seen too much, not to know the evil consequences of such system. Goods are sold at such exorbitant prices, that the Indian gets a mere shadow for his peltries, &c. The Indians see no white people but traders and sellers of whiskey; and of course, judge us all by them—they consequently hold us, and always will, in contempt; as inferior to themselves, as they have reason to do—and they neither fear no respect us.[19]

Whether his constant agitation with Indian politics or just his lack of business sense was responsible, Houston's trading operations did not make him wealthy, as he had dreamed. The story of the Indian trade is the story of men who came to the Indian country poor and left with vast fortunes, and yet Houston left a poor man. The story of Houston's departure on a straggly pony may be legendary, but his negotiations with New York financier James Prentiss and other financial interests in the East are concrete proof that the possible wealth of the Indian trade escaped Houston, and that Houston left for Texas seemingly poorer than when he came to the Cherokees.[20]

[19] George Catlin, *Illustrations of the Manners, Customs and Condition of the North American Indians in a Series of Letters and Notes Written during Eight Years of Travel and Adventure among the Wildest and Most Remarkable Tribes Now Existing,* II, 83.

[20] George Creel, *Sam Houston, Colossus in Buckskin*, pp. 61–62; see also the series of letters from SH to James Prentiss, Sam Houston, *The Writings of Sam Houston,* Amelia W. Williams and Eugene C. Barker (eds.), I, 197–266 *passim.*

14. The Wigwam Neosho

> Within three-quarters of a mile of each other, on the old Military Road, a branch of the Texas Road between Okay and Fort Gibson [Oklahoma], are the two locations [known as the Scott Place and the Boling Place] most historians name, each for good reasons, as the site of the Wigwam Neosho. It was at Wigwam Neosho that Sam Houston lived for three years between 1829 and 1833.
>
> Phil Harris, "Exact Site of Wigwam Neosho Is Sought," *Muskogee Daily Phoenix,* September 20, 1964

> Well, now [Grant] Foreman told me that the Scott place was not the location and, if the evidence he had was correct, then the location was on the Boling place. During the Texas Centennial in 1936 some gentlemen came up here from Texas looking for the Wigwam Neosho and Foreman told them, that from his evidence and research, the Boling site was it.
>
> Q. B. Boydstun, Interview, October 10, 1964

An "old settler" in the Fort Gibson-Okay area was amazed at the number of people who came to inquire of him as to the exact location of the Sam Houston house known as the Wigwam Neosho. He finally remarked, upon being pressed for more and more details, that Sam Houston was there and that seemed, to him, all that mattered. The attitude of most early historians was that of the old settler.[1] That Sam Houston lived at Cantonment Gibson was known to all.[2] Only in re-

[1] Alfred M. Williams, "Houston's Life among the Indians," *Magazine of American History,* X (November, 1883), 406. "With her he took up as his wife, and removed west of Grand River, opposite Fort Gibson, where he made a clearing which still remains, and erected a log cabin, which was burnt during the war."

[2] Grant Foreman, "Fort Gibson Happenings," *Muskogee Daily Phoenix,* December 27, 1931. "He acquired a house about three miles northwest of Fort Gibson which he calls 'Wigwam Neosho' and where he carried a stock of goods for sale to the Indians."

cent years has the interest in knowing the precise point at which the Houston home was located become an obsession, with this point considered to the virtual exclusion of any other historical question of Houston's stay with the Cherokees.[3] At least six possible sites have been defended as the "exact" location of the Houston home. Of these sites, only two are strongly defended: the first is known as the "Boling Place" and the second is known as the "Scott Place."

The general area of the location of the Wigwam Neosho is well known. This was recorded in a letter from Captain George Vashon, Cherokee agent, to President Andrew Jackson in September of 1830. Vashon wrote: ". . . Gen S. Houston & a Mr. Drenen a Mercht of Nashville appear[s] to be connected in trade . . . in the Cherokee country & within 3 miles of this post."[4] Houston's official biographer in his *Authentic Memoir* located the site even more precisely as "between the Grand River and the Verdigris [River]."[5]

Perhaps the clearest general location of the Wigwam Neosho is given by Grant Foreman in his pamphlet *Down the Texas Road*:

> The Texas Road entered this settlement [Three Forks] on the banks of the Verdigris River and then continued down the stream to where it crossed the Arkansas River between the mouths of the Verdigris and Grand.
>
> A branch of the road, however, pursued a southeasterly course for six miles to Fort Gibson where it crossed the Grand River. About midway down this road Sam Houston established himself for three years in a house which he called "Wigwam Neosho."
>
> He was conveniently located, being near the boat landing at Three Forks and equally near the landing at Fort Gibson and the company of Army officers with whom he found congenial companionship.[6]

[3] This renewed interest was analyzed in Phil Harris, "Exact Site of Wigwam Neosho Is Sought," *Muskogee Daily Phoenix,* September 20, 1964. The authors are also victims of this craze. See Jack Gregory and Rennard Strickland, "Historic Archeology: Locating Sam Houston's Cherokee Trading Post," *The Northwest Arkansas Archaeological Society Amateur,* IV (August, 1965), 3–6.

[4] George Vashon to AJ, September 12, 1830, in Grant Foreman, *Pioneer Days in the Early Southwest,* p. 195.

[5] C. Edwards Lester, *The Life of Sam Houston: The Only Authentic Memoir of Him Ever Published,* p. 55.

[6] Grant Foreman, *Down the Texas Road,* p. 11.

The confusion as to the exact location of this trading post results from at least three factors: First, few of the maps made by the government during these years showed the location of the trading posts which were not attached to settlements. Second, the land in this area was not owned individually, but was owned in common by the entire Cherokee Nation, with no recording as to who was occupying any given section. And finally, the foundations upon which a conclusion must be based are the recollections of "old settlers," who are three to four generations removed from the days when Sam Houston lived at Cantonment Gibson.

A detailed investigation of the map collections of the Library of Congress, the Bureau of Indian Affairs, and the War Department has never revealed a contemporary map showing the location of Houston's Wigwam.[7] The Foreman collection of photostats of these maps show the location of the Texas or Military Road between 1828 and 1834 but show no trading posts.[8] Thus, the only contemporary account is the short statement by Agent Vashon that the Wigwam was about three miles from Cantonment Gibson.

The land upon which Houston built his Wigwam was a part of the general dominion of the Cherokee Nation and was never owned by him. The records of the Oklahoma Land Offices and the county recorders date from the distribution of Indian lands in the early twentieth century and are of no value in placing the person who occupied a piece of land in 1830.[9]

To rely upon the memory and "hearsay" of individuals as to the location of a piece of property is, at best, risky. When the property was occupied for only three years, it is dangerous. When the occupancy was over 130 years prior to the investigation, it is foolhardy. And yet virtually the only sources available as to the exact location of the Wigwam Neosho are these interviews.

Grant Foreman investigated the question during the 1920's and

[7] Carolyn Thomas Foreman, Interview, July 3, 1964.

[8] Fort Gibson, Official Maps and Military Surveys, GFP, GRL; and Cantonment Gibson, Plans and Diagrams of the Original Buildings, GFP, GRL.

[9] Muskogee County, Records of Land Transactions, County Clerk's Office, Muskogee County Court House, Muskogee, Oklahoma; and Wagoner County, Records of Land Transactions, County Clerk's Office, Wagoner County Court House, Wagoner, Oklahoma.

early 1930's and reached the conclusion that the exact location of the Sam Houston house was on what is known as the "Boling Place." The Texas Centennial Commission, upon the recommendations and findings of Grant Foreman, is said to have accepted this location.[10] Others have reached this same conclusion.[11] The Boling Place is pictured in the Official Map of the Works Project Administration, which was drawn by Thomas Meagher under the supervision of Dr. Foreman.[12]

Perhaps, instead of engaging in a controversy over the exact location of this site, historians should take the approach Marquis James chose in his biography *The Raven* of seeking to find what life was like at the Wigwam Neosho.

> [T]here was peace and tranquility at the Wigwam Neosho where the Raven established his bride. This dwelling place was near the Neosho River, a little above Cantonment Gibson, and thirty miles from the lodge of Oo-loo-te-ka. Houston bought or built a large log house and set out an apple orchard. There he lived in style, transacting his affairs and entertaining his friends.[13]

However, if the exact site of the Wigwam Neosho is to be established, there is no reason to reject Foreman's conclusion that the Wigwam Neosho was located on the Boling Place. In fact, evidence and tradition substantiate Foreman's position.

In truth, the origin of the Scott Place as the site dates only from the beginning of the twentieth century and a series of articles in a Fort Gibson newspaper, which contained a number of historical inaccuracies, such as placing Houston at the home of Chief Journeycake instead

[10] Carolyn Thomas Foreman, Interview, July 3, 1964. Q. B. Boydstun, Interview, October 10, 1964.

[11] Don Boling, Interview, July 4, 1964.

[12] From the small map in G. Foreman, *Down the Texas Road,* p. 11, it appears as if the site might be the "Scott Place." However, the larger map compiled by Grant Foreman and drawn by Thomas Meagher (reproduced in this volume) clearly shows the site as the "Boling Place." Note the schoolhouse, which still stands on the Boling Road. "The Three Forks," Map, Prepared by the Works Project Administration under the direction of Grant Foreman. Drawn by Thomas Meagher, OIA.

[13] Marquis James, *The Raven: A Biography of Sam Houston,* p. 152. There is considerable controversy over whether Houston planted a pear or an apple orchard.

ap 2. THE THREE FORKS COUNTRY, GRANT FOREMAN MAP. Drawn May 8,
38, by Thomas F. Meagher, of the WPA Indian-Pioneer History Project.

of John Jolly.[14] Mrs. George West, whose family included one of the Cherokee "Ambassadors" or delegates to the Washington Treaty Conference of 1866, recalls this period as the first definite mention of the Scott Place as the site for the Wigwam Neosho. She has concluded: "My father went to dances at the Scott Place . . . but it was not known at that time [when he was a boy] as the home of Sam Houston. I couldn't be sure that it was the Sam Houston place. . . . I couldn't really say, one way or the other."[15]

It is unquestioned that the Wigwam Neosho was located almost exactly "half-way" between Cantonment Gibson and the Three Forks settlement on an "ideal spot at a curve in the Texas Road, near a fork in the lanes."[16] At such a spot in the field on the Boling Place are large foundation stones, which have been smoothed and which are identical to those in the foundation of the Boling house, which still stands and which tradition insists was built from the foundation of the Wigwam Neosho.[17] From this spot, where the foundation stones still rest, the curve and fork in the Texas Road are only a few feet.

Digging on the Boling site has produced large quantities of trading materials, including copper awls, beads, and pipes. In addition, pieces of import China and glass have also been found. The Bolings have taken larger pieces of iron and china from the fields. The whole area is so filled with these "store goods" that it was obviously the site of a commercial establishment. The Scott site has never produced such quantities of trading materials.

An additional factor which has added to the confusion was the presence of a number of small houses in the immediate area and the remains of several other "cabins."[18] The house on the Scott Place, ac-

[14] *Fort Gibson Post,* October 15, 1904.

[15] Mrs. George West, Interview, August 16, 1964.

[16] Carolyn Thomas Foreman, Interview, June 22, 1964.

[17] See generally Noel Ballard, *Muskogee Daily Phoenix,* October 28, 1951.

[18] A picture of a house thought to be the Sam Houston home was sent to Miss Nettie Wheeler of Muskogee and is in her collection of materials on "Wigwam Neosho." This house, investigation proved, was in the town of Fort Gibson. There are also the "remains" of a group of cabins, which some claim are the buildings of Houston's home, on Julian Fite's "Sam Houston Ranch." These, however, are some distance from the Texas Road. Mrs. Carolyn Thomas Foreman, whose wit and memory are as keen at ninety-six as when she accompanied her husband to the sites, remembers visiting a site with Dr. Fore-

cording to many old settlers, was the Wigwam Neosho. It is known, however, that the Wigwam was either burned or torn down during, or immediately after, the Civil War. Alfred M. Williams, who came to the Indian Territory after the Civil War for the purpose of learning the facts of Houston's stay with the Cherokees, talked to Houston's associates who were still living. Williams recorded the fact that the Wigwam Neosho was destroyed: "[H]e . . . removed to the west of Grand river, opposite Fort Gibson, where he made a clearing, which still remains, and erected a log cabin, which was burnt during the war."[19]

Mabel Washburn Anderson, also basing her conclusion upon contemporary "remembrances" concluded: "At the beginning of the Civil War the log house where Sam Houston resided was still standing, and was pointed out to strangers as a landmark of interest and curiosity. It was torn down later, and rebuilt, and is still standing at the present time."[20]

Mrs. West has identified the house on the Scott Place as the one in which she lived, but has refused to say whether it was the Wigwam Neosho. However, she has stated that the house, according to her father, was neither burned nor torn down.[21] The Scott Place, if we accept the Williams and Anderson information, cannot be the Wigwam Neosho.

The house on the Scott site was destroyed in 1943 by a tornado, but was photographed earlier by the Historic American Buildings Survey. The Survey made "no conclusion" concerning the house.[22] In fact, it has been reported that the Commission was told, at the time of the survey, that this "was probably not the house."[23] Unfortunately the Works

---

man when the "Houston House" was standing. This could possibly be either the reconstructed Boling House (although not likely), the "Scott Place," or other similar cabins in the area.

[19] Williams, "Houston's Life among the Indians," p. 406.

[20] Mabel Washburn Anderson, "Old Fort Gibson on the Grand," *Twin Territories Magazine,* IV, No. 9 (September, 1902), 252–253.

[21] Mrs. George West, Interview, August 16, 1964.

[22] American Homes Survey, *Historic American Homes,* p. 187. See also Phil Harris, "Houston Wigwam Neosho Location Studied," *Muskogee Sunday Phoenix and Times Democrat,* April 23, 1967.

[23] Dr. T. L. Ballenger, professor emeritus of history at Northeastern State College, Tahlequah, Oklahoma, accompanied Grant Foreman to the site with the photographers. According to Dr. Ballenger, Foreman made this statement.

Project Administration Historical Survey of "The Military Road and Fort Gibson" did not consider the question of the site of the Houston home.[24]

An interesting comparison of statements of the individuals interviewed in connection with the Historical Survey and Interview programs conducted by the Works Project Administration reveals the frustration of seeking the location from such records. Mrs. D. D. Hitchcock remembered:

> I knew well the house where Sam Houston lived, about one-half mile across Grand River from Fort Gibson; I sometimes when passing, drank from the well there, and admired the great tall pear tree, which was said to have been planted by Sam Houston—[and] is I believe, still living and bearing fruit, it must now be nearly one hundred years old.[25]

While Dr. G. W. West recollected:

> Sam Houston . . . came back dressed in full Indian dress. A man by the name of Shaw was with him. Sam Houston sent his man down the Grand River to build a cabin. It was a one room cabin, made of rough logs, and they lived down there for a long time. I have been in this cabin. I suppose it is still standing.[26].

One of the most valuable of the interviews on the location of the Wigwam Neosho was conducted by Noel Ballard, feature writer for the *Muskogee Daily Phoenix* and *Times Democrat.* The interview and its results were reported by Phil Harris, city editor of the *Muskogee Daily Phoenix,* himself a man who has stimulated interest in the controversy by his well-researched and reasoned articles on Houston's life among the Cherokees. Harris reported:

Ballenger, however, is not certain that this could not be the "Wigwam Neosho." Interview, July, 1964.

[24] "Military Road and Fort Gibson." Survey conducted by Buchanan Plusche for the Oklahoma Historical Survey, Writer's Project of the Works Project Administration, OIA. However, see John W. Morris and Edwin C. McReynolds, *Historical Atlas of Oklahoma,* p. 33. Professors Morris and McReynolds show remarkable precision in locating the Wigwam Neosho.

[25] Mrs. D. D. Hitchcock cited in *Old Fort Gibson,* a small booklet with no publisher or publication date. A copy may be found in the Indian Archives of the Oklahoma Historical Society.

[26] "Indian-Pioneer Papers," Typescript of Interviews of the Works Progress Administration, Vol. 29, p. 228, OIA, PC, UOL.

The late Charley Fox Taylor of Okay, whose grandmother, Lenzia Kell, once owned the Boling place, always said he had been told by his grandmother that the farm was the site of Houston's Wigwam Neosho . . . In a feature article in the *Muskogee Phoenix* and *Times-Democrat,* dated October 28, 1951 . . . Ballard left no doubt that he accepted the Boling place as the site for Wigwam Neosho.[27]

On the basis of the physical facts available and the evidence given in interviews plus his own understanding of Houston's life in the Cherokee Nation, Grant Foreman reached the conclusion that "the Scott place was not the location . . . and the location was on the Boling place."[28] Today, without the information of individuals closer to Houston's year among the Cherokees, but with many years of additional consideration, this conclusion of Grant Foreman remains sound. The most probable location of the Wigwam Neosho is the site on the Boling farm about two and one half miles from Fort Gibson and two and three fourths miles from Okay, Oklahoma.[29]

[27] Phil Harris, "Exact Site of Wigwam Neosho Is Sought," *Muskogee Daily Phoenix,* September 20, 1964, and see also Noel Ballard, *Muskogee Daily Phoenix,* October 28, 1951.

[28] Carolyn Thomas Foreman, Interview, July 3, 1964. See also Grant Foreman, WPA Map, May 8, 1938. Q. B. Boydstun, Interview, October 10, 1964.

[29] The authors are indebted to Phil Harris as well as Miss Nettie Wheeler and Mr. Horace C. Boren, who have done detailed research and field interviews. There has been some suggestion that a set of "plans" and an undated WPA document establish the Scott site as the location. This document, however, is inconsistent with both the Williams and Washburn contemporary reports and with the official Grant Foreman-WPA Indian-Pioneer History Project Map. See Phil Harris, "Houston Wigwam Neosho Location Studied," *Muskogee Sunday Phoenix and Times Democrat,* April 23, 1967. A Site Committee appointed by the Oklahoma Historical Society includes W. B. McIntosh, Earl Boyd Pierce, R. M. Mountcastle, and Q. B. Boydstun. The Committee has stressed that "no designation will be made until all historical evidence is in and has been evaluated." This is reassuring since an appropriation of $15,000 by the Oklahoma State Legislature for the purchase of three historical sites including the Wigwam Neosho has produced rumors that the Scott site might be selected because it could be more easily purchased. However, the authors' most valuable interviews were with the Oklahoma Indian historian, Carolyn Thomas Foreman, to whom we owe our greatest debt. Her ideas were invaluable to the authors in suggesting new books to read, settlers to interview, and sites to visit. Work on Sam Houston's years with the Cherokees would have been impossible without Mrs. Foreman's assistance.

15. Speculation in Indian Lands and Rations

> Tell my dear little God daughter that I must make a fortune, and give her, a marriage portion, and that is some fifty cows and calves, in *this* country.
>
> Sam Houston to John H. Houston, June 28, 1830, *Writings,* V, 4

For all his merchant and professional activities, Houston was a speculator who constantly dreamed of making a fortune. Some even suggest that his resignation from the governorship of Tennessee was staged so that he could come to the Indian country to capitalize on Jackson's plans for the removal of the Cherokees.[1] His letter to "my little God daughter" in which he promised "a marriage portion" of "some fifty cows and calves" is typical of Houston's dreaming.[2]

The purchase of the Grand Saline by Houston was one of his most fantastic bits of speculation. He wrote his friend and business associate John Van Fossen, in New York, saying that "I am just about to make a grand purchase of Salt Springs, and trust in God that I will be in a way to 'do well,' My fortune must not *wane* it must *full*, if I live and meet my deserts (in my humble opinion) . . ."[3]

Colonel A. P. Chouteau controlled a spring which contained one of the richest salt deposits in the area. To a western Indian community the salt spring was almost as important as water itself. Such springs were the center of community life and tribesmen came to them from hun-

[1] The rumors of the causes of Houston's resignation were so widespread that the exact origin of any one of them is hard to pinpoint. This seems to have first appeared in 1830, when Houston was a bidder on a government ration contract.

[2] SH to John H. Houston, June 28, 1830, Sam Houston, *The Writings of Sam Houston,* Amelia W. Williams and Eugene C. Barker (eds.), V, 4.

[3] SH to John Van Fossen, August 22, 1830, Houston, *Writings,* I, 187–188.

dreds of miles away. The operation of a salt spring was one of the quick ways to wealth and power on the frontier.[4]

Under the Osage Treaty of June 2, 1825, James, Paul, Henry, Anthony, Amelia, and Schemehunga, the Osage children of Chouteau, were each assigned one section of 640 acres of land. This land was the most valuable in the Osage Nation, and included in the allotments of Anthony and Amelia was much of the east side of the Grand River, encompassing the Grand Saline or salt deposit. On September 1, 1830, this land was deeded to Sam Houston, David Thompson, and John Drennan. In consideration of $3,000, half in cash and half in goods, Chouteau, acting as guardian for his Osage children, transferred this property. In addition to the $1,500 in cash, payment was made of one negro slave boy valued at $500 and $1,000 worth of merchandise to be selected from the Wigwam Neosho, including blankets, "first and second rate Mackinaws and French Mackinaws," valued at "twenty-five per cent advance upon cost and carriage."[5]

Individuals familiar with the character of the Chouteaus have suggested that Houston and Chouteau were maintaining a joint operation. It is true that Houston seems never to have profitably operated the saline, despite his boasts that the salt works would make a fortune. That he never realized its potential in production was noted by Richard M. Hannum, the Quapaw subagent in Arkansas, who observed that Houston "owned a valuable saline on Neosho . . . about twenty-five miles from Fort Gibson," which if put in complete operation "would produce immense quantity of salt."[6]

Houston's speculation on the land around the Grand Saline, how-

[4] See generally Grant Foreman, "Salt Works in Early Oklahoma," *The Chronicles of Oklahoma,* X (December, 1932), 474–500; Josiah Gregg, *Commerce of the Prairies,* II, 186.

[5] The sale of the Chouteau Saline to Sam Houston was a favorite topic with Grant Foreman. The documents dealing with this transaction were collected by Foreman and the material dealing with this salt-works speculation is from his work, unless otherwise indicated. Grant Foreman, "Some New Light on Houston's Life among the Cherokee Indians," *The Chronicles of Oklahoma,* IX (June, 1931), 143–148; Grant Foreman, *Pioneer Days in the Early Southwest,* pp. 188, 194–195, 260.

[6] Richard M. Hannum, "Letter from Quapaw Sub-Agent." *Arkansas Gazette,* May 27, 1833.

ever, seems to have paid off in quite "a tidy profit from his investments." The price was so good that over one hundred years later "the thirty dollars per acre paid to Houston by his grantee is more than the same land would bring today under a valid title."[7]

The deed from Houston to John C. McLemore and M. H. Howard, which is one of the earliest recorded conveyances of land in Oklahoma, sets out the essential facts of the sale of a portion of this land.

> Know all men by these presents that I Samuel Houston of the State of Tennessee, for and in consideration of the sum of Six thousand five Hundred Dollars . . . do Give, Grant, Bargain, Sell, alien, Convey to . . . John C. McLemore and M. H. Howard . . . One third part of a certain tract . . . below the Grand Saline (Known by the name of "Chouteau's Saline").[8]

Other portions of this land near the Grand Saline were sold by Houston. Although there is no deed for this sale, Governor Stokes seems to have thought that the remainder of the land was sold to Thompson and Drennan of Nashville. None of Houston's purchasers profited from this land, because the land was owned by the Cherokee Nation under the treaty of 1828 and could not legally have been sold by Chouteau or purchased from the Cherokee Nation or owned individually.

Hope of fast profit from the sale and the difficulty of locating a buyer brought James K. Polk into the transaction. Polk, later President of the United States, was issued a power of attorney to locate a buyer in Tennessee. A second power of attorney was later issued to Polk because "there was a likelihood that the Genl. Government would propose to pay the owners for it." Howard was so dissatisfied with his purchase that he wrote Polk:

> I would be truly glad that Some disposition could be made of the above named property as I understand the Indians are much averse to its being owned or used by the Whites . . . I have been informed by several that the above property would be of immense value if properly managed, but it is too far beyond my reach to pay much attention to it.[9]

The land upon which the saline itself was built had been transferred

[7] Foreman, "Some New Light," p. 145.
[8] Foreman, "Some New Light," pp. 144–145.
[9] Foreman, "Some New Light," pp. 147–148.

from the Osages to the Cherokees by the treaty of 1828. The agents felt that personal interest in this salt work and the land around it prompted Houston in 1830 to accompany the Cherokees to Washington, where he pushed for full ratification of the treaty provisions and expulsion of the Osages from this land.[10]

The operation of the salt works became the business of Captain John Rogers, Houston's brother-in-law. By the fall of 1832, when Washington Irving visited Chouteau, operation of the saline had been completely transferred to Rogers. Irving describes the home and the salt works in his journal:

> Ride to Saline—Major Rogers' house—he and his wife Cherokee half-breeds—he absent at Cherokee council—which has been in session four weeks, being discordant—Mrs. Rogers fine-looking woman—her son a tall, fine-looking young man, married to a handsome, tall half-breed. Log house with piazza—locust trees—Saline in valley—bubbling springs.[11]

The saline was operated quite profitably by Rogers, who maintained it until it was taken from him and transferred by somewhat questionable legislation to a brother of the Cherokee Chief John Ross. At the height of his operations, Rogers was working over one hundred salt kettles both day and night. A portion of the Grand Saline was being rented to others, and the remaining area was valued at over $100,000. In the early 1830's Rogers refused almost $40,000 for his interest and the assets of his salt works.[12]

Houston's attempt to obtain an Indian ration contract was not as successful as his speculation in Osage lands. Unquestionably, the rations provided for the Indians were insufficient and of an inferior quality. Houston had written of the enormous profits which the agents, acting as contractors, made on these sales in his Tah-lohn-tus-ky and Standing

[10] Vashon to Cass, January 4, 1832, OFT, OIA.

[11] Washington Irving, *The Journals of Washington Irving,* William P. Trent and George S. Hellman (eds.), pp. 132–133.

[12] The Rogers salt works were described by most of the early travelers in the Indian Territory, and most of these reports have been published. However, there is a considerable amount of unpublished material in the Official Report of the Cherokee Saltworks Investigation, "Cherokee Saltworks File," OVF, OIA.

Bear articles in the *Arkansas Gazette*. The picture is even more vividly described in *Authentic Memoir*:

> One charge which he made against the agents [was] proved incontrovertibly. . . . They had been contractors for furnishing Indian rations; and through their injustice or delinquency, some of the Indians had died of starvation, and to multitudes only a scanty and insufficient supply had been issued. These rations were issued at but one point in the two Nations [Creeks and Cherokees], which compelled the emigrants, as they had not had the benefit of a crop to locate in the most unhealthy parts of the country, for there only their rations could be obtained. This prevented their establishment and creation of homes in the new country, to which they had emigrated.[13]

The War Department advertised proposals to furnish rations for emigrant Indians through a public announcement made on February 18, 1830, by Thomas L. McKenney; bids were to be submitted by March 20. Since Houston was in Washington with the Cherokees at this time, he enlisted the support of New York financier John Van Fossen, his friend Benjamin Hawkins, and Congressman Robert Selden Rose of New York.

In a letter to Van Fossen written from Baltimore in April of 1830, Houston detailed the plans of submitting the bids for the ration contracts. He concluded the letter with a request that they all act in good faith in dealing with the ration contracts:

> To act in good faith with all parties, and to get just as much from the Government as will indemnify us for the use of the capital employed, and the labor bestowed, is what I wish; and further, to do ample justice to the Indians in giving to them full ration, and of good quality, should we get the contract, must be regarded as a "sine qua non" with us.[14]

Van Fossen submitted a bid of thirteen cents per ration. Twelve other bids were submitted, ranging from eight to seventeen cents per ration of one and a quarter pounds of fresh beef, or one pound of fresh pork, with two quarts of salt to every hundred rations. While several bids were lower than Houston's, his bid proposed to raise the

[13] C. Edwards Lester, *The Life of Sam Houston: The Only Authentic Memoir of Him Ever Published,* p. 57.

[14] SH to Van Fossen, April 4, 1830, Houston, *Writings,* I, 148.

quality of food and to deliver it to the Indians at points closer to their villages.[15]

Charges and countercharges were made against Houston, Secretary of War Eaton, and President Jackson. Luther Blake, the Creek agent, was the lowest bidder, and testified before a House Committee that Houston had requested that he withdraw his bid and join Houston in the higher bid, which would enable each to make more money. When Eaton did not let the contracts go to the lowest bidder, it was charged that he favored Houston. Finally, Eaton refused to accept any bids because no removal bill had been passed by the Congress, but the general political agitation against Houston and Jackson seems to be the reason that no contract was awarded.[16]

After his return to the Wigwam Neosho in the summer of 1830, Houston wrote to Secretary of War Eaton defending himself and his action. He also took this chance to attack many of the ration-contract holders:

> By authority from your Department, it has been stated, that I had sought to impose upon the Government on account of Indian Rations . . . And Sir, by the last advises it is understood here that Colonel Crowell was waiting . . . to take the contract . . . "privately" and . . . to withdraw his bid, as it was the lowest . . . and then the bid of . . . *another partner* would get it! . . . [I]t is most probable, that my next epistle will meet the public eye! The judgment will then belong to others, the Vindication, to myself![17]

[15] Houston, *Writings,* I, 149, 152, 187.

[16] See Houston, *Writings,* I, 149. A Congressional investigation was made of the charges of fraud and corruption. The reports are generally inconclusive. Reports of Committees, House of Representatives, First Session, Twenty-second Congress, V, Document 502. For excerpts from these reports combined with a short analysis see Grant Foreman, *Pioneer Days in the Early Southwest,* pp. 185–188.

[17] SH to JE, June 13, 1830, also JE to SH, July 28, 1830, G. Foreman, "Some New Light," pp. 141–142.

16. Gone to Texas

G.T.T.—the three letters were written on the doors of abandoned houses in the South and meant "gone to Texas"; and for any man to go to Texas in those days meant his moral, mental, and financial dilapidation.

Lecture, W. C. Evans, Professor of History, Northeastern State College, Tahlequah, Oklahoma

Houston had "gone to Texas"—the dream which he had envisioned as his destiny had come to pass.[1] In mid-November of 1832 the man who was to become President of the Republic of Texas left the Cherokee Indians headed for Texas, telling officials at Fort Gibson that he was on his way to visit with the Southern and Western Indians. Houston did visit these tribes and encouraged them to come to Cantonment Gibson to talk peace with the War Department's officials, but going to Texas was Houston's long-range plan.

In Washington with the Cherokees in the spring of 1832, Houston corresponded with New York financier James Prentiss about Texas. On April 8, Houston wrote to Prentiss, "If my presence should be required by those *interested*; it will be convenient for me . . . with very little delay (say a few days) to repair to Texas. . . . I have concluded to visit Texas, at all events this spring or summer."[2]

By May, Prentiss was anxiously inquiring when Houston could leave for Texas,[3] and by June they had signed an agreement by which Hous-

[1] Perhaps the best-told story of the parting of Diana Rogers and Sam Houston is found in George Creel, *Sam Houston, Colossus in Buckskin,* pp. 61–62.

[2] SH to JP, April 8, 1832, Sam Houston, *The Writings of Sam Houston,* Amelia W. Williams and Eugene C. Barker (eds.), I, 200–201.

[3] SH to JP, Houston, *Writings,* I, 266.

ton promised to go to Texas to purchase land interests.[4] During the spring Houston wrote not of his Cherokee friends but of Texas. He was anxious to reach Texas during the summer because he felt that a delay might produce serious consequences involving both England and Spain.[5] Being pressed for information "about Texas" and compelled to remain "close mouthed," Houston found his anxiety increased by the news of activity in Texas.[6]

Lack of funds, the congressional charges and investigation of the Stanbery caning, and the Indian ration-contract controversy delayed the summer departure for Texas. By early July, plans for the summer trip had been abandoned and Houston decided to visit his two sanctuaries of friendship—the Hermitage, where Jackson would meet him, and the Indian country near Cantonment Gibson, where the Cherokees were awaiting his return.[7]

Arriving in Nashville on the sixteenth of August, Houston dispatched to Prentiss another letter, in which he spoke of his dreams of Texas, "Thousands would flock there from this country, if the Government were settled, but will not venture without it!" There should be someone "with a view, to [make] changes, which are necessary, and must [take] place. [He reported that] several persons have said . . . that I was looked for, and earnestly wished for by the Citizens of Texas."[8]

Houston met with President Jackson at the Hermitage, where they unquestionably discussed Texas. There is only limited evidence to support the assertion that Houston was going to Texas as a revolutionary agent of the United States, but Jackson, nonetheless, appears interested in the trip. A considerable group of historians believe that Jackson either gave or loaned Houston $500 for the trip.[9]

Poverty always haunted Houston and even at the time of his death

[4] "Agreement between Houston and Prentiss," June 1, 1832, Houston, *Writings,* I, 229–230.

[5] SH to JP, June 9, 1832, Houston, *Writings,* I, 234–235.

[6] Letters, SH to JP, June 13, 1832; June 16, 1832; June 20, 1832; June 28, 1832, Houston, *Writings,* I, 237, 240, 243, 248.

[7] SH to JP, July 10, 1832, Houston, *Writings,* I, 257–258.

[8] SH to JP, August 18, 1832, Houston, *Writings,* I, 263–264.

[9] For a discussion of this controversy see Marion Karl Wisehart, *Sam Houston: American Giant,* p. 655 n.

he was a man of limited wealth. Prentiss had delayed payment of the promised financing despite Houston's constant demands. Houston finally concluded that their financial schemes had collapsed and demanded return of his note and agreement from Prentiss.[10]

In order to travel among the Indians in Texas, Houston was issued a passport, which reached him while he was in Nashville. It was issued at the request of President Jackson and probably presented to him personally by Jackson. The passport written by Acting Secretary of War John Robb on August 6, 1832, was a "request [to] all the Tribes of Indians, whether in amity with the United States, or as yet not allied to them by Treaties, to permit safely and freely to pass through their respective Territories, General Sam Houston, a Citizen of the United States."[11]

Still bound for Texas, Houston left the Hermitage, intent on journeying to Cantonment Gibson and the Indians. The purpose of his trip among the Cherokees was to maintain their friendship for the coming revolution in Texas. "The people," he wrote when describing the settlers in Texas, "look to the Indians on Arkansas as auxilaries, in the event of a change—so I will pass that way and see my *old friends*."[12]

Houston arrived at Cantonment Gibson on October 8, Washington Irving arrived on October 9,[13] and Houston, Arbuckle, and Irving spent a night together discussing the events of the day. Plans for the trip to Texas would have been an appropriate topic, but, perhaps at Houston's request, no recording or notes of this talk were made in either *A Tour on the Prairies* or Irving's personal journals.[14]

From the eighth of October until late November, Houston remained in the Gibson area to plan his trip and put his affairs in order. By the legendary accounts, Houston is said to have deeded the Wigwam Neosho to his Indian wife, Diana Rogers, and to have presented her with his two slaves. This tradition is subject to serious doubt, since

[10] SH to JP, September 15, 1832, Houston, *Writings,* I, 266.
[11] Passport, SH, August 6, 1832, Houston, *Writings,* IV, 11.
[12] SH to JP, August 18, 1832, Houston, *Writings,* I, 265.
[13] Henry Ellsworth to Lewis Cass, October 9, 1832, OFN, OIA.
[14] Washington Irving, *A Tour on the Prairies,* pp. 16–20; Washington Irving, *The Western Journals of Washington Irving,* Francis McDermott (ed.).

Cherokee citizens never owned land individually, and a power of attorney of Diana's in favor of Sam Houston was not issued until the next spring. Houston's abandonment would, under tribal law, have transferred the fields and improvements to her regardless of any gift.[15]

Houston said good-bye to Diana and left for Texas with United States Marshall Elias Rector, who went with him as far as the Red River. Traditionally, they drank away the hours on horseback, with Houston riding a small donkey or tailless mustang. Houston is said to have persuaded Rector to exchange horses with these words:

> This damned bob-tail pony is a disgrace. He is continually fighting flies, and has no means of protecting himself, and his kicks and contortions render his rider ridiculous. I shall be the laughter of all of Mexico. I require a steed with his natural weapon, a flowing tail, that he may defend himself against his enemies as his master has done . . . you *must* trade.[16]

Houston, according to another part of this same legend, is supposed to have rubbed the stubble of his beard in a gesture of contemplation. Rector then handed his razor to his companion.

"General," Rector said, "I wish to give you something before we separate and I have nothing that will do as a gift except my razor."

"I accept this gift," Houston said, "and mark my words, if I have luck this razor will some day shave the chin of the President of a Republic."[17]

Of his coming to Texas, Houston like to tell a story, which was saved and repeated by his friend Major Goree. "While he lived among the Cherokees, the raven, whenever he saw that bird, would fly in the

[15] An Act Relative to Breach of Marriage, "Furthermore if a white man should leave his wife, without just cause such white man shall be tried for such act, before the Judge, and if convicted, he shall pay the woman left, for all damages done her for breach of marriage and for deceiving her. The amount of damages to be decided by the Judges."

Piney, Approved—John Jolly
September 24, 1824 Black Coat, Chiefs

Cherokee Nation, *Laws of the Cherokee Nation Adopted at Various Times,* p. 171; Cherokee Nation, *Laws of the Cherokee Nation, 1808–1835,* p. 6; A. H. Murchison, "Intermarried Whites in the Cherokee Nation between the Years 1865 and 1887," *The Chronicles of Oklahoma,* VI (September, 1928), 298.

[16] Creel, *Sam Houston,* pp. 60–61.

[17] Marquis James, *The Raven: A Biography of Sam Houston,* p. 186.

direction of Texas, and he at last determined to follow the course of his flight."[18]

Although Houston traveled throughout Texas, he always said that he was a Texan as soon as he crossed the Red River. His feeling of an awaiting destiny is clearly expressed in his *Authentic Memoir*:

> . . . a single glance at the resources of this new country, and the character and condition of its population, satisfied him that a great destiny awaited . . . and in imagination he already saw a new commonwealth rising into power. He was still in the morning of life—here was a new field for achievement, where all the bold elements of his character could find full play. Once embarked on the stream of a revolution, the world would learn, at last, the character of the man it had hunted from society, and history and time would pronounce his eulogy.[19]

[18] A. W. Terrell, "Recollections of General Sam Houston," *The Southwestern Historical Quarterly,* XVI (October, 1912), 132–133.

[19] C. Edwards Lester, *The Life of Sam Houston: The Only Authentic Memoir of Him Ever Published,* p. 65.

17. Cherokee Emperor of Texas

It has been communicated to me that you had the *illegal enterprise* in view of conquering Texas; that you had declared that you would, in less than two years, be *emperor* of that country, by conquest. . . . and that the physical force to be employed was the Cherokee Indians!

Andrew Jackson to Sam Houston, June 21, 1829, in Henderson Yoakum, *History of Texas,* I, 307

[General Houston] . . . abdicated the government of Tennessee . . . to domiciliate himself among the Indians . . . [A]ll Mexico has been long since compassed, in the imagination and ardent desire, by the grasping enterprise of certain piratic American citizens; and that too under the connivance of Andrew Jackson. The same FATE [as Aaron Burr] would probably have fallen to the lot of HOUSTON, but for the protection he enjoyed under the dynasty of his patron. . . . General Jackson . . .

Robert Mayo, *Political Sketches of Eight Years in Washington,* pp. 118–167

Even before Houston had reached the Indian country rumors of a plot masterminded by him and designed to conquer Texas by military force were circulating in Washington. Houston, according to these stories, planned to build an Indian alliance and make himself the "Emperor of Texas." The rumors became so persistent and widespread that official Washington began to give them credence. While their exact nature varied with the group in which they were circulating, the one common feature was that Houston planned an Indian Federation, which would by military conquest make him the emperor of an independent nation south of the Red River in the country belonging to Mexico.

The President was connected in these rumors with plans to revolutionize Texas with a Cherokee army by "Adams . . . and many other contemporaries [who] believed that President Jackson secretly encouraged a filibuster against Texas by the agency of Sam Houston, his friend and former protégé."[1] Jackson's political opposition remembered statements the President had made in 1824 as a senator in the hearings on Mexico "that the United States ought to have spared no means to obtain it; and . . . that the way to get the territory was to occupy it and after taking possession enter into treaties."[2] Horace Greeley, Henry A. Wise of Virginia, and historians J. F. H. Claiborne, Henry Bruce, and Richard Stenbery accepted the rumors of a "Jackson-Houston scheme."[3]

In 1839 Dr. Robert Mayo published a book, *Political Sketches of Eight Years in Washington*, which developed his thesis "of the conspiracy of General Houston to dismember the Mexican dominions and the connivance of President Jackson to give it effect."[4] Mayo had in 1830 written to President Jackson of a conversation in which Houston "descanted on the immense fields for enterprise in the Indian settle-

[1] Richard Stenbery, "The Texas Schemes of Jackson and Houston, 1829–1836," *The Southwestern Social Science Quarterly*, XV (December, 1934), 229.

[2] For text of Jackson's statement see Stenbery, "The Texas Schemes," p. 229, and authorities cited therein.

[3] For a general sampling of these opinions see Llerena B. Friend, *Sam Houston: The Great Designer*, pp. 37–55, and authorities cited therein. John Quincy Adams, *Speech of John Quincy Adams, of Massachusetts, upon the Right of the People, Men and Women, To Petition; on the Freedom of Speech and of Debate in the House of Representatives of the United States; on the Resolutions of Seven State Legislatures, and the Petitions of More Than One Hundred Thousand Petitioners, Relating to the Annexation of Texas to This Union*, pp. 103–104; Horace Greeley, *The American Conflict: A History of the Great Rebellion in the United States of America, 1860–64*, I, 150; J. F. H. Claiborne, *Mississippi, as a Province, Territory and State, with Biographical Notices of Eminent Citizens*, p. 431; Henry A. Wise, *Seven Decades of the Union: The Humanities and Materialism*, p. 149; Henry Bruce, *Life of General Houston*, p. 80; see also Marquis James, *The Raven: A Biography of Sam Houston*, pp. 261–263.

[4] Robert Mayo, *Political Sketches of Eight Years in Washington*, pp. 177–178. The publisher describes Mayo as "author of an Inaugural Thesis on the Sensorium . . . Compiler of an Epitome on Ancient Geography; and a New System of Mythology; Compiler of the Pension Laws . . . by desire of the Secretary of War . . . 1832." For a short biographical sketch of Robert Mayo examine James Grant Wilson and John Fiske (eds.), *Appleton's Cyclopedia of American Biography*, IV, 277.

ment . . . as a stepping stone, in Texas";[5] later that same year Mayo visited the White House to discuss these rumors with the President.

Dr. Mayo's original letter was returned to him by General Jackson in 1836 along with a copy of a "Special Alphabet" code, which the conspirators had written and Mayo had obtained from Mr. Hunter, "a bona fide agent." The letter was published in *Eight Years in Washington*:[6]

TO GENERAL ANDREW JACKSON

President of the United States:

. . . Some time in the month of February last . . . shortly after General Samuel Houston arrived . . . I was introduced to him at Brown's hotel . . . [O]ur frequent interviews, and his confidence in my serving his ends . . . induced him to avow to me [his plan] . . . He descanted on the immense fields for enterprise in the Indian settlement beyond the Mississippi and through that as a stepping stone, in Texas . . . I learnt from him these facts and speculations, viz:

That he was organizing an expedition against Texas; to afford a cloak to which, he had assumed the Indian costume, habits, and associations, by settling among them, in the neighbourhood of Texas. That nothing was more easy to accomplish, than the conquest and possession of that extensive and fertile country, by the co-operation of the Indians in the Arkansas Territory, and recruits among the citizens of the United States. That in his view it would hardly be necessary to strike a blow to wrest Texas from Mexico. That it was ample for the establishment and maintenance of a separate and independent government from the United States . . .

I am, very respectful, your obedient servant,

R. Mayo

Washington City, D.C. Dec. 2, 1830

Mayo became disillusioned with Jackson and convinced that he was a "piratic conspirator" after the President delivered a speech concluding that "the unfortunate and unfounded suspicions in regard to our disposition [toward Mexico] . . . have been . . . entirely removed."[7]

[5] Mayo to AJ, December 2, 1830, reprinted in Mayo, *Political Sketches*, pp. 119–122.

[6] The letter, of which this is only a short excerpt, is discussed in considerable detail by Mayo. For the entire letter see Mayo, *Political Sketches*, pp. 119–122.

[7] AJ, "Second Annual Message to Congress," December 7, 1830, James D. Richardson (comp.), *Messages and Papers of the Presidents*, III, 1070.

Mayo's surprise at this statement and Jackson's subsequent conduct was clearly expressed in his presentment "of the entire affair before the public." Of Jackson's conduct Mayo asks:

> Did he do . . . any thing . . . Did he not on the contrary, entertain General Houston . . . while he sojourned at Washington, maturing his schemes and fomenting an affray with a member of Congress . . . still pretending to be an "Indian alien"? Did the president take any steps to make inquiry into this matter . . . No, but he prompted Houston in all his disorderly conduct . . .
>
> General Jackson must have been actuated by some extraordinary SECRET impulses connected with the *inception* and *prosecution* of the nefarious, wicked, and piratical enterprise of General Houston against the integrity of the Mexican dominions. . . .
>
> General Jackson, the patron of General Houston, was one of the most active confederates of Aaron Burr, and was so deeply interested in Burr's trial as to devote to a personal attendance during the whole or great part of its tedious progress of three or four months.[8]

Whether or not Jackson was involved in the "schemes" for Texas, he was certainly not ignorant of the maneuvering of General Houston or of the charges against him. In addition to the letter from Mayo, Jackson received letters from both friends and enemies, such as one from Duff Green, who forwarded a report written by Congressman Marable announcing that Houston had declared "he would conquer Mexico or Texas, and be worth two million in two years."[9]

Jackson's secretary, Andrew Jackson Donelson, received a letter from his brother reporting that Houston was not deranged with jealousy over his wife Eliza Allen, but was obsessed with a "grand scheme" for revolutioning Texas. Houston, Donelson recalled, had told him that William Wharton went to Texas as his agent and would notify him when "everything was properly arranged."[10] Z. N. Morrell re-

[8] Mayo, *Political Sketches,* pp. 128, 153, 167.

[9] John Spencer Bassett, *Life of Andrew Jackson,* II, 667; John Spencer Bassett (ed.), *Correspondence of Andrew Jackson,* V, 532; John Wharton to SH, cited in Sarah Barnwell Elliott, *Sam Houston,* p. 38; Alfred M. Williams, *Sam Houston and the War of Independence in Texas,* p. 75; Wise, *Seven Decades of the Union,* p. 148; Stenbery, "Texas Schemes," p. 230.

[10] Stanley F. Horn (ed.), "Holdings of the Tennessee Historical Society," *Tennessee Historical Quarterly,* III (December, 1944), 349–351; Friend, *Sam Houston,* pp. 50–51.

membered a story told him by his friend McIntosh, a deacon of the Baptist church in Nashville, that Houston confided in the deacon a plan to renew his contacts with the Cherokees and, with their aid and the assistance of his friends from Tennessee, to establish "a little two horse republic" of which he would be the first president.[11]

Read in the light of these statements a letter written by Houston's business associate, John Van Fossen, on August 3, 1832, has additional significance. Van Fossen wrote Houston:

> . . . that I do not believe that the portion of country will long continue its allegiance to the Mexican Government, and I would much rather see it detached through your agency, as the consequences could not fail to be highly favorable to your interest, than to learn that the object had been effected through any other means, or even to learn that it had become the property of the United States on the most favorable terms of purchase.[12]

Houston denied these rumors even before he had reached the Cherokee Nation, for the charges seemed so serious that he addressed himself to them in a letter written to President Jackson from Little Rock, Arkansas Territory. Denying any knowledge of the exact nature of the rumors, Houston eloquently refuted charges of a plot designed to injure the United States:

> This remark is induced, by the fact . . . that you have been assured that I meditated an enterprise calculated to injure, or involve my country [he began]. To you any suggestion on my part would be idle . . . ridiculous—You Sir, have witnessed my conduct from boyhood thro life. You have seen my private and my official acts—to these I *refer* you—To what woud they all amount, and for what would I live? but for my honor, and the honor and safety of my country? Nothing![13]

Jackson appeared so moved by Houston's reply that he quickly answered he did not believe the rumors, but added that Houston should consider locating in Arkansas. From Jackson's letter it is obvious that he intended to continue watching, in case the rumors were true. In con-

[11] Z. N. Morrell, *Flowers and Fruits in the Wilderness: Or, Forty-Six Years in Texas and Two Winters in Honduras,* p. 20; Friend, *Sam Houston,* p. 51.

[12] John Van Fossen to SH, August 3, 1832, in William Carey Crane, *Life and Select Literary Remains of Sam Houston,* pp. 48–49.

[13] SH to AJ, May 11, 1829, Sam Houston, *The Writings of Sam Houston,* Amelia W. Williams and Eugene C. Barker (eds.), I, 132–134.

cluding his letter, the President ridiculed the scheme in tones which suggest that his purpose was more to discourage the scheme than to assure Houston of Presidential confidence in his integrity. Jackson wrote:

It has been communicated to me that you had the *illegal enterprise* in view of conquering Texas; that you had declared that you would, in less than two years, be *emperor* of that country, by conquest . . . I must have really thought you deranged to have believed you had such a wild scheme in contemplation; and particularly when it was communicated and that the physical force to be employed was the Cherokee Indians![14]

Jackson was not yet convinced that Houston did not have an illegal plan in mind or wanted to provide evidence that he had no part in the plan should it fail. Houston was placed under military surveillance, his mail was opened and read, and reports were sent to the War Department by Houston's traveling companion, Haralson. Jackson was either so uncertain of Houston's motives or so anxious "that it might appear in the future as 'proof' that he had not connived at Houston,"[15] that he wrote a detailed memorandum concerning Houston in his daybook:

May 21, 1829—recd from Genl. Duff Green an extract of a letter (Doctor Marable to Genl. G) containing declaration of Gov. Houston, late of Tennessee, that he would conquer Mexico or Texas, and be worth two million in two years, &c. Believing this to be the effusion of a distempered brain, but as a precautionary measure I directed the Secretary of War to write and enclose to Mr. Pope, Govr of Arkansas, the extract, and instruct him if such illegal project should be discovered to exist to adopt prompt measures to put it down and give the government the earliest intelligence of such illegal enterprise with the names of all those who may be concerned therein.[16]

[14] AJ to SH, June 21, 1829, Henderson Yoakum, *History of Texas, from Its First Settlements in 1685 to Its Annexation to the United States in 1846,* I, 307.

[15] See the thesis developed in Richard Stenbery, "Jackson, Anthony Butler, and Texas," *Southwestern Social Science Quarterly,* XIII (December, 1932), 264–286; Stenbery, "Jackson, Buchanan, and the 'Corupt Bargain' Calumny," *Pennsylvania Magazine of History and Biography,* LVIII (January, 1934), 61–85; Stenbery, "Jackson's Neches Claim, 1829–1836," *The Southwestern Historical Quarterly,* XXXIX (April, 1936), 255–274; Stenbery, "Texas Schemes," p. 229.

[16] Jackson's Manuscripts, "Executive Book," Library of Congress, cited in Stenbery, "Texas Schemes," p. 230.

A letter from Andrew Jackson to William S. Fulton concerning Houston's Cherokee Empire created a "whodunit" problem in Washington in 1837.[17] Jackson had written a letter to Fulton, secretary of the Arkansas Territory, stating that there appeared to be no evidence of such a plot but asking that Houston be kept under surveillance and that action be taken if necessary. Somehow, either by accident ("enclosed by mistake") or by "theft,"[18] the letter reached Mayo. He interpreted the statement that "no movements have been made nor have any facts been established which would require or would justify the adoption of official proceedings against individuals implicated" as proving Jackson's connivance in the scheme.[19] It was thought by others that the letter was never mailed or was deliberately misaddressed so as never to reach Fulton, since "it was calculated to explain . . . if Houston's success in the enterprise should . . . necessitate explanations by the President of his own failure to uphold the neutrality law."[20]

Despite denials, evidence strongly suggests that Houston was contemplating an empire for the Indian Nation. Perhaps it was a "Rocky Mountain Alliance" or a Columbia River Nation instead of an empire in Mexico, but he spoke often of an empire—an empire won with the help of his Indian allies. Some say it was idle talk, that there was no plan; yet H. Haralson wrote that the "Rocky Mountain Alliance" was more than an idle plan. In a letter which is offered as proof that Haralson was a spy for the Jackson administration as well as a traveling companion, the plans to visit the Rockies are set forth. "[G]en Houston and myself . . . arrived at this place [Cantonment Gibson] on our way to the Rocky Mountains. The weather becoming hot we concluded to defer it until the fall of the year. In the fall I will return to this place on my way to the Rocky Mountains."[21]

[17] Friend, *Sam Houston,* pp. 52–54. The entire Fulton letter is found in Mayo, *Political Sketches,* p. 125. A foldout facsimile is also included in the Mayo book.

[18] Mayo claimed the letter had been included by mistake in the papers returned to him by Jackson. Jackson insisted that this letter plus an entire file of correspondence had been stolen. Friend, *Sam Houston,* pp. 52–54; Stenbery, "Texas Schemes," pp. 231–238.

[19] AJ to Fulton, December 10, 1830, Mayo, *Political Sketches,* p. 125.

[20] Stenbery, "Texas Schemes," p. 234.

[21] H. Haralson to JE, June 22, 1829, GSHBF, GRL. See also H. Haralson to JE, June 24, 1829, OFN, OIA.

Charles Noland, who was in Little Rock at the time of Houston's arrival, noted that Governor Houston was already looking West and was not the least likely to remain an exile in the Indian nation. "He wishes to go to the Rocky Mountains, to visit that tract of country . . . He came with a rifle on his shoulder. General Jackson will certainly persuade him to come back from the woods."[22]

It is easy to dismiss Houston's interest in Texas during this period as only secondary to his major occupation as "an agent for the Cherokees and for certain New York interests!" But to claim that the current interest in Texas was "a mere interlude in his Indian life" ignores a number of facts bearing on his long association with the dream of a Texas empire.[23]

Houston is said to have conceived of the idea of locating the Cherokees in Northern Mexico as early as 1818, when he became convinced that the Indians would never be free from white encroachment, as long as they remained within the United States. The northern provinces of Mexico seemed to Houston the most logical place for the Cherokees to establish their nation. When one of the chiefs of the Cherokees, known as Bowles, or "The Bowl," became dissatisfied with his life at his new home located in the United States territory north of the Red River, he called upon Houston to assist him in obtaining a patent of land from the Mexican government. Thus it is asserted that in 1818, with the assistance of Sam Houston, the Cherokees obtained a tract of land approximately thirty by sixty miles in an area north of Nacogdoches, Texas, within the area owned by Mexico.[24]

Houston's personal interest in Texas is recorded as early as 1822, when he joined a group in applying for grants of land in Texas. These applications, which required a guarantee of willingness to develop and

[22] Charles F. M. Noland to William Noland, May 11, 1829, Lewis Berkley Papers (Photographic copy in Archives Collection, University of Texas Library), quoted in Friend, *Sam Houston*, pp. 23–24.

[23] Allen Johnson and Dumas Malone (eds.), *Dictionary of American Biography*, IX, 264.

[24] This suggestion is made in Carolyn Thomas Foreman, "Texanna," *The Chronicles of Oklahoma*, XXXI (Summer, 1953), 178. However, the authors have found no concrete documentation for this suggestion. It is known that Houston was assisting the Western Cherokees during this period and that he had assisted in obtaining lands in Arkansas.

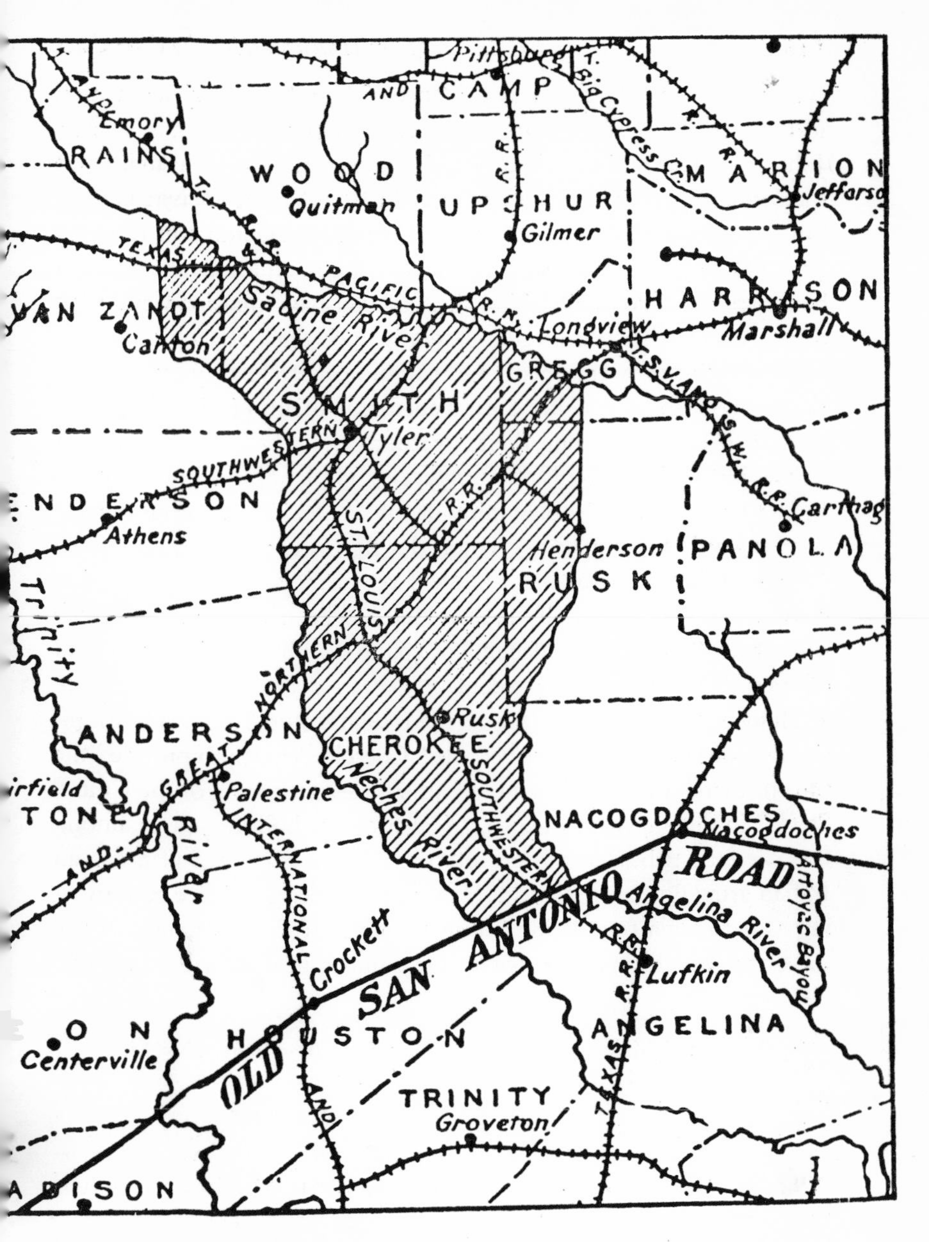

Map 3. THE CHEROKEE LAND GRANT IN TEXAS. Courtesy Texas State Library.

colonize the patents, are clear evidence of Houston's early speculation in the growth of Texas.[25] In fact, many of Houston's friends, such as John A. Wharton, had migrated to Texas and were anxious to interest the former governor in locating there. In 1829 Wharton invited Houston to come to Texas and settle.[26] Thomas Hart Benton sent Houston copies of two pamphlets which he had written "on our South Western boundary" and counseled him, ". . . if you have ulterior views your *tongue* and *pen* should dwell incessently upon these . . . topics."[27] The citizens of Texas were openly campaigning in 1832 to interest either Houston or Houston's old political enemy, William (Billy) Carroll, in coming to Texas to become their governor.[28]

The birth of Houston's active interest and planning for Texas came in 1829, the year of the beginning of his "exile." Texas seems to have been his only topic of conversation during his early months with the Cherokees, since "throughout most of the year . . . no matter in what company he found himself . . . Sam Houston invariably brought up the subject of Texas as an independent country with himself at the head of it as king, emperor, or president."[29]

Houston is said to have "put on the Indian costume . . . that he might shelter himself" and to have become a Cherokee citizen to provide "the plea of being a foreigner, and not amenable to the laws of the United States" in dealing with Mexico.[30] His efforts at building peace among the Western tribes have been interpreted as a part of a plan for an Indian army united to fight in Texas.[31] He appears to have been moving as if to lay a foundation for an Indian confederation, and "at the successful conclusion of that effort we find him standing as a white

[25] Johnson and Malone, *Dictionary of American Biography,* IX, 264.

[26] Johnson and Malone, *Dictionary of American Biography,* IX, 264; see Wharton to SH, June 2, 1832, Houston, *Writings,* I, 230–231.

[27] Thomas H. Benton to SH, August 15, 1829, Houston, *Writings,* I, 140.

[28] Houston contemplated returning to Tennessee. See SH to Major William B. Lewis, May 20, 1830, Houston, *Writings,* I, 151–152, also, SH to John Houston, December 2, 1832, VI, 1–2; Friend, *Sam Houston,* pp. 28–29.

[29] Owen P. White, *Texas: An Informal Biography,* p. 70.

[30] Mayo, *Political Sketches,* p. 166.

[31] White, *Texas,* p. 71. For an excellent summary discussion of these activities see Grant Foreman, *Pioneer Days in the Early Southwest,* p. 204.

chief at the head of a potential army of as many as ten thousand red warriors."[32]

That the scheme of an Indian confederation composed of these thousands of warriors was neither as "deranged" or "wild" as Jackson had suggested, was shown by a federation of Indians who joined Texas colonists in the ill-fated Fredonia Rebellion against Mexico in 1826–1827. "From the best information twenty-three . . . tribes [to assist with the revolution] had united in one political body,"[33] of which the Cherokees, with whom the Republic of Fredonia entered treaties in December of 1826, were the largest. The Fredonia Republic and the Indian federation against Mexico suffered from lack of organization, leadership, and internal power struggles, even among the Cherokees, but the potential fighting force of an Indian confederation was amply demonstrated by this experiment.[34]

An Indian empire in Texas would have been compelling to any man, but to Houston, with his love of the dramatic, belief in divine uncontrollable destiny, and conviction that the only hope for salvation of the Indian was a land outside the control of the United States, it was a magnet. Houston looked "upon himself as their future white chief, the head to be of a great, warlike nation of redmen."[35] His dream of a "retreat" for the Indians was expressed to Alexis de Tocqueville, whom he met on a steamboat headed for New Orleans in December of 1831. This famous French traveler viewed Houston as having the "unfortunate characteristic of popular sovereignty," but recorded Houston's prediction that "the Indian nations of the South will find a refuge and civilize themselves there."[36]

Houston envisioned himself as a Caius Marius, his favorite historical character, at the head of a Cherokee army.[37] Marius, a Roman general and statesman noted for his patience and recovery from setbacks,

[32] White, *Texas,* p. 71.

[33] *Arkansas Gazette,* March 27, 1827.

[34] *Courier des Natchitoches,* June 2, 1827; General Gaines to Colonel Zachery Taylor, March 14, 1827, cited in Yoakum, *History of Texas,* I, 245–250.

[35] White, *Texas,* p. 75.

[36] George W. Pierson, *Tocqueville in America,* p. 390.

[37] This story is most clearly presented in Marion Karl Wisehart's *Sam Houston: American Giant,* pp. 116–117.

fascinated Houston, who had carried a copy of *The Life of Caius Marius* with him to the Cherokees and who, even as a boy, is said to have compared himself to Marius.[38] When drunk, Houston quoted Marius, and on the boat coming to the Indian country declared himself to be an American Marius.

Marius was an exile like Houston, and following his exile organized an army out of peasants and demoralized soldiery, dealing two major defeats to foreign invaders. Houston doubtless saw himself as Marius in exile and considered the Cherokee Indians to be his peasant soldiery. While visiting in Nashville, Houston had himself painted as Marius, a gesture interpreted as an announcement to the world of his intention to return to power. Houston is said to have told the artist, "Paint me as Marius barefooted in the ruins of the city of Carthage." Today a copy of this painting known as *Houston as Marius* hangs in the Texas State Capitol on the west wall of the Senate gallery.

There is more than mere speculation of Houston's plans for the Cherokee Indians. His intention to use the Indians, if needed, as a military force in Texas is recorded in his own correspondence. In 1832, when Houston had definitely announced his plans to go to Texas, he wrote to his New York associates that he would go to Texas by way of Cantonment Gibson and his old friends the Cherokees. "The people," he wrote when describing the settlers in Texas, "look to the Indians on [the] Arkansas as auxiliaries, in the event of a change."[39]

The early maneuverings for the organization of the Indian auxiliaries were never recorded, perhaps because Houston's mail was constantly subjected to inspection by the Indian agent, military officials, and representatives of Mexico.[40] President Jackson later wrote that "we had had, ever since the intimation of his [Houston] being regarded as unfriendly to the existing government of Mexico a secret agent watching his movements and prepared to thwart any attempts to organize within the United States a military force to aid in the revolution of Texas."[41]

Proof of Houston's dependence upon his Indian friends is seen as the names of his associates in the days at Cantonment Gibson, his In-

[38] SH to Sam Houston, Jr., April 7, 1860, Houston, *Writings,* VIII, 8.
[39] SH to JP, August 18, 1832, Houston, *Writings,* I, 263–264.
[40] White, *Texas,* p. 75.
[41] AJ to Butler, Bassett, *Correspondence of Andrew Jackson,* V, 221.

dian trading activities, and his Indian social life appear in early Texas history. Houston's interest in locating the Cherokees in Texas is too well known to be questioned. Even the most conservative commentators have observed that "Samuel Houston himself . . . was using his friendship with the Creeks and Cherokee to enlist them on the side of Texas in her contest with Mexico."[42]

In fact, his relationship with the Cherokees was so notorious that they were known in Texas as "Houston's pet Indians" and along with the Creeks and Choctaws were encouraged to actively participate in the struggles with Mexico. This is an interesting contrast with the Alabama-Coushatta tribes of Southern Texas, whom Houston encouraged to remain outside the struggle, explaining "that by their not taking sides, the winner of the war, whether Texan or Mexican, would have no grievance against the 'redman'."[43]

Ironically, one of Houston's lieutenants in raising an Indian army was Hugh Love, who had been an agent and Indian trader among the Cherokees and Creeks from 1828 to 1832, when he operated a trading post at the Three Forks settlement under a license issued by Major George Vashon. Serious accusations were made between Love and Houston in the Tah-lohn-tus-ky series in the *Arkansas Gazette,*[44] but in 1836 Houston "detached Col. Hugh Love to Nacogdoches for the purpose of raising an auxiliary corps to the Main army, three hundred or more Indians of the Cherokees, Delaware, Shawnee, Kickapoo, and any other friendly tribes." If the Indians agreed to serve six months, Love was authorized by Houston to pay them "Seven Thousand Dollars to be equally divided among the individuals engaged," and to offer "one-half of all property taken by them." Houston regarded this Indian brigade as "the most efficient auxiliary corps to the main army that can be raised."[45]

Another long-time associate of Houston's, Benjamin Hawkins, who was an educated mixed-blood Creek, who was married to a half-breed, and who had been associated with Houston in his trading post at the

[42] G. Foreman, *Pioneer Days,* p. 232.

[43] Prairie View Malone, *Sam Houston's Indians,* p. 21.

[44] See generally the excerpts from *The Arkansas Gazette,* in Houston, *Writings,* I, 161, 163, 170, 173.

[45] SH to Governor Henry Smith, January 17, 1836, Houston, *Writings,* I, 342.

Wigwam Neosho, came to Texas. Hawkins had speculated with Houston in gold mining, in the ill-fated attempts to secure Indian rations contracts, and in several other schemes. At Houston's invitation, Hawkins brought the Creek chieftain, Opothleyahola, to Texas and induced him to enter into negotiations for the purchase of a large tract of land north of Nacogdoches, for which a preliminary payment of over $20,000 was made by the Creeks. The Creeks owed a balance of $80,000 on the purchase.[46]

Houston's purpose in bringing five thousand Creeks to Texas through Hawkins' work is clearly outlined in a letter to Andrew Jackson:

> During the last spring, two men, one . . . Archibald Hotchkiss . . . and Benjamin Hawkins, a quarteroon Creek Indian, made a contract with Apothleyahola [sic], and other chiefs of the Creek nation, who were at this place, to procure for them a grant of land which had been made by the Mexican government! . . . In consideration of which the Indians were to pay to them the sum of one hundred thousand dollars. An arrangement was made by which they actually received from the Indians at New Orleans the sum of twenty thousand dollars! . . . Since then they have returned to Texas, and Hawkins has recently left this country for the United States, with the avowed and manifest intention of introducing into Texas not less than five thousand Creeks, so soon as it will be possible for them to reach here. The residue of the nation to join them as soon as they can remove to this country.[47]

Of those who came to Texas, the individual most closely associated

[46] See Houston, *Writings,* I, 205; Kenneth Wiggins Porter, "The Hawkins Negroes Go to Mexico," *The Chronicles of Oklahoma,* XXIV (Spring, 1946), 57; "Muskogee and Environs," Map drawn by Winnifred Clark and Grant Foreman, Foreman Room, Public Library, Muskogee, Oklahoma; Yoakum, *History of Texas,* II, 328; G. Foreman, *Pioneer Days,* pp. 205–206; *Arkansas Gazette,* August 20, 1828. It is thought that Hawkins was killed by a band of Cherokees. G. Foreman has recorded the following document. "September 15, 1835. F. Thorn, President; T. J. Rush, Secretary. *Resolved,* that General Houston be appointed to make such steps as he may deem necessary in attempting to arrest the progress of one Benjamin Hawkins, who, we have every reason to believe, is attempting to introduce a body of Indians from the United States into Texas." "Proceedings of Vigilance Committee, Nacogdoches," cited in *Pioneer Days,* p. 205.

[47] SH and others to AJ, September 11, 1835, Houston, *Writings,* I, 299–302.

with Houston's days among the Cherokees was Lieutenant Peter Harper. Harper was a "partner" of Houston's at the Wigwam Neosho with his father-in-law, James Rogers, who supplied trade goods, while Harper, himself, assisted in the operations of the Wigwam. Harper was a soldier at San Jacinto, was discharged a second lieutenant on April 27, 1836, and in 1838 received a headright of land from the Nacogdoches County Board of Land Commissions.[48] Harper was Houston's chief agent in enlisting the support of the Indians. "The plans of conquest in contemplation by Sam Houston in Texas, undoubtedly had in mind the use of certain of his Indian friends among the Cherokees and Creeks. Through Lt. Peter Harper . . . he undertook to get in touch with the Indian Chiefs to the north."[49] Houston sent Harper, accompanied by Kendall Lewis, who had also been in the Cantonment Gibson area, to Opothleyahola with a letter which Houston knew would reach the Indian agents in the United States.[50] The reaction to this letter was immediate and violent.

The Cherokees and Creeks appeared anxious for war against the Mexican government, and the situation so alarmed William Armstrong, the acting superintendent of Indian Affairs for Arkansas, that he wrote to the commissioner of Indian Affairs: "The Creeks as well as the Cherokees have a great disposition to engage in the contest between the Texans and the Mexicans, and there are those among them, more especially the Cherokees, who are secretly encouraging such a design."[51]

Armstrong felt that legal action should be brought against Houston and Harper, but was restrained by order of the War Department from taking any action or making any interference against the plotting in Mexico. Nonetheless, he requested that Samuel Hall, the United States district attorney for Arkansas, consider the violation of the Intercourse Acts.

I enclose a letter signed Saml Houston to Lt. Peter Harper . . . Should you deem this an infraction of the Intercourse Law of 1834 you will please have writ issued against Harper who is now in the Cherokee Nation. There

[48] Biographical information on Peter Harper is gathered in Houston, *Writings,* II, 51, and IV, 448–449.

[49] Carolyn Thomas Foreman, Interview, July 3, 1964.

[50] Note the explanation in Houston, *Writings,* II, 49–51.

[51] Armstrong to C. A. Harris, May 10, 1837, Houston, *Writings,* II, 50.

is a disposition with some individuals to alienate the confidence of the Creeks and Cherokees from the United States and to enlist them in the present contest now going on between the Texans & Mexicans.[52]

Others from the days in the Cherokee Nation were enlisted in the aid of the struggling young Republic. Houston summoned Colonel James B. Marcy from Fort Jessup in August of 1838 to bring troops to stop a rebellion of Mexicans and Indians in the region of Nacogdoches.[53] The Dawsons[54] and Baylors,[55] who had been associates of Houston at Cantonment Gibson, were involved in the Texas settlement, as was Kendall Lewis. The Fieldses,[56] Benges, B. H. Smith,[57] Corn Tassle, and Oosoota had come to Texas.[58] "The influence . . . that brought these Indians to Texas was obviously . . . Houston."[59]

Houston's strongest ally in Texas was "The Bowl," or Bowles, whom he had helped locate in the area in 1818. Bowles was always ready to provide military assistance for Houston, and in commemoration of their friendship Houston presented Bowles with a hat, a suit of clothing, and a sword. It was Bowles with whom Houston signed the Texas-Indian Treaty, and Bowles who was the head of the associated band of Indians.[60]

[52] Armstrong to Hall, May 10, 1837, Houston, *Writings,* II, 50–51.

[53] Carolyn Thomas Foreman, "Colonel James B. Marcy, *The Chronicles of Oklahoma,* XIX (June, 1941), 119.

[54] *Arkansas Gazette,* April 15, 1829, and May 6, 1829; for the later career of Dawson see Edwin C. McReynolds, *The Seminoles,* pp. 253–254.

[55] SH to John Houston, June 24, 1829, Houston, *Writings,* II, 12; *Cherokee Advocate,* November 25, 1893.

[56] Emmett Starr, *History of the Cherokee Indians,* p. 558; *Daily Oklahoman,* September 27, 1931.

[57] See Chapter 7, "Indian Peacemaker." It is generally agreed that "Smith taught school in the employ of Captain John Rogers . . . and then went to Texas in the company with Sam Houston." "Indian-Pioneer Papers," Typescripts of Interviews of the Works Progress Administration, XXCI, 433, OIA, PC, UOL.

[58] An interesting comparison can be made between the accounts of John Drew, listing individuals in the Fort Gibson area between 1829 and 1833, and the names of Cherokees who later signed the Texas Treaty. John Drew Papers and Accounts, GRL.

[59] G. Foreman, *Pioneer Days,* p. 206.

[60] See generally Starr, *History of the Cherokee Indians,* pp. 187–224; Texas-Cherokee Treaty, Dorman Winfrey and James M. Day (eds.), *Texas Indian Papers,* I, 14–17.

The military conquest of Mexico eliminated the need for an "Indian auxiliary,"and the succession of Mirabeau B. Lamar to the Presidency of the Republic of Texas assured the triumph of the white forces, which had always opposed emigration of Indians, thus signalling the end of Houston's dream of an Indian empire in Texas.[61] Lamar, a native Georgian possessing the traditional hatred of his state for the red man, used rumors of a Cherokee-Mexican alliance as an excuse to attack the Texas Cherokees and drive them from their lands. Lamar's defeat of the Cherokees was so overwhelming that Bowles, who died in the battle, may have been more fortunate than his fellow tribesmen. *The Northern Standard,* October 14, 1843, pictures Bowles' band:

> The remnant of the Cherokees who were there, were in a most distressed condition. The family of Bowles who were all there, would not come into camp until the Commissioners purchased clothes for the women and children. Accustomed to the decencies of life, they were unwilling to show themselves to civilized people in their state at that time . . . we find . . . them . . . lately robbed of the very last vestige of property by a people which ranks itself a nation, free, powerful, and proud, but which is far beneath these Indians.[62]

It was an ironic twist in the career of Sam Houston that he should find his destiny in Texas without his Cherokee friends and brothers. The attack upon the Cherokees was not made until Houston had left Texas for a conference in the United States, but, upon his return, Houston denounced the action of Lamar and his associates for what he considered breaking faith with their Indian allies. Houston never forgave the committee responsible for the expulsion of the Cherokees, and as late as 1855, when he was serving as United States senator from Texas, he spoke with bitterness of Lamar's extermination policy.

> I well remember . . . we had peace . . . The declaration was made . . . that they would kill "Houston's pet Indians" . . . The Cherokees had been very friendly when Texas was in consternation, and the men and women were fugitives from the myrmidons of Santa Anna . . . they had aided our

[61] Lamar to Bowles, Winfrey and Day, *Texas Indian Papers,* I, 61–66, Item 34.

[62] Charles DeMorse, Editorial, *The Northern Standard* (Clarksville, Arkansas), October 14, 1843.

people, and given them succor—and this was the recompense. They were driven from their homes and left desolate. What was the consequence? Every Indian on the border from the Red River to the Rio Grande took the alarm. They learned that extermination was the cry, and hence it was that the flood of invasion came upon our frontier and drenched us with blood.[63]

[63] SH, Speech, January 29, 31, 1855, quoted in Starr, *A History of the Cherokee Indians,* p. 222; also SH, "On an Increase of the Army, and the Indian Policy of the Government," January 29, 31, 1855, Houston, *Writings,* VI, 111–154.

A Conclusion

> These men [Houston and Jackson] lived at a time when the whole theory of government of the United States was in a state of flux, but whether we now regard them as right or wrong, they were giants in those days.
>
> Paul I. Wellman, *Magnificent Destiny*

In 1829 Sam Houston saw a raven flying west and followed it to the Cherokee country, describing himself as "the most unhappy man . . . living"; "a man in the darkest, direst hour of human misery." In 1833 Houston left the Cherokees, predicting that he might soon be "President of a Republic," since he was "looked for and earnestly wished for by the Citizens of Texas." The interlude between 1829 and 1833—Houston's years with the Cherokees—has been called a "blot upon his life." Far from being a blot, this interlude spent with the Cherokee Indians was one of the most important periods in Houston's public career.

These years were more than a pastoral sojourn in which the former governor of Tennessee spent idyllic hours selling beads and cloth and drinking on the banks of a stream with a beautiful Indian maiden. Many of Houston's basic attitudes—attitudes reflected in his policies as President of the Republic of Texas, United States senator, and governor of Texas—were formulated during these "missing years." Statements from the Cherokee period are re-echoed in public statements and speeches throughout his Texas career.

Houston's contributions to the Indian administration are, moreover, among his most significant achievements. Reforms instituted in the Agency System, many resulting from Houston's Tahlontuskee and Standing Bear articles and his personal testimony to President Jackson, were basic and long-lasting. Treaties and agreements negotiated with Houston's assistance provided a stable basis for Indian-White relations along the Southwestern frontier. Furthermore, the peace established on the North Texas boundary enabled the struggling Republic to follow a policy free from the fear of Indian attack.

To suggest that Houston's years with the Cherokees were but a dress rehearsal for the drama that followed in Texas ignores too many facts. To suggest that Houston divorced himself from the civilized world, planning to become a Cherokee, is equally shortsighted. Evidence substantiates the conclusion that Sam Houston came to the Cherokees a rejected man—a man hoping to rebuild a public career. Houston, no doubt, knew of the opportunities awaiting an ambitious man in Texas. He was equally aware of the potential of an army composed of his Indian friends. When the Stanbery caning provided him with a "national platform," Houston was ready. The raven, his bird of destiny, flew south to Texas and Houston could only follow it—as he had followed it to the Cherokee country.

APPENDIX: HOUSTON CHRONOLOGY, 1829–1833

1829

January 22—Eliza Allen and Samuel Houston married at Gallatin, Tennessee, by Dr. William Hume.

January 30—Houston announces as a candidate for re-election as governor of Tennessee.

April 9—Houston and wife are separated; letter written to John Allen about marriage.

April 15—Colonel J. Love writes Andrew Jackson that Houston will leave for Arkansas Territory to reside with the Indians.

April 16—Houston resigns as governor.

April 16–23—Houston remains in seclusion after being refused baptism by Dr. Hume and Obadiah Jennings of the Nashville Presbyterian Church.

April 23—Houston accompanied to packet *Red Rover* by Sheriff Willoughby Williams and Dr. John Shelby.

April 23–May 9—In the company of H. Haralson, Houston travels from Nashville to Little Rock by way of Cairo, Memphis, Helena, mouth of White River. Meets Jim Bowie on ship.

May 9–13—Houston stays in Little Rock talking and dreaming of his "Rocky Mountain" alliance; writes to Jackson denying rumors of plan to be "Cherokee Emperor of Texas" and offers assistance in Indian peacemaking.

May 15—Houston, Haralson, and John Litton in Fort Smith drunkenly join in a "Bacchian Celebration."

May 22—Daniel Donelson writes to President Jackson's secretary that Houston resigned as a part of a plan to revolutionize Texas.

Late May—Houston reunited with the Cherokees at Tahlontuskee, home of his adopted father, John Jolly.

Early June—Houston goes to Chouteau's trading post and with H. Haralson and Dr. Neil accompanies a party of Osages to their villages.

June 22—At Cantonment Gibson, Houston witnesses a memorial of the Creek chiefs to be sent to President Jackson.

June 24—From Cantonment Gibson, Houston sends Creek memorial to President Jackson by request of "Governor McIntosh" of the Creeks;

recommends Chouteau to Jackson and again offers to assist in peace negotiations. Writes letter to John H. Houston recommending Dr. Baylor as "worthy of your friendship."

June 25—Houston writes to Jackson from Cantonment Gibson concerning Major Anthony's answer to the Creek memorial.

July 7—Houston attends Dance and Talk at Maynard Bayou, Cherokee Nation, as John Jolly's representative, but fails to persuade against war.

July 18–21—Houston visits with Captain and Mrs. McClellan at the Choctaw Agency, where he met "an old Choctaw Chief," who told him of his complaints.

July 22—At Fort Smith, Arkansas Territory, Houston writes Secretary of War Eaton on behalf of the Choctaws.

August 12–September 19—Houston suffering "from a long spell of fever," probably malaria, from which he rested in Jolly's home at Tahlontuskee ("Cherokee Nation, in Arkansas").

September 19—At Tahlontuskee, Houston writes Jackson of "renewed health" and interest in politics; rejects Jackson's plan to locate in Arkansas, but may go to Natchez.

October 21—Houston becomes Cherokee citizen by admission letter issued at Tahlontuskee.

October 29—Houston present at allotment payment on north side of Arkansas above Fort Smith when "specie-certificates" instead of gold issued.

December 3—Letter of instructions to Andrew Jackson from John Jolly is written by Sam Houston at Tahlontuskee.

Mid-December—Houston leaves for Washington to represent the Cherokee Nation.

December 28—On board the "Steam Boat Amazon . . . passing near to the Borders of . . . Tennessee," where Houston announces that "the hour of anguish has passed by."

1830

January 1—Shawneetown, Illinois, *Gazette* reports that "Governor Houston passed . . . for Washington, accompanied by three Indian Chiefs."

January 4—John Rogers, Jr., sends additional instructions to Houston, Walter Webber, and John Brown, who "some several weeks since . . . left here for Washington."

January 11—Houston visits in Fredricktown, Maryland.

January 12—Houston arrives in Baltimore.

January 13—Houston takes up residence in Washington at the Brown Hotel.

Late January—Andrew Jackson enthusiastically receives Sam Houston at a reception for the diplomatic corps.

January–April—Houston in Washington as unofficial Cherokee ambassador; Cherokees negotiate on annuities, survey of land, removal of Eastern Cherokees, and Osage disputes.

February 18—Thomas McKenney of the War Department advertises for bids on contracts to furnish Indian food rations.

March 4—The *Cherokee Phoenix* reports that Houston, who is "now at Washington, has abandoned entirely assumption of the Indian costume and habits, and mingles in social intercourse and gaiety as freely as formerly."

April 1—In Washington, Houston formally aligns himself with the Cherokee merchants in a letter written to Eaton on behalf of Walter Webber. Houston also executes a letter of credit in Webber's favor.

April 4—At Baltimore, Houston writes to his associate John Van Fossen about bids for Indian ration contract.

April–July—Controversy over alleged fraud by Houston, Secretary of War Eaton, and even President Jackson. Committee hearings held.

May 18 and 20—On the "Steam Boat Nashville . . . Mouth of White River," where Houston is "just ready to start for Cantonment Gibson."

May 29—Houston is a member of the commission to settle Osage-Delaware disputes which submits formal report to Secretary of War Eaton.

June 13—At the Wigwam Neosho, Houston withdraws his application for Sutlers Post at Cantonment Gibson, defends position in Indian ration conflict, and announces intent to begin a series of articles in the *Arkansas Gazette.*

June 22—First issue of Houston's newspaper column appears in the *Arkansas Gazette* signed "Tah-lohn-tus-ky."

June 28—At Wigwam Neosho, Houston announces his intent to open his store "soon."

June 29—Reply to Houston's article on Indians in the *Arkansas Gazette.*

July 1—On behalf of the Cherokees, Houston writes to Major McCombe in Washington in order to obtain a land survey.

July 7—Second article, "The Creek Indians," appears in the *Arkansas Gazette.* Answer to *Arkansas Gazette* articles appear.

July 20—Arbuckle reports return of Cherokees from Texas border war and notes that Houston prevented Creeks from joining the Cherokees in this war.

July 21—From the Wigwam Neosho, Houston writes Arbuckle of intent to open store, of the arrival of a shipment of whiskey, and of his exemption as a Cherokee citizen from the license and Intercourse Acts. Reply to Houston in *Arkansas Gazette.*

July 23—From Cantonment Gibson, Houston again argues that as a "Cherokee Citizen" he is free to trade. Arbuckle writes to secretary of war for an opinion.

July 28—Eaton writes to Houston at Fort Gibson explaining the circumstances which caused the rejection of Indian ration bids and denying any intended reflection on Houston's integrity.

August 4—Another answer to Houston appears in the *Arkansas Gazette*, written by Hugh Love, a trader of Three Forks, with whom Houston is later associated in Texas.

August 14—Houston's "In Defense of the Indians" by Standing Bear published in the *Arkansas Gazette.*

August 22—At Wigwam Neosho, Houston writes concerning supply contract and of his intention "to make a grand purchase of Salt Springs." Acknowledges the Tah-lohn-tus-ky articles.

September 1—Houston and several associates purchase the Grand Saline and the land surrounding it from the Osage children of A. P. Chouteau.

September 8—"The Indians!!!" for the *Arkansas Gazette* appears.

September 11—G. P. Randolph, acting secretary of war, officially denies Houston's position on obtaining a trader's license.

October 20—A letter signed "Tekatoka" addressed to the Standing Bear, alias General Samuel Houston, appears in a supplement to the *Arkansas Gazette.*

December 7—At Wigwam Neosho, Houston writes to General William Hall concerning a publication on his marriage to Eliza Allen called a "Report from a committee of some citizens of Summer County."

December 8—The *Arkansas Gazette* issues Houston's defense to "Tekatoka" in a supplement to the paper.

December 15—Houston sends a letter from Wigwam Neosho to Andrew Jackson recommending Captain Nathaniel Pryor for the position of subagent to the Osages.

December 21—Attorney General John MacPherson Berrien issues opinion that adopted Cherokee citizens cannot trade without a license.

December 23—Houston writes from Wigwam Neosho to the editor of the *Arkansas Advocate* in defense of Secretary of War Eaton.

Date uncertain—Houston offers to serve on a commission with Colonel Arbuckle and Colonel Chouteau "to treat with the Pawnees and to make peace between them."

1831

Date uncertain—Houston writes a poem to an unnamed "young lady . . ."

February 16—Letter "To the Editor of the *Arkansas Advocate*" from Houston written in defense of Secretary Eaton's Indian ration-contract proposals.

March—Osages offer to meet with Creeks for peace negotiation, with Houston as one of the negotiators.

March–August—Houston represents his brother-in-law John Rogers in a controversy over Rogers' dismissal as Cherokee interpreter.

May 10—Creek and Osage treaty signed at Cantonment Gibson. Sam Houston is one of the witnesses.

May 18—Houston at Cantonment Gibson, when the Cherokee-Osage treaty is signed.

May 28—*Cherokee Phoenix* reports Houston's defeat in Cherokee elections and states that he is considering moving to the Choctaw Nation.

June—Matthew Maury records a plan of Houston's "to establish a colony . . . at the mouth of the Columbia," for which Houston predicted, "I should get plenty of settlers."

June 2—Houston officially asks for reinstatement of Captain John Rogers as Cherokee interpreter.

July 6—Houston sells a "third interest" in his purchase of the Grand Saline.

July 13—Houston issues a satirical proclamation in answer to attacks made on him about his marriage of Eliza Allen.

August–September—Houston returns to Baker County, Tennessee, and is at his mother's bedside when she dies.

October 20—Houston attends annuity payment at the Cherokee Agency.

December 27—Houston boards steamboat on which Tocqueville and Beaumont are passengers. Tocqueville observed that "Mr. Houston embarked on our vessel to go to New Orleans. We encountered him the twenty-seventh of December at the mouth of White River, where we had stopped to set ashore the Choctas [Choctaws]; he was riding a superb stallion."

December 27–December 31—Conversations between Tocqueville and Houston continue to include observations of the Indians. This material is basis of Tocqueville's *The Present State and Probable Future of the Indians.*

1832

January 1—Houston departs from steamboat in New Orleans on way to Washington.

January 4—Houston's controversy with missionaries reaches climax when Cherokee agent writes to secretary of war that all instructions for removal of Union Mission were written by Houston and should be ignored.

February 5—In Washington with the Cherokee delegation, Houston invites friend to visit him at Brown Hotel.

March–September—Houston corresponds with New York financier James Prentiss expressing his intention to go to Texas.

April–July—Houston and Stanbery controversy before the House of Representatives.

April 2—Remarks of William Stanbery appear in the *National Intelligencer* alleging fraud by Houston and Eaton.

April 3—Houston writes to Stanbery asking for an explanation of remarks made by the Congressman.

April 13—Houston and Stanbery meet on the street and the "caning" occurs.

April 18—Case of Samuel Houston before the House of Representatives begins. Houston is interrogated.

May 7—Houston addresses House of Representatives in his own behalf. Francis Scott Key continues as Houston's attorney.

Early June—Houston in New York to negotiate for trips to Texas.

June 1—Agreement is reached in New York between Houston and Prentiss by which "Houston agrees to proceed to Texas as soon as convenient and to purchase . . . land."

June 2—John Wharton writes to Houston to insure him that his conduct toward Stanbery "has been approved by a large majority" and invites him to come to Texas.

June 10—Houston returns to Washington from New York and writes to Charles F. M. Noland in search of traveling companion to accompany him to Texas.

June 12—Houston offers all his correspondence on the Indian ration contract to a Congressional subcommittee.

June 22—Houston called and sworn before special Congressional subcommittee.

June—Houston and acting Secretary of War Robb discuss plans for Houston to visit Indians in Texas area.

July 9—Houston takes case to public in answer to Stanbery.

July 25—Washington, Undersecretary of War Robb and Houston reach agreement on excursion to Southern Comanches and other tribes.

August 6—Robb issues passport to Houston requesting "all tribes of Indians . . . to permit [Houston] safely and freely to pass through their . . . Territories . . ."

August 16–September 15—In Nashville, Houston making plans for departure to Texas; meets with President Jackson.

August 18—Houston "rides to the Hermitage this evening [to] . . . see the Old Chief, General Jackson." Jackson said to have given or loaned Houston money for trip to Texas at this meeting.

September 15—At Nashville, Houston demands return of notes from Prentiss and announces plans to "cast my bread upon the waters" in Texas.

September—Albert Pike questions Houston's motives in going to Texas.

September–November—Period of intensified enforcement of Trade and Intercourse Acts. Whiskey supplies of Houston's partners seized. No indictments brought against them, and the goods restored.

October 8—Houston arrives at Cantonment Gibson.

October 9—Houston meets with Washington Irving at Gibson.

October 10—Washington Irving takes "ride with Col. Arbuckle, Gen. Houston to Col. Chouteau's . . ."

Mid-November—Houston leaves for Texas from Cantonment Gibson to "visit among the Indian tribes."

December 1—Houston writes of arrival at Fort Towson "a few days since" and outlines plans for trip through Indian country.

December 2—Houston remains at Fort Towson, where "health and spirits . . . good, . . . habits sober, and . . . heart straight." Writes cousin to "ask Miss Bell to play . . . 'Auld lang sine'. . . . Its notes would even reach me in the Indian's wigwam and reclaim me to the civilized world again."

December 10—Henderson Yoakum's *History of Texas* places Houston crossing Red River and entering Texas.

December 24—Sam Houston's application for headrights in Texas colony "with the object of acquiring lands for establishing myself" approved by Stephen Austin.

1833

February 13—Houston is in Natchitoches, Louisiana, where he writes a report to Fort Gibson on his Indian visits and outlines plans of tribes to come to Fort Gibson for Stokes Conference. Houston writes to Jackson about the prospects for Texas.

May 28—Houston returns to Fort Gibson, but finds the commissioners absent on official business and can not make his report.

June 27—Diana Gentry executes a power of attorney in favor of Samuel Houston.

July 31—At Hot Springs, Arkansas Territory, Houston reports on trip to the Indian tribes in Texas which began from Fort Gibson in November of 1832.

October 4—At Natchitoches, Louisiana, Houston writes for his expenses on trip from Fort Gibson to "wilderness as a Special Agent."

October 4–5—War Department acknowledges agreement with Houston in June of 1832 and on July 25, 1832, but rejects claim for expenses as "Special Agent" to Indians.

November 30—Houston files petition for a divorce from Eliza Allen in the "Free State of Coahuila and Texas, District of Ayish."

SOURCES

Manuscripts: Letters, Papers, and Journals

Andrus, Thekla, N. "Sam Houston and the Indians." M.A. thesis, Texas College of Arts and Industries, 1950. (Not examined by the authors.)

Arbuckle, Matthew. Papers (Photostats). Sam Houston Biographical Files, and Grant Foreman Typescripts, Reference Library, Thomas Gilcrease Institute, Tulsa, Oklahoma.

Arkansas River Steamboat Records. "Arkansas File Box," Indian Archives, Oklahoma Historical Society, Oklahoma City, Oklahoma.

Boyce, Annie M. "A Red Man's Foster Son." M.A. thesis, Southwest Texas State College, 1939. (Not examined by the authors.)

Clark, William. Letters. Grant Foreman Typescripts, Reference Library, Thomas Gilcrease Institute, Tulsa, Oklahoma.

Drew, John. Papers and Accounts. Reference Library, Thomas Gilcrease Institute, Tulsa, Oklahoma.

Foreman, Carolyn Thomas. Letters. "Arkansas File Box," Indian Archives, Oklahoma Historical Society, Oklahoma City, Oklahoma.

Foreman, Grant. Letters. "Arkansas File Box," Indian Archives, Oklahoma Historical Society, Oklahoma City, Oklahoma.

———. Notebooks. Indian Archives, Oklahoma Historical Society, Oklahoma City, Oklahoma.

Houston, Sam. Papers (Originals and Photostats). Sam Houston Biographical Files, and Grant Foreman Typescripts, Reference Library, Thomas Gilcrease Institute, Tulsa, Oklahoma.

———. Selected Articles and Typescripts. Sam Houston Biographical File, Reference Library, Oklahoma Historical Society, Oklahoma City, Oklahoma.

Houston, Temple. Articles and Typescripts. Vertical File, Biographical Files, Reference Library, Oklahoma Historical Society, Oklahoma City, Oklahoma.

"Indian-Pioneer Papers." Typescripts of Interviews of the Works Progress Administration. 116 vols. Copies in Indian Archives, Oklahoma Historical Society, Oklahoma City, Oklahoma, and Phillips Collection, University of Oklahoma Library, Norman, Oklahoma.

Irving, Washington. "Western Journals." Notebook 6, Irving Collection, Public Library, New York City.

Jolly, John. Letters written for. Grant Foreman Typescripts, Reference Library, Thomas Gilcrease Institute, Tulsa, Oklahoma.

———. Letters written for. Grant Foreman Notebooks and "Cherokee Leaders" File, Indian Archives, Oklahoma Historical Society, Oklahoma City, Oklahoma.

Meigs, Return Jonathan. Papers. Grant Foreman Typescripts, Indian Archives, Oklahoma Historical Society, Oklahoma City, Oklahoma.

Rogers, Captain John. Papers. Grant Foreman Typescripts, Reference Library, Thomas Gilcrease Institute, Tulsa, Oklahoma.

Rogers, Nan Hainey (Mrs. W. C.). Letters. Cherokee Collection, Sequoyah Rogers, Tulsa, Oklahoma.

Strickland, Rennard. "From Clan to Court: The Cherokee Legal System Emerges," Unpublished Typescript, Law School Library, University of Virginia.

Sutler's Papers. Grant Foreman Typescripts, Reference Library, Thomas Gilcrease Institute, Tulsa, Oklahoma.

Washburn, Cephas. Journals. Grant Foreman Notebooks, Indian Archives, Oklahoma Historical Society, Oklahoma City, Oklahoma.

Weaver, William. Scrapbook. Microfilm Division, Library, University of Arkansas.

Webber, Walter. Papers (Typescripts). Biographical Files, Indian Archives, Oklahoma Historical Society, Oklahoma City, Oklahoma.

Indian Tribal Records, Documents, and Laws

"Cherokee Agency." Letters Received by the Office of Indian Affairs. Microfilm Publications, The National Archives of the United States, Washington, D.C.

"Cherokee Agency, West." Letters Received by the Office of Indian Affairs. Microfilm Publications, The National Archives of the United States, Washington, D.C.

Cherokee Leaders Files. Grant Foreman Typescripts, Indian Archives, Oklahoma Historical Society, Oklahoma City, Oklahoma.

Cherokee Nation. *Laws of the Cherokee Nation Adopted by the Council at Various Times.* Tahlequah, Cherokee Nation: *Cherokee Advocate* Office, 1852.

———. *Laws of the Cherokee Nation, 1808–1835.* Tahlequah, Cherokee Nation: *Cherokee Advocate* Office, 1854.

———. *Treaties between the United States of America and the Cherokee*

Nation from 1785. Tahlequah, Cherokee Nation: National Printing Office, 1870

Cherokee Saltworks Investigation. Official Report. "Cherokee Saltworks File," Foreman Vertical File, Indian Archives, Oklahoma Historical Society, Oklahoma City, Oklahoma.

Cherokee Tribal Letters. Grant Foreman Typescripts, Reference Library, Thomas Gilcrease Institute, Tulsa, Oklahoma.

Cherokee West. Removal Papers. Grant Foreman Typescripts, Reference Library, Thomas Gilcrease Institute, Tulsa, Oklahoma.

"Choctaw Agency, West." Letters Received by the Office of Indian Affairs. Microfilm Publications, the National Archives of the United States, Washington, D.C.

"Creek Agency, West." Letters Received by the Office of Indian Affairs. Microfilm Publications, The National Archives of the United States, Washington, D.C.

Creek Memorials. Sam Houston Biographical Files, Reference Library, Thomas Gilcrease Institute, Tulsa, Oklahoma.

Osage Letters. Grant Foreman Typescripts, Reference Library, Thomas Gilcrease Institute, Tulsa, Oklahoma.

Osage Records (Typescripts). Indian Archives, Oklahoma Historical Society, Oklahoma City, Oklahoma.

Land Records, Maps, and Surveys

American Homes Survey. *Historic American Homes*. Washington: Private Printing, 1939.

Cantonment Gibson. Plans and Diagrams of the Original Buildings. Grant Foreman Photostats, Reference Library, Thomas Gilcrease Institute, Tulsa, Oklahoma.

Fort Gibson. Official Maps and Military Surveys. Grant Foreman Photostats, Reference Library, Thomas Gilcrease Institute, Tulsa, Oklahoma.

"Military Road and Fort Gibson." Survey conducted by Buchanan Plusche for the Oklahoma Historical Survey, Writer's Project of the Works Project Administration, Indian Archives, Oklahoma Historical Society, Oklahoma City, Oklahoma.

"Muskogee and Environs." Map. Drawn by Winnifred Clark and Grant Foreman. Foreman Room, Public Library, Muskogee, Oklahoma.

"Muskogee Area." Map. Drawn by Thomas Meagher. Oklahoma Map Collection, Reference Library, Thomas Gilcrease Institute, Tulsa, Oklahoma.

Muskogee County. Records of Land Transactions. County Clerk's Office, Muskogee County Court House. Muskogee, Oklahoma.

"The Three Forks." Map. Prepared by the Works Project Administration under the direction of Grant Foreman. Drawn by Thomas Meagher. Indian Archives, Oklahoma Historical Society, Oklahoma City, Oklahoma.

Wagoner County. Records of Land Transactions. County Clerk's Office, Wagoner County Court House. Wagoner, Oklahoma.

Books, Pamplets, and Articles

Abel, Annie H. "The History of Events Resulting in Indian Consolidation West of the Mississippi," *Annual Report of the American Historical Association for the Year 1906.* Washington: Government Printing Office, 1908.

———. *The Slaveholding Indians.* 3 vols. Cleveland: The Arthur H. Clark Company, 1915.

Adair, James. *The History of the American Indian.* London: Privately Printed for E. and C. Dilly, 1775.

Adams, John Quincy. *Speech of John Quincy Adams, of Massachusetts, upon the Right of the People, Men and Women, To Petition; on the Freedom of Speech and of Debate in the House of Representatives of the United States; on the Resolutions of Seven State Legislatures, and the Petitions of More Than One Hundred Thousand Petitioners, Relating to the Annexation of Texas to This Union.* Washington: Gales and Seaton, 1838.

Allen, Albert H. (ed.). *Arkansas Imprints 1821–1876.* New York: Published for the Bibliographical Society of America, P. R. Bowker Company, 1947.

Allsop, Fred W. *History of the Arkansas Press.* Little Rock: Parke-Harper, 1922.

Anderson, Mabel Washburn. "Old Fort Gibson on the Grand," *Twin Territories Magazine,* IV, No. 9 (September, 1902), 117.

Atkinson, M. Jourdan. *Indians of the Southwest.* San Antonio: The Naylor Company, 1958.

Bartram, William. *Travels through North and South Carolina, Georgia, East and West Florida, the Cherokee Country, the Extensive Territories of the Muscogules, or Creek Confederacy, and the Country of the Chactaws; Containing an Account of Those Regions, Together with Observations on the Manners of the Indians, 1791* (Naturalist Edition as edited by Francis Harper). New Haven: Yale University Press, 1958.

Bass, Althea. *Cherokee Messenger.* Norman: University of Oklahoma Press, 1936.

———. *The Story of Tullahassee*. Oklahoma City: Semco Color Press, Incorporated, 1960.

———. "Talking Stones—John Howard Payne's Story of Sequoyah," *The Colophon,* Part Nine (1932).

Bassett, John Spencer (ed.). *Correspondence of Andrew Jackson.* 7 vols. Washington: Carnegie Institution of Washington, 1926–1935.

———. *Life of Andrew Jackson.* New York: The Macmillan Company, 1916.

Berry, Louise. "Oklahoma's National Cemetery," *My Oklahoma Magazine*, I (August, 1927), 26, 60–61.

Blackwell, Jessie Dawson. *Families of Samuel Dawson and Polly Ann Rogers.* N.P.: Private Printing, n.d. (Copies in Reference Library, Thomas Gilcrease Institute, and Cherokee Collection of Sequoyah Rogers, Tulsa, Oklahoma.)

Bolton, Herbert E. "New Light on Manuel Lisa and the Spanish Fur Trade," *The Southwestern Historical Quarterly*, XVII (June, 1913), 61–66.

Boney, F. N. "The Raven Tamed," *The Southwestern Historical Quarterly*, LXVIII (July, 1964), 90–92.

"Book Reviews and Notices," *The Southwestern Historical Quarterly*, XXIII (January, 1920), 228.

Brown, David. "Views of a Native Indian, as to the Present Condition of His People," *The Missionary Herald*, XXI (November, 1825), 354–355.

Brown, John P. "Eastern Cherokee Chiefs," *The Chronicles of Oklahoma*, XVI (March, 1938), 3–35.

———. *Old Frontiers: The Story of the Cherokee Indians from Earliest Times to the Date of Their Removal to the West, 1838*. Kingsport, Tennessee: Southern Publishers, Incorporated, 1938.

Bruce, Henry. *Life of General Houston*. New York: Dodd, Mead and Company, 1891.

Bryan, George S. *Sam Houston*. New York: The Macmillan Company, 1917.

Byington, Cyrus. *A Dictionary of the Choctaw Language*. Edited by John R. Swanton and Henry S. Hablen. Smithsonian Institution, Bureau of American Ethnology, Bulletin 46. Washington: Government Printing Office, 1915.

Campbell, W. P. "Sam Houston in Indian Territory," *Historia Quarterly*, VIII (July, 1919), 1–4.

———. "More about Houston in Oklahoma," *Historia Quarterly*, VIII (October, 1919), 6–8.

Carter, Clarence E. (comp. and ed.). *The Territorial Papers of the United States*. 24 vols. Washington: Government Printing Office, 1934–1959.

Catlin, George. *Illustrations of the Manners, Customs, and Condition of the North American Indians in a Series of Letters and Notes Written during Eight Years of Travel and Adventure among the Wildest and Most Remarkable Tribes Now Existing*. 2 vols. London: Henry G. Bohn, 1851.

Claiborne, J. F. H. *Mississippi, as a Province, Territory and State, with Biographical Notices of Eminent Citizens*. Jackson: Power and Barksdale, 1880.

Coit, Margaret. *John C. Calhoun*. Boston: Houghton Mifflin Company, 1950.

"Colonel John Nicks, Report of Placing a Marker in the National Cemetery at Fort Gibson," *The Chronicles of Oklahoma,* X (December, 1932), 553–555.

Corkran, David H. *The Cherokee Frontier: Conflict and Survival, 1740–62*. Norman: University of Oklahoma Press, 1962.

Cornelius, Elias. *The Little Osage Captives: An Authentic Narrative*. Boston: Private Printing, 1822.

Covington, James W. "Sam Houston: Interpreter of Indian Strategy," *The Chronicles of Oklahoma,* XXXI (Summer, 1953), 212–214.

Crane, William Carey. *Life and Select Literary Remains of Sam Houston of Texas*. Philadelphia: J. B. Lippincott and Company, 1884.

Creel, George. *Sam Houston: Colossus in Buckskin*. New York: Cosmopolitan Book Corporation, 1927.

Cunningham, Hugh T. "A History of the Cherokee Indians," *The Chronicles of Oklahoma,* VIII (September, 1930), 291–314, 407–440.

Davis, John B. "The Life and Work of Sequoyah," *The Chronicles of Oklahoma,* VIII (June, 1930), 149–180.

Davis, Louise. "The Mystery of the Raven," *The Nashville Tennessean,* August 5, 12, 19, 1962.

Debo, Angie. *The Road to Disappearance*. Norman: University of Oklahoma Press, 1941.

Debo, Angie, and John M. Oskison (eds.). *Oklahoma: A Guide to the Sooner State*. Compiled by Workers of the Writers Program of the Works Project Administration. (American Guide Series.) Norman: University of Oklahoma Press, 1941.

DeShields, James T. *Border Wars of Texas*. Lioga, Texas: The Herald Company, 1912.

Donaldson, Thomas. "The George Catlin Indian Gallery in the United States National Museum (Smithsonian Institution) with Memoirs and

Statistics." *Annual Report. July 1885*. Board of Regents of the Smithsonian Institution. Part II. Appendix (V). Washington: Government Printing Office, 1886.

Duncan, Robert L. *Reluctant General: The Life and Times of Albert Pike*. New York: E. P. Dutton and Company, Incorporated, 1961.

Eggan, Fred (ed.). *Social Anthropology of North American Tribes*. (Enlarged edition.). Chicago: University of Chicago Press, 1955.

Elliott, Sarah Barnwell. *Sam Houston*. Boston: Small, Maynard and Company, 1900.

Ellsworth, Henry Leavitt. *Washington Irving on the Prairie, or a Narrative of a Tour of the Southwest in the Year 1832*. Edited by Stanley T. Williams and Barbara D. Simpson. New York: American Book Company, 1937.

Featherstonhaugh, G. W. *Excursion through the Slave States, from Washington on the Potomac to the Frontier of Mexico*. 2 vols. London: John Murray, 1844.

Ferber, Edna. *Cimarron*. Garden City: Doubleday-Doran ,1930.

Flanagan, Sue. *Sam Houston's Texas*. Austin: University of Texas Press, 1964.

Foreman, Carolyn Thomas. "The Armstrongs of Indian Territory," *The Chronicles of Oklahoma*, XXX (Autumn, 1952), 292–308, 420–453.

———. "Captain David McNair and His Descendants," *The Chronicles of Oklahoma*, XXXVI (Autumn, 1958), 270–281.

———. "The Cherokee Gospel Tidings of Dwight Mission," *The Chronicles of Oklahoma*, XII (December, 1934), 454–469.

———. "Colonel James B. Marcy," *The Chronicles of Oklahoma*, XIX (June, 1941), 119–128.

———. "A Creek Pioneer," *The Chronicles of Oklahoma*, XXI (September, 1943), 271–279.

———. "Early History of Webbers Falls," *The Chronicles of Oklahoma*, XXIX (Winter, 1951–1952), 444–483.

———. "Fairfield Mission," *The Chronicles of Oklahoma*, XXVII (Winter, 1949–1950), 373–388.

———. "General John Nicks and His Wife, Sarah Perkins Nicks," *The Chronicles of Oklahoma*, VIII (December, 1930), 389–406.

———. "Journal of a Tour in the Indian Territory," *The Chronicles of Oklahoma*, X (June, 1932), 219–256.

———. "The Lighthorse in the Indian Territory," *The Chronicles of Oklahoma*, XXXIV (Spring, 1956), 17–43.

———. "Military Discipline in Early Oklahoma," *The Chronicles of Oklahoma*, VI (June, 1928), 140–144.
———. *Oklahoma Imprints*. Norman: University of Oklahoma Press, 1936.
———. *Park Hill*. Muskogee: Star Printery, 1948.
———. "Texanna," *The Chronicles of Oklahoma*, XXXI (Summer, 1953), 178–188.

Foreman, Grant. *Advancing the Frontier, 1830–1860*. Norman: University of Oklahoma Press, 1934.
———. "The Centennial of Fort Gibson," *The Chronicles of Oklahoma*, II (June, 1924), 119–128.
———. *Down the Texas Road*. (Historic Oklahoma Series, No. 2.) Norman: University of Oklahoma Press, 1936.
———. *Fort Gibson: A Brief History*. (Historic Oklahoma Series, No. 1.) Norman: University of Oklahoma Press, 1936.
———. "Fort Gibson Happenings," *Muskogee Daily Phoenix*, December 27, 1931.
———. "Historic Phases of the Grand River Valley," *The Chronicles of Oklahoma*, XXV (Summer, 1947), 141–152, 172.
———. *A History of Oklahoma*. Norman: University of Oklahoma Press, 1942.
———. *Indian Removal: The Emigration of the Five Civilized Tribes of Indians*. Norman: University of Oklahoma Press, 1932.
———. *Indians and Pioneers: The Story of the American Southwest before 1830*. Norman: University of Oklahoma Press, 1936.
———. *Muskogee and Eastern Oklahoma*. Muskogee, Oklahoma: Chamber of Commerce, n.d.
———. "Nathaniel Pryor," *The Chronicles of Oklahoma*, VII (June, 1929), 152–163.
———. *Pioneer Days in the Early Southwest*. Cleveland: The Arthur H. Clark Company, 1926.
———. "River Navigation in the Early Southwest," *The Mississippi Valley Historical Review*, XV (June, 1928), 34–55.
———. "Salt Works in Early Oklahoma," *The Chronicles of Oklahoma*, X (December, 1932), 474–500.
———. *Sequoyah*. Norman: University of Oklahoma Press, 1938.
———. "Some New Light on Houston's Life among the Cherokee Indians," *The Chronicles of Oklahoma*, IX (June, 1931), 139–152.

Foster, George E. *Se-Quo-Yah: The American Cadmus and Modern Moses*. Philadelphia: Office of Indian Rights Association, 1885.

Friend, Llerena B. *Sam Houston: The Great Designer*. Austin: University of Texas Press, 1954.

Gabler, Ina. "Lovely's Purchase and Lovely County," *The Arkansas Historical Quarterly*, XIX (Spring, 1960), 31–39.

Garrison, George P. (ed.). "Diplomatic Correspondence of the Republic of Texas," *American Historical Association Annual Report*. 3 vols. Washington: Government Printing Office, 1908–1911.

Gearing, Fred. *Priests and Warriors*. Memoirs of the American Anthropological Association. Vol. 64, No. 5, Part 2, Memoir 93 (October, 1962).

Goodpasture, Albert V. "The Paternity of Sequoyah," *The Chronicles of Oklahoma*, I (October, 1921), 12–130.

Gould, Charles N. *Oklahoma Place Names*. Norman: University of Oklahoma Press, 1933.

Greeley, Horace. *The American Conflict: A History of the Great Rebellion in the United States of America, 1860–64*. 2 vols. Hartford: O. D. Case and Company, 1865–1867.

Green, Rena Maverick (ed.). *Samuel Maverick, Texan: 1803–1870*. San Antonio: Private Printing, 1952.

Gregg, Josiah. *Commerce of the Prairies*. 2 vols. New York: H. G. Langley, 1844.

Gregory, Jack, and Rennard Strickland. "Historic Archeology: Locating Sam Houston's Cherokee Trading Post," *The Northwest Arkansas Archaeological Society Amateur*, IV (August, 1965), 3–6.

Guild, John C. *Old Times in Tennessee*. Nashville: Travel, Eastman and Howell, 1878.

Hall, Benjamin F. (comp.). *Official Opinions of the Attorneys General of the United States Advising the President and Heads of Departments in Relation to Their Official Duties; and Expounding the Constitution, Subsisting Treaties with Foreign Governments and with Indian Tribes, and the Public Laws of the Country*. 2 vols. Washington: Robert Farnham, 1852.

Hannum, Richard M. "Letter from Quapaw Sub-Agent," *Arkansas Gazette*, May 27, 1833.

Harbour, Emma Estill. "Annual Meeting of the Oklahoma Historical Society," *The Chronicles of Oklahoma*, XII (June, 1934), 123–129.

Hargrett, Lester. *A Bibliography of the Constitutions and Laws of the American Indians*. Cambridge: Harvard University Press, 1947.

Harmon, George Dewey. *Sixty Years of Indian Affairs*. Chapel Hill: University of North Carolina Press, 1941.

Harris, Phil. "Exact Site of Wigwam Neosho Is Sought," *Muskogee Daily Phoenix*, September 20, 1964.

———. "Houston's Life with Cherokees," *Muskogee Sunday Phoenix and Times Democrat*, February 21, 1965.

———. "Play on Houston Life Soon," *Muskogee Sunday Phoenix and Times Democrat*, February 14, 1965.

———. *This Is Three Forks Country*. Muskogee, Oklahoma: Hoffman Printing Company, 1965.

Heard, Irma Celestine. "Lover's Leap—A Legend," *My Oklahoma Magazine*, I (April, 1927), 37–38.

Hitchcock, Ethan Allen. *A Traveler in Indian Territory*. Edited by Grant Foreman. Cedar Rapids: The Torch Press, 1930.

Horn,Stanley F. (ed.). "Holdings of the Tennessee Historical Society: An Unpublished Photograph of Sam Houston," *Tennessee Historical Quarterly*, III (December, 1944), 349–351.

Houston, Sam. *The Autobiography of Sam Houston*. Edited by Donald Day and Harry Herbert Ullom. Norman: University of Oklahoma Press, 1954.

———. *The Writings of Sam Houston*. Edited by Amelia W. Williams and Eugene C. Barker. 8 vols. Austin: University of Texas Press, 1938–1943.

Houston, Samuel R. *Brief Biographical Accounts of Many Members of the Houston Family*. Cincinnati: Elm Street Printing Company, 1882.

Hynds, Alexander. "General Sam Houston," *The Century Magazine*, XXVIII (August, 1884), 494–506.

Irving, Washington. *The Journals of Washington Irving*. Edited by William P. Trent and George S. Hellman. Boston: The Bibliophile Society, 1919.

———. *A Tour on the Prairies*. Annotated by Joseph B. Thoburn and George C. Wells. Oklahoma City: Harlow Publishing Company, 1955.

———. *The Western Journals of Washington Irving*. Edited by Francis McDermott. Norman: University of Oklahoma Press, 1944.

Jacobs, Wilbur R. (ed.). *Indians of the Southern Colonial Frontier, the Edmond Atkins Report and Plan of 1755*. Columbia: University of South Carolina Press, 1954.

James, Bessie. *Six Foot Six*. (Children's Book.) Indianapolis: Bobbs-Merrill Company, 1934.

James, Marquis. "On the Trail of Sam Houston," *The Texas Monthly*, VI (July, 1930), 1–8.

———. *The Raven: A Biography of Sam Houston*. New York: Blue Ribbon Books, 1929.

Johnson, Allen, and Dumas Malone (eds.). *Dictionary of American Biography.* 20 vols. New York: Charles Scribner's Sons, 1928–1937.

Kennedy, John F. *Profiles in Courage.* New York: Harper & Brothers, Publishers, 1956.

Keppler, Charles (ed.). *Indian Affairs, Laws and Treaties.* 2 vols. Washington: Government Printing Office, 1903.

King, V. O. "The Cherokee Nation of Indians," *The Quarterly of the Texas Historical Association,* II (July, 1898), 58–72.

Knight, Oliver. "Cherokee Society under the Stress of Removal, 1820–46," *The Chronicles of Oklahoma,* XXXII (Winter, 1954–1955), 414–428.

Lackey, Vinson. *The Chouteaus and the Founding of Salina, Oklahoma's First White Settlement—1796.* Tulsa, Oklahoma: Tulsa Printing Co., 1961.

Lamar, Mirabeau B. *The Papers of Mirabeau Buonaparte Lamar.* Edited by Charles A. Gulick, Jr. 6 vols. Austin: VonBoeckmann-Jones, 1921–1927.

Langford, Ella Molly. *Johnson County, Arkansas, the First Hundred Years.* Clarksville, Arkansas: Private Printing, 1921.

Lester, C. Edwards. *Life and Achievements of Sam Houston, Hero and Statesman.* New York: Hurst and Company, 1883.

———. *The Life of Sam Houston: The Only Authentic Memoir of Him Ever Published.* Philadelphia: G. G. Evans, 1860.

———. *Sam Houston and His Republic.* New York: Burgess-Stringer Company, 1846.

Litton, Gaston. "The Principal Chiefs of the Cherokee Nation," *The Chronicles of Oklahoma,* XV (September, 1937), 253–270.

Lowrie, Walter, Matthew St. Clair Clarke, and Walter S. Franklin (eds.). *American State Papers: Documents, Legislative and Executive of the Congress of the United States.* 38 vols. Washington: Gales and Seaton, 1832–1834.

Lucas, Jim. "Fort Gibson Grave Recalls Romance of Houston and Cherokee Maid," *Muskogee Daily Phoenix,* September 29, 1935.

Lucke, Jessie R. "Correspondence concerning the Establishment of the First Arkansas Press," *The Arkansas Historical Quarterly,* XIV (Summer, 1955), 161–171.

Lumpkins, Wilson. *The Removal of the Cherokee Indians from Georgia.* 2 vols. New York: Dodd, Mead, and Company, 1907.

McKenney, Thomas L. *History of Indian Tribes of North America.* 2 vols. text, 2 vols. plates. Philadelphia: D. Rice and Company, 1865.

McReynolds, Edwin C. *The Seminoles.* Norman: University of Oklahoma Press, 1957.

Malone, Prairie View. *Sam Houston's Indians.* San Antonio: The Naylor Company, 1960.

Manning, W. R. (ed.). *Diplomatic Correspondence of the United States: Inter American Affairs, 1831–1860.* 12 vols. Washington: Carnegie Endowment for International Peace, 1932–1939.

Mayo, Robert. *Political Sketches of Eight Years in Washington.* Baltimore: Fielding Lucas, Jr., 1839.

Meserve, John Bartlett. "Chief Opothleyahola," *The Chronicles of Oklahoma,* IX (December, 1931), 439–453.

Mooney, James. "The Cherokee Ball Play," *American Anthropologist,* III (April, 1890), 105–132.

———. "Myths of the Cherokees," *Nineteenth Annual Report.* Smithsonian Institution, Bureau of American Ethnology. Washington: Government Printing Office, 1897–1898.

———. *The Swimmer Manuscript.* Revised, Completed, and Edited by Frans M. Olbrechts. Smithsonian Institution, Bureau of American Ethnology, Bulletin 99. Washington: Government Printing Office, 1932.

Morrell, Z. N. *Flowers and Fruits in the Wilderness: Or, Forty-Six Years in Texas and Two Winters in Honduras.* (4th ed.). Dallas: W. G. Scarff and Company, 1886.

Morris, John W., and Edwin C. McReynolds. *Historical Atlas of Oklahoma.* Norman: University of Oklahoma Press, 1965.

Morrison, William B. *Military Posts in Oklahoma.* Oklahoma City: Harlow Publishing Company, 1936.

Muckleroy, Anna. "The Indian Policy of the Republic of Texas," *The Southwestern Historical Quarterly,* XXV (April, 1922), 229–260; XXVI (July, 1922), 1–29; XXVI (October, 1922), 128–148; XXVI (January, 1923), 184–206.

Murchison, A. H. "Intermarried Whites in the Cherokee Nation between the Years 1865 and 1887," *The Chronicles of Oklahoma,* VI (September, 1928), 299–327.

Newcomb, W. W., Jr. *The Indians of Texas: From Prehistoric to Modern Times.* Austin: University of Texas Press, 1961.

Nuttall, Thomas. *A Journal of Travels into the Arkansas Territory during the Year 1819, with Occasional Observations on the Manners of the Aborigines.* Edited by Reubin Gold Thwaites. Early Western Travels Series, Volume XIII. Cleveland: The Arthur H. Clark Company, 1905.

O'Beirne, H. F. *Leaders and Leading Men of the Indian Territory.* 2 vols. Chicago: American Publishers Association, 1891.

Oglesby, Richard E. *Manuel Lisa and the Opening of the Missouri Fur Trade.* Norman: University of Oklahoma Press, 1963.

Old Fort Gibson. Fort Gibson, Indian Territory: Private Printing, n.d. (Copy in Indian Archives, Oklahoma Historical Society, Oklahoma City, Oklahoma.)

Olgin, Joseph. *Sam Houston: Friend of the Indian.* (Children's Books). Boston: Houghton Mifflin Company, 1958.

Orr, Lyndon. *Famous Affinities of History.* 4 vols. in one. New York: Harper and Brothers Publishers, 1912.

"Osages," *The Missionary Herald,* XXV (April, 1829), 123–126.

Oskison, John M. *A Texas Titan.* Garden City: Doubleday, Doran and Company, 1929.

Owen, Narcissa. *Memoirs of Narcissa Owen, 1831–1907.* Washington: Private Printing, 1907.

Paine, Thomas. *Rights of Man.* New York: The Heritage Press, 1961.

Parker, Thomas Valentine. *The Cherokee Indians.* New York: The Grafton Press, 1907.

Paschal, George W. "Last Years of Sam Houston," *Harper's New Monthly Magazine,* XXXII (April, 1866), 630–635.

Pierson, George W. *Tocqueville in America.* Garden City: Anchor Books, 1959.

Pilling, James Constantine. *Bibliography of the Iroquoian Language.* Smithsonian Institution, Bureau of American Ethnology. Washington: Government Printing Office, 1888.

Porter, Kenneth Wiggins. "The Hawkins Negroes Go to Mexico," *The Chronicles of Oklahoma,* XXIV (Spring, 1946), 55–58.

Prucha, Francis Paul. *American Indian Policy in the Formative Years.* Cambridge: Harvard University Press, 1962.

Reagon, John. H. "A Conversation with Governor Houston," *The Quarterly of the Texas State Historical Association,* III (April, 1900), 279–281.

———. "The Expulsion of the Cherokees from East Texas," *The Quarterly of the Texas State Historical Association,* I (July, 1897), 38–46.

"Report of Annual Meeting of the Oklahoma Historical Society," *The Chronicles of Oklahoma,* XXII (June, 1934), 123–129.

Richardson, James D. (comp.). *Messages and Papers of the Presidents.* 10 vols. Washington: Government Printing Office, 1896–1899.

Ridge, John. "The Cherokee War Path," Annotated by Carolyn Thomas

Foreman. *The Chronicles of Oklahoma*, IX (September, 1931), 233–263.

Ross, Joshua. "My Countrymen, the Cherokees," *Twin Territories Magazine*, II (October, 1899).

Royce, Charles C. "The Cherokee Nation of Indians." *Fifth Annual Report.* Smithsonian Institution, Bureau of American Ethnology. Washington: Government Printing Office, 1887.

Sabin, Edward L. *With Sam Houston in Texas.* Philadelphia: J. B. Lippincott and Company, 1916.

"Sam Houston," *The Baconian Magazine*, VII, No. 2 (February, 1904).

Schlesinger, Arthur M., Jr. *The Age of Jackson.* Boston: Little, Brown and Company, 1945.

Seymour, Flora Warren. *Indian Agents of the Old Frontier.* New York: D. Appleton-Century Company, 1941.

———. *Sam Houston, Patriot.* New York: Century Company, 1930.

Shearer, Ernest. "The Mercurial Sam Houston," *The East Tennessee Historical Society's Publications*, No. 35 (1963), 3–20.

Skarritt, Preston. "The Green-Corn Ceremonies of the Cherokees," *National Intelligencer*, April 4, 1849.

Smith, W. R. L. *The Story of the Cherokees.* Cleveland: The Church of God Publishing House, 1928.

Starkey, Marion L. *The Cherokee Nation.* New York: Alfred A. Knopf, 1946.

Starr, Emmett. *Cherokee "West" 1794–1839.* Claremore, Oklahoma: Private Printing, 1910.

———. *An Early History of the Cherokees.* Kansas City: Private Printing, 1916.

———. *History of the Cherokee Indians.* Oklahoma City: The Warden Company, 1921.

Stenbery, Richard. "Jackson, Anthony Butler, and Texas," *The Southwestern Social Science Quarterly*, XIII (December, 1932), 264–286.

———. "Jackson, Buchanan, and the 'Corrupt Bargain' Calumny," *Pennsylvania Magazine of History and Biography*, LVIII (January, 1934), 61–85.

———. "Jackson's Neches Claim, 1829–1836," *The Southwestern Historical Quarterly*, XXXIX (April, 1936), 255–274.

———. "The Texas Schemes of Jackson and Houston, 1829–1836," *The Southwestern Social Science Quarterly*, XV (December, 1934), 229–250.

Stuart, John. *A Sketch of the Cherokee and Choctaw Indians.* Little Rock: Woodruff and Pew, 1837.

Terrell, A. W. "Recollections of General Sam Houston," *The Southwestern Historical Quarterly,* XVI (October, 1912), 113–136.

Thoburn, Joseph B. "Centennial of the Tour on the Prairies," *The Chronicles of Oklahoma,* X (September, 1932), 426–433.

Thoburn, Joseph B., and Muriel H. Wright. *Oklahoma: A History of the State and Its People.* 4 vols. New York: Lewis Historical Publishing Company, Incorporated, 1929.

"Tragic Romance of General Sam Houston and Talhina Rogers," *The American Indian,* IV, No. 9 (June 20, 1930), 10.

Van Zandt, Howard F. "The History of Camp Holmes and Chouteau's Trading Post," *The Chronicles of Oklahoma,* XIII (September, 1935), 316–337.

Walker, Robert S. *Torchlight to the Cherokees.* New York: The Macmillan Company, 1931.

Wardell, Morris L. *A Political History of the Cherokee Nation, 1838–1907.* Norman: University of Oklahoma Press, 1938.

———. "Protestant Missions among the Osages," *The Chronicles of Oklahoma,* II (September, 1924), 285–297.

Washburn, Cephas. *Reminiscences of the Indians.* Richmond: Presbyterian Committee of Publications, 1869.

Wellman, Paul I. *Magnificent Destiny.* Garden City: Doubleday and Co., 1962.

Westbrook, Harriette Johnson. "The Chouteaus," *The Chronicles of Oklahoma,* XI (September, 1933), 786–797, 943–966.

White, Lonnie J. "Arkansas Territorial Indian Affairs," *The Arkansas Historical Quarterly,* XXI (Autumn, 1962), 193–212.

White, Owen P. *Texas: An Informal Biography.* New York: G. P. Putnam's Sons, 1945.

White, Robert H. (ed.). *Messages of Governors of Tennessee.* 4 vols. Nashville: Tennessee Historical Commission, 1952.

Williams, Alfred M. "Among the Cherokees," *Lippincott's Magazine,* XXVII (February, 1881), 195–203.

———. "Houston's Life among the Indians," *Magazine of American History,* X (November, 1883), 401–408.

———. *Sam Houston and the War of Independence in Texas.* Boston: Houghton-Mifflin Company, 1935.

Williams, Amelia, and Bernhardt Wall. *Following General Sam Houston.* Austin: Steck Company, 1935.

Williams, Samuel C. "Christian Missions to the Overhill Cherokees," *The Chronicles of Oklahoma,* XII (March, 1934), 66–73.

———. "The Father of Sequoyah: Nathaniel Gist," *The Chronicles of Oklahoma,* XV (March, 1937), 3–200.

Williams, Thomas Benton. *The Soul of the Red Man.* N.P.: Private Printing, n.d. (Copies in Grant Foreman Room, Muskogee, Oklahoma, Public Library, and Reference Library, Oklahoma Historical Society, Oklahoma City, Oklahoma.)

Wilson, James Grant, and John Fiske (eds.). *Appleton's Cyclopedia of American Biography.* 6 vols. New York: D. Appleton and Company, 1887–1900.

Wilson, William. "Talihina's Grave," *The Fort Gibson Post,* July 21, 1904.

Winfrey, Dorman. "Chief Bowles of the Texas Cherokees," *The Chronicles of Oklahoma,* XXXII (Spring, 1954), 29–41.

Winfrey, Dorman, and James M. Day (eds.). *Texas Indian Papers.* 4 vols. Austin: Texas State Library, 1958–1961.

Winkler, Ernest W. "The Cherokee Indians in Texas," *The Quarterly of the Texas State Historical Association,* VII (October, 1903).

Wise, Henry A. *Seven Decades of the Union: The Humanities and Materialism.* Philadelphia: J. B. Lippincott and Company, 1872.

Wise, Jennings. *The Red Man in the New World Drama.* Washington: W. F. Roberts Company, 1931.

Wisehart, Marion Karl. *Sam Houston: American Giant.* Washington: Luce, Incorporated, 1962.

Woldert, Albert. "The Last of the Cherokees in Texas, and the Life and Death of Chief Bowles," *The Chronicles of Oklahoma,* I (June, 1923), 179–226.

Wright, Muriel H. "Early Navigation and Commerce along the Arkansas and Red Rivers in Oklahoma," *The Chronicles of Oklahoma,* VIII (March, 1930), 65–88.

———. *Springplace, Moravian Mission.* Guthrie, Oklahoma: Co-operative Publishing Company, 1940.

Yoakum, Henderson. *History of Texas, from Its First Settlements in 1685 to Its Annexation to the United States in 1846.* 2 vols. New York: J. S. Redfield, 1855.

Newspapers

A. *Cherokee Language Newspapers*

Cherokee Advocate (Tahlequah, Indian Territory), February 20, 1845; April 2, 1846; November 25, 1893.

Cherokee Phoenix (New Echota, Georgia), March 27, 1828; June 24, 1829; March 4, 1830; December 11, 1830; May 28, 1831.

B. *Newspapers of General Circulation*

Arkansas Advocate (Little Rock), February 16, 1831.

Arkansas Gazette (Little Rock), February 10, 1827; March 27, 1827; April 17, 1827; May 29, 1827; March 5, 1828; July 21, 1828; August 20, 1828; January 6, 1829; April 15, 1829; May 6, 1829; May 20, 1829; June 22, 1830; June 29, 1830; July 7, 1830; July 21, 1830; August 4, 1830; August 11, 1830; August 14, 1830; September 8, 1830; October 5, 1830; August 3, 1831; May 27, 1833.

Arkansas Gazette (Supplement), March 5, 1829; January 16, 1829; May 20, 1829; October 20, 1830; December 8, 1830.

Courier des Natchitoches, January 2, 1827; January 30, 1827; March 13, 1827.

Daily Oklahoman (Oklahoma City), March 9, 1924; September 27, 1931.

Dallas Morning News, January 10, 1937.

Fort Gibson Post (Indian Territory), July 21, 1904; October 15, 1904.

Gallatin Newspaper (Tennessee), April 28, 1830.

Kentucky Reporter (Lexington), 1831.

Louisville Courier Journal, January, 1878.

Muskogee Daily Phoenix, January 5, 1924; June 5, 1924; May 30, 1926; December 27, 1931; January 3, 1932; January 10, 1932; January 17, 1932; January 31, 1932; February 7, 1932; February 11, 1932; February 14, 1932; January 10, 1933; January 17, 1933; September 29, 1935; October 28, 1951; September 20, 1964; February 14, 1965; February 21, 1965.

Muskogee Sunday Phoenix and Times Democrat, February 14, 1965; February 21, 1965; April 23, 1967.

Muskogee Times Democrat, January 24, 1904; May 10, 1904; May 19, 1904; May 27, 1904; August 9, 1904; August 30, 1904; January 1, 1909; April 27, 1915; September 26, 1919.

Nashville Banner and Nashville Whig, April 23, 1830; July 13, 1831.

Nashville Republican, April 17, 1829.

The Nashville Tennessean, August 5, 1962; August 12, 1962; August 19, 1962.

National Intelligencer (Washington, D.C.), April 2, 1832; April 4, 1849.

Niles' Weekly Register (Baltimore), X (1816), 16, 127; June 2, 1827; July 20, 1827; May 9, 1829; May 16, 1829; May 29, 1830; August 27, 1831.

Northern Standard (Clarksville, Arkansas), October 14, 1843.

Tulsa World, November 1, 1925; January 3, 1932.

United States Telegraph (Washington, D.C.), 1831.

Interviews

Ballenger, T. L. (Tahlequah, Oklahoma), July, 1964.

Boling, Don (Fort Gibson, Oklahoma), July 4, 1964.

Boydstun, Q. B. (Fort Gibson, Oklahoma), October 10, 1964.

Carselowey, James (Adair, Oklahoma), December 23, 1964.

Foreman, Carolyn Thomas (Muskogee, Oklahoma), June 22, 1964; July 3, 1964; August 20, 1964; August 24, 1964.

Garrett, Judge Claude (Muskogee, Oklahoma), August 26, 1964.

Langston, Robert (Fort Gibson, Oklahoma), October 10, 1964.

Rogers, Sequoyah (Tulsa, Oklahoma), July 12, 1964; July 18, 1964.

Ward, Mrs. Gail (Muskogee, Oklahoma), June 26, 1964; July 23, 1964.

West, Mrs. George (Wagoner, Oklahoma), August 16, 1964.

Wright, Muriel H. (Oklahoma City, Oklahoma), July, 1964.

INDEX